HE RESCUES VIETNAM

Phil Marshall

DMZ Dustoff 7-1-1

1969

II

"DMZ Dustoff Vietnam"

and

"Dustoff & Medevac Vietnam"

Also by Phil Marshall

ISBN-10: 150614148X
ISBN-13: 978-1506141480

DEDICATION

To the helicopter crews of the United States Military in Vietnam. We were, oh, so young, but, oh, so talented and very, very dedicated. We got that way by flying several hours a day in combat, making 30 or 40 take-offs and landings some days.

Our flight school motto was "Above the Finest", a tribute to the Warriors on the ground. It was those Warriors who were the very reason for our existence. We were there for them. Because of that, we are all still brothers today, decades later.

CONTENTS

No risk, no reward.

(That pretty well sums up helicopter rescues flown in any combat.)

"We knew what was going on back in the States…the riots, the protests, the 'free love'… but we had more important things to worry about; like surviving and getting back home to the REAL world!"

Author unknown

Front Cover photo by Ed Iacobacci

DMZ Dustoff Medic

Veteran of Lam Son 719

(Hueys of the 237th Medical Detachment)

Back Cover photo by Phil Marshall

Thank you to Dan Gower of the Dustoff Association for helping me locate some of the crewmembers that you will read about.

INTRODUCTION

Welcome to "Helicopter Rescues Vietnam", the third in a series of books that documents the Dustoff and Medevac missions that we flew as youthful Huey, Loach and Cobra helicopter crews in Vietnam. The first two volumes are titled "DMZ Dustoff Vietnam" and "Dustoff & Medevac Vietnam".

The radio call sign "Dustoff" was chosen at random very early in the Vietnam War for the medevac Huey helicopters with the red crosses. They were assigned the specific duty of rescuing wounded soldiers from the battlefields, rendering assistance whenever possible and they were also utilized for patient transportation between medical facilities. The crew normally consisted of 2 pilots, a crewchief (riding mechanic, so to speak, who was usually assigned to maintain the aircraft that he flew in) and a medic. Occasionally, when a mission was known ahead of time to be particularly dangerous, a Patient Protector would ride along. This could be the closest guy to the aircraft with a weapon when the mission came in. "Jump in, Dude, you're going with us!"

The 101st Airborne Division Dustoff Hueys and the 1st Cavalry Division, call sign "Medevac", Hueys carried M60 door guns and a Door Gunner for a crew of 5.

Although the Geneva Convention did not allow us to carry offensive weapons, these M60s were considered by those two units to be *defensive* weapons. Thus, only a very small percentage (perhaps 10%?) of Hueys displaying the Red Cross carried these somewhat heavy machine guns. The rest of the hand painted red cross Hueys were unarmed except for personal, hand carried weapons which were very rarely fired by the crews.

The call sign of Dustoff seemed appropriate for these missions of mercy and the name stuck throughout the war and continues today, decades later, throughout the US Army worldwide. Although some units preferred the call sign "Medevac", all the missions were performed the same. Often unarmed, the aircraft and youthful crews who manned them were there to remove the sick, wounded, dying or dead warriors from further harm. It is noted here that anytime a helicopter crew rescued wounded warriors, it was considered a Medevac mission. Not only were just Army warriors picked up by Army helicopters. It was this author's experience to medevac US Marines, Vietnamese soldiers, Vietnamese civilians, enemy Prisoners of War and even wounded guard dogs.

In this book, you will read stories by the men who flew those missions, like Dustoff pilot Fred McKellar, who tells of the time he could not get gunship cover for a hot (insecure) hoist mission, a hoist mission being perhaps the most dangerous thing we did as Medevac crews. Hovering over the tree tops and dropping a cable down to pull the wounded to safety. We were an incredibly tempting target for the enemy by executing this maneuver.

"I was calling on the radio on Guard frequency and the only aircraft that said they could help was two Air Force F4 Phantom jets. They quickly located me and although I could not see them, I heard them whoosh by, then pull pretty much straight up and I couldn't figure out why they didn't fire their machine guns at the targets. About that time, two napalm canisters exploded in front of us and I immediately felt the heat. Next thing I knew, two more canisters exploded in front of us. We didn't take any fire at all after that, and we completed our pickup but when we got back, the Maintenance Officer wanted to know what the hell we did to blister the paint on the front of our Huey!"

You will also read about some of the men on the ground that we rescued or were involved in our rescues. I received this email from a veteran whom I now consider a good friend:

I'm Don Alsbro, president of Lest We Forget, LWF, and I wanted to write a letter complimenting you on your book. I was very interested in your presentation at our event at Benton Harbor (Michigan) and on our trip to Vermont I started reading your book and couldn't put it down. I finished it in a couple of days. As I mentioned when I was talking to the American Huey 369 personnel that one of my Viet Nam (VN) tours was with the 11th Aviation Group, 1st Cav and I spent a year around choppers. In addition to my regular job as Civil Affairs for 11th Avn Gp I was the Club Officer for our Red Hawk Officers Club and I found that pilots can drink when they're off duty. I have a lot of respect for the VN pilots, especially the 20 year old pilots. I have a grandson who graduated from ROTC last year and is now at Fort Rucker becoming a chopper pilot. I'm going to send the book to him as I think he will be able to relate to it. Apparently he just had his instrument test. Thanks for doing the presentation and sharing your story.

Don Alsbro

Or the mission by Lieutenant Colonel (Retired, then a First lieutenant) Gary Brink, a Dustoff pilot that was in the 237th Medical Detachment with me. When I used gentle persuasion, relentlessly applied (thanks for the idea, Bob Hamilton) to get a mission out of Gary, he offered me via email that he had one but could not remember who the crew was:

"Phil,

You are right that I have not found the papers. The mission was on (I think) Dec 10, 1969. The mission was to attempt to respond to a UH-1H that had been shot down with a LRRP team on board. It was undetermined if there was any survivors, but they thought so. The location was on Rocket Ridge just south of the DMZ. I am not sure at all who was on board with me except I believe Adams was my copilot. *(Authors note: It was not Walt 'Itchy Pink" Adams. In country, Walt picked up a rash all over his body, hence the nickname "Itchy Pink".)* The medic is actually the hero of the story and I am totally embarrassed that I cannot remember who it was. We made the approach to the crash site and began to take a lot of fire so I pulled in behind a knoll. The medic ran down to see if anyone was alive. As soon as he started running to the aircraft he began to be shot at. It was like a movie in that as he was running the puffs of dust were churning up behind his heels. He tried to get to the aircraft and thought there was someone alive. The fire got so much that he had to retreat back to the aircraft. We could not stay any longer so I got out of there. We then called in gunships and discussed going back in and how we would better use the terrain to approach it. So we went back in, attempting to be in a better spot not to receive more fire and the medic again ran down the hill. Checked the soldiers there and found them to be dead. We then attempted to get out without being shot down. Fortunately, while taking a hail of fire, we got out safely. When we got back, we were told that we had landed on the regimental headquarters of the NVA. I remember feeling like a tank in full defilade when we were avoiding getting shot at.

There you are. The thumb nail story. I received the Distinguished Flying Cross when I got back in the US, but always felt the medic was the true hero and not sure if he got anything.

Take care,

Gary"

(Author's note: As of this writing, we are still trying to determine who the medic was so he can be recognized for the credit he deserves.)

Each of the following missions that I have accumulated for this book are designed to be stand alone stories. Most have been authored by me from interviews with the participants, but many have different authors...the participants themselves. Therefore, the astute reader will notice some duplication of information among the stories as these contributing authors wanted to document some of the most important events in their lives, their helicopter rescue missions. With their permission, I am sharing those life-changing events with you as they shared them with me.

From the internet, I offer this humorous, but not too far from the truth, piece:

LETTER ON WHETHER TO BECOME AN AIR FORCE PILOT... OR A NAVAL AVIATOR.

The piece is written by Bob Norris, a former Naval aviator who also did a 3 year exchange tour flying the F-15 Eagle. He is now an accomplished author of entertaining books about U.S. Naval Aviation including "Check Six" and "Fly-Off".

In response to a letter from an aspiring fighter pilot on which military academy to attend, Bob replied with the following:

Young Man,

Congratulations on your selection to both the Naval and Air Force Academies. Your goal of becoming a fighter pilot is impressive and a fine way to serve your country. As you requested, I'd be happy to share some insight into which service would be the best choice. Each service has a distinctly different culture. You need to ask yourself "Which one am I more likely to thrive in?"

USAF Snapshot: The USAF is exceptionally well organized and well run. Their training programs are terrific. All pilots are groomed to meet high standards for knowledge and professionalism. Their aircraft are top-notch and extremely well maintained. Their facilities are excellent. Their enlisted personnel are the brightest and the best trained. The USAF is homogenous and macro. No matter where you go, you'll know what to expect, what is expected of you, and you'll be given the training & tools you need to meet those expectations. You will never be put in a situation over your head. Over a 20-year career you will be home for most important family events. Your Mom would want you to be an Air Force pilot...so would your wife. Your Dad would want your sister to marry one.

Navy Snapshot: Aviators are part of the Navy, but so are Black Shoes (surface warfare) and Bubble Heads (submariners). Furthermore, the Navy is split into two distinctly different Fleets (West and East Coast). The Navy is heterogeneous and micro. Your squadron is your home; it may be great, average, or awful. A squadron can go from one extreme to the other before you know it. You will spend months preparing for cruise and months on cruise. The quality of the aircraft varies directly with the availability of parts. Senior Navy enlisted are salt of the earth; you'll be proud if you earn their respect. Junior enlisted vary from terrific to the troubled kid the judge made join the service. You will be given the opportunity to lead these people during your career; you will be humbled and get your hands dirty. The quality of your training will vary and sometimes you will be over your head. You will miss many important family events. There will be long stretches of tedious duty aboard ship. You will fly in very bad weather and/or at night and you will be scared many times. You will fly with legends in the

Navy and they will kick your ass until you become a lethal force. And some days - when the scheduling Gods have smiled upon you - your jet will catapult into a glorious morning over a far-away sea and you will be drop-jawed that someone would pay you to do it. The hottest girl in the bar wants to meet the Naval Aviator. That bar is in Singapore.

Bottom line, son, if you gotta ask...pack warm & good luck in Colorado.

P.S.: Air Force pilots wear scarves and iron their flight suits.

P.S.S. And oh yes, the Army pilot program, don't even think about it unless you got a pair bigger than basketballs. Those guys are completely crazy.

Let me explain a little bit about the Huey helicopter as pictured on the front of this book. The Huey was developed due to the success of the Bell OH-13 helicopter that was used in Korea. Originally designed as a scout helicopter, this is the one that many are so familiar with from the movie and television series M*A*S*H. The OH-13 did what it was designed to do very well but when you saw it in the movies or on television carrying the wounded outside of the cockpit in those little pods, that's all that helicopter could do. It barely had enough power to lift the pilot and those two patients. Not one thing more.

Bell OH-13 Sioux helicopter in Korea.

Plus, the patients were picked up at a forward aid station and flown back to a hospital; the wounded in Korea were rarely, if ever, picked up at the site of injury as we could do in Vietnam. Yes, there were some daring rescues of downed pilots by helicopter during the Korean war but for the most part the casualties of battle were not picked up by helicopter until they had been stabilized. The only real problem with the OH-13 was that once the patients were put on the outside of the helicopter, there was no one and no way to tend to them, thus, the need for them to be somewhat stabilized.

However, the Army especially realized the value of the helicopter for casualty evacuation and thereby sought a helicopter capable of carrying a medic and crew chief in an enclosed cabin with an all-weather capability flown by two pilots. Because the gas turbine engine had been perfected by the 1950s, it was part of the requirement for the new utility helicopter.

Fortunately for everyone involved, Bell helicopter's winning design of the Helicopter Utility design 1, HU-1, Iroquois, far exceeded the needs of the Army. The original designation of HU-1 is what gives us the nickname of the helicopter, "Huey". HU-1 looked like "Huey" and even though the designation was changed to UH-1, Utility Helicopter 1, it never lost the moniker of Huey. And hardly anyone outside of Army Aviation even knows that it is officially designated as Iroquois, not Huey.

All Army helicopters are named after Native American tribes. Chinook, Apache, Lakota, Cheyenne, Cayuse, Tarje and even the OH-13 Sioux just to name a few. However, for you trivia buffs, there is one Army helicopter, and only one, that is not named for a Native American tribe. In fact, it was designed specifically for the Vietnam war. As I give presentations throughout the year to different organizations and groups, both veteran groups and school groups, very rarely does someone know the answer even among Vietnam veteran groups. If you know the answer, you are the exception. If you don't know the answer, read on...

The answer is the Cobra. The Cobra gunship that was flown in Vietnam used virtually the same powertrain as the Huey. Today, as this book is written, the Marines are still purchasing brand new Cobras with twin engines, rather than Vietnam War Cobras that only had one engine, and using them very effectively. They're also buying brand new Huey helicopters with twin engines and four rotor blades instead of the Vietnam Huey with one engine and two rotor blades. You go Marines, I love you guys and gals.   OORAH!

One further point I would like to make. This book is written over 40 years after these missions were flown. Sometimes memories will differ between the same parties who were there or witnessed an event. It happens today; minutes after an accident, perhaps, witnesses will remember events differently. It's part of our humanity.

More than once during these interviews, someone would very emphatically tell me about a mission and as they were recalling the details, they would say something like "No , wait, that was a different mission, this is what happened." Please realize that we flew hundreds of missions, sometimes several a day, and in our minds, some could and did run together. But again, these stories are as accurate and correct as possible, and I will assure you, the reader, that if there is an inconsistency, it does not affect the overall content in the least. These missions did happen the way you will read about them. So if you spot an inconsistency, please forgive the storyteller as they are doing the best that they can to sort out some horribly stressful events, many of which could have been, or were, fatal.

Finally for this introduction, I would like to dispel a couple of myths about the Vietnam War:

- Fact: 2/3 of the men who served in Vietnam were <u>volunteers.</u> 2/3 of the men who served in World War II were <u>drafted.</u>
- Approximately 70% of those killed in Vietnam were volunteers, not draftees.

- Fact: 86% of the men who died in Vietnam were Caucasians/Latinos, 12.5% were black, 1.2% were other races. 79% had a high school education or better. This is virtually the identical population mix of the United States at the time, point being that blacks and non-high school diploma warriors were not "cannon fodder".

- Fact: The average age of an infantryman (Military Occupational Specialty, MOS, 11B) serving in Vietnam to be 19 years old is a myth, it is actually 22. The average man who fought in World War II was 26 years of age. Again, 19 year olds were not "cannon fodder".

- Fact: The average infantryman in the South Pacific during World War II saw about 40 days of combat in <u>four</u> years. The average infantryman in Vietnam saw about 240 days of combat in <u>one</u> year thanks to the mobility of the helicopter. Doesn't make the Vietnam Infantryman any better, just different.

- Fact: The American soldier did not lose the War in Vietnam, we were brought home in 1973. South Vietnam fell to the North in 1975, long after the Americans left. Same thing is happening in Iraq and Afghanistan, I suppose our politicians will never learn.

There are more myths but I just wanted to highlight a few of the more common.

I hope you enjoy this book.

Phil Marshall, Author

Mission 1

"When I Have Your Wounded"

The Legacy of Major Charles Kelly

By Captain Richard "Dick" Anderson and Major General Patrick H. Brady

As a brand new Warrant Officer helicopter pilot "wanna be", I showed up at the flight line Day 1 with the others in my flight school class where we were assigned three at a time to an instructor pilot. Virtually all of our instructor pilots were Chief Warrant Officers, CWOs, who had flown at least one tour in Vietnam already. As two of my classmates and I sat around the table with our Instructor Pilot, IP, we listened intently to his every word. In the middle of this instructional, another Warrant Officer Instructor walked by and our IP said to us "There walks a dead man, he flew Dustoff." The three of us students had been in the Army long enough that we knew what Dustoff was...unarmed Huey helicopters flying into the proverbial heat of battle to pick up the wounded. Dustoff crews were known to suffer over 3 times the number of casualties as other helicopter missions, according to some sources.

"There walks a dead man, eh?" I thought. I knew right then that I wanted nothing to do with flying unarmed helicopters. I wanted to fly gunships, to go in with weapons blazing and something to defend myself with, not this stupid stuff of flying unarmed helicopters in combat. So I devoted all of my energy and concentration on being the best helicopter pilot I could be so I could fly guns.

When we left Mineral Wells, Texas, (Fort Wolters, a former World War II Training Camp) after the first five months of our flight training, we headed to Southeast Alabama and Fort Rucker for our final four months of training. Shortly upon arrival we were told by the flight instructors that those of us with the top 20% of flight grades would receive gunship training, commonly referred to as Gun School. The remaining 80% would learn formation flying before receiving orders for Vietnam.

While I do not know exactly where I finished in those flight grades, I was in the top 20% and 24 of us students began a two week instructional period learning about the weapons used on the Huey and Cobra helicopters. We were instructed on the XM−21 weapons system which included a seven pod, 2.75 inch rocket launcher and also on the 6000 round per minute minigun, both of which were mounted on each side of the aircraft. Other aircraft weapon systems that we trained on in this school included the grenade launcher, which is a large flexible ball on the nose of the aircraft which fires small hand grenades. This grenade launcher became known as a "Chunker" due to the noise the weapon made as it fired one round about every second. These were virtually the same rounds that our ground troops used in the hand-held M79 grenade launcher. We trained with live ammunition on firing ranges, flying patterns that we would utilize in combat.

I mention all of this because the ammunition we were firing was not cheap. During this very intensive and expensive training, as students we became quite proficient with the weapons. However, in the infamous wisdom of the military, all of this was for naught for some of us.

During our Friday night full Company formation of approximately 150 students we were given pertinent information that we needed and we were informed as to who had passes for the weekend and who did not. After all information was disseminated, the commander called out 24 names, mine included, and told us to remain after the formation was dismissed. As the rest of the company was leaving the area , those of us that had to stay looked at each other and the general conversation was something like "What the heck did we do?" and "Are we in trouble?" We soon found out.

The 24 of us were told that after graduation from flight school in a few weeks, we had orders to go to Fort Sam Houston in San Antonio, Texas, for a five week medevac Dustoff course. We were all going to be Dustoff pilots! I remember walking back to the barracks and telling my roommate "That's it. I'm not going to make it back, they're sending me to Dustoff school." To this day, I have no idea why we were selected, as about half of us selected for Dustoff training were in the gun school. I would LIKE to think there was a reason we were chosen but even after all this time, I have no idea why. As it turned out, it was the best thing that could have happened to me. But at the time I thought it was my death notice.

Soon after we arrived at Fort Sam Houston, we began to hear the name Major Charles Kelly. The more we heard the more we realized that this man was considered to be the father of Dustoff. While he certainly was not the first, he left a legacy that remains to this day. Simply put, Kelly set the standard. No compromise, no rationalization, no hesitation. Fly the mission. Now. He became the embodiment of Dustoff, the one you would want to come for you regardless of the situation. After you read this mission, you will better understand why he is so highly regarded by those of us who flew Dustoff and Medevac missions.

Much has been written about Major Charles L. Kelly, you can look up several references to him on the internet. Therefore, I will spare you many of the minute details for now. In the very early days of Dustoff, many commanders failed to see the value of dedicated medevac helicopters and crews. Instead, these same commanders whose duties included caring for the well-being of their men, they were more concerned about their helicopters. As the Hueys first began arriving in Vietnam, the first 6 were assigned as medevac helicopters. As other Hueys began to arrive, there became a shortage of parts for these A-Model, Alpha Model, Hueys, as more and more aircraft became available but the replacement parts were slow to arrive.

Those early Hueys seem to have had problems with the starter/generator, an electric motor that was mounted on the helicopter in such a way that in one position, it was the only starter for the helicopter and with a flip of a switch on the overhead panel, it became a standby generator. Easy enough, but as these starter/generators began to fail, commanders demanded that the medevac units strip their Hueys of the starters so the troop transports could have them. In fact, there is a tale of starting one Dustoff aircraft and while it was running, the starter was removed and placed on another Huey so IT could be started. Thus, the struggle to even get Dustoff "off the ground" so to say.

Major Kelly and those before him fought to keep these Hueys with the red cross in the air, and Kelly was determined to show the value of dedicated air ambulances.

Every night he would fly a route through the Mekong Delta to look for casualties. He had a routine route of about a dozen points and as he neared each one he would call and ask if they had any casualties. He would just call and ask if everything was okay and if there were no patients to pick up he would tell them I will see you tomorrow night. Of course he was over hostile territory, and he would fly this 400+ mile route in a blacked out condition. Every night. And all of this was in addition to his daytime duties as commander and pilot of the 57th Medical Detachment. Major Kelly knew that he had to sell the idea of dedicated medical evacuation helicopters and this was one way he could do it.

On 1 July 1964, everything changed. Major Kelly's copilot this day was Capt. Richard "Dick" Anderson; this was the day we lost Major Charles Kelly. He was killed doing what he did best, flying Dustoff missions.

Questions that I have had in mind all these years were "How was Major Kelly killed? What really happened?" There are several accounts, but none that I had found included statements from any of the crew. As the proverbial luck would have it, at an American Huey 369 event a few years ago, I had the pleasure of an unexpected introduction to Captain Dick Anderson. All of us were rather busy at the time, so I did not have a chance to really talk with him, but I recently asked him how the one bullet could have killed Major Kelly, didn't they have armored seats on their aircraft? They were flying an early B Model Huey, did it still have the standard seats? His answer was that, no, they didn't have the standard seat, they had armored seats but the round came through the open left cargo door and hit Major Kelly in the side of his chest, entering his heart and killing him virtually instantly.

Anderson told me "It was a beautiful day, lots of sunshine, about as nice as they got in Vietnam. I remember it was just before noon." As the aircraft was touching down, they were told by the men on the ground to "Leave the area now! You're taking fire!" on the radio. The already published accounts tell how Major Kelly said the words that have become the catchphrase of Dustoff, "Not until I have your wounded".

Immediately upon landing, Kelly took that fatal bullet and called out "My God" when he was hit. He instinctively pulled up on the collective pitch to take off but then gave the aircraft full left cyclic, causing the aircraft to roll onto it's side with the rotor blades beating themselves to pieces against the ground. Anderson said " The maneuver was pretty violent and I had no time whatsoever to react. When one flew with Major Kelly you were not to touch the controls while he had them. Most pilots had a standard operating procedure of both pilots on the controls when going into an insecure landing zone. One pilot flying and the other light on the controls in case the pilot that was flying was wounded, exactly what happened in this case. But not Major Kelly. When you were flying with him you did not touch the controls unless he gave them to you.

When the aircraft went on its side, I was knocked unconscious. Apparently I came to rather quickly and right away I wondered what was going on. There was blood on my helmet visor and face shield and at first I thought that I had been hit. But then I realized the blood was coming from Major Kelly who was still strapped in his seat above me since we were laying on my side of the aircraft. The engine was still running even though we were laying on our side; I closed the throttle completely but the engine continued to run. I then shut off the fuel and the engine finally died; there was no post crash fire whatsoever. Of that I am certain because had there been a post crash fire I would have been burned and I was not burned. I climbed out of my seat and released Kelly's seatbelt which of course allowed him to fall on top of me. Luckily, the crew chief, PFC Pickstone and the medic, unfortunately I have forgotten his name, were uninjured although Capt. H W Giles, the doctor that was with us, suffered a broken leg. All of us exited through the open cargo door that was now serving as a skylight. I remember

I was pretty much the one who pushed Major Kelly's body through the opening. We immediately began looking for the weapons that we carried with us but could not find any. Apparently they were laying on the ground underneath the aircraft.

An L-19 fixed wing forward air controller pilot who had shown us the landing zone called out "Dustoff has been shot down" over the radio. Some accounts say that we were receiving fire just before we landed or as we were touching down. As far as I know, we were not being fired on until that one round, the aircraft took no hits whatsoever. There was just the one round that struck Major Kelly.

The aircraft was recovered by a CH 37 helicopter and because it was so badly damaged it was taken to the boneyard. In fact, I went to the aircraft later and removed some pieces of it and there were no bullet holes in it anywhere. The tail number was 63-08591. One other thing, when we were finally rescued, we did take enemy fire at that time. The home unit of the injured Special Forces guy that we were picking up never did show up."

Major Dick Anderson.

(Author's note. According to the database of the Vietnam Helicopter Pilots Association, VHPA, Major Kelly was killed "On a mission... to pick up a slightly wounded Special Forces person." Anderson recalled "That was the rub. The guy had a bandage on his wrist and was going on R and R, Rest and Relaxation. The mission was called in as 'urgent' when it was not, Kelly's death was so needless." Also according to the VHPA database, the accident

summary for 63-08591 includes this note: "Major Kelly was the 57th Med's third Commanding Officer and is known as the 'Father of Dustoff'. Much has been written about the profound effect his death had on the business of dedicating helicopters to the medevac operations." The entry goes on to say "Many believe 'the legend of Dustoff' was born out of his death." The aircraft was written off as a total loss.

Lastly, Dick Anderson offers this bit of information. "I was rated as both a fixed wing and rotary wing pilot at the time. A couple of weeks after Major Kelly's death, I was assigned to a (Fixed Wing) Caribou unit that rotated us every few weeks between Vietnam and Thailand. I spent the last six months of my tour with this unit and enjoyed it very much. It was certainly a lot less stressful than flying Dustoff, but I would not trade my time with the 57th Med for anything."

Following is an excerpt from Major General Patrick Brady's book "Dead Men Flying", reprinted here with his permission:

Toward the end of June 1964, the command was changing hands. General Stilwell was leaving as commander, U.S. Army Support Command, Vietnam, and Kelly came to town to attend the farewell dinner. I was having lunch that day with Kelly when we got word that a ship had gone down up north and a pilot was killed. I asked for his name. Kelly wondered why I wanted to know that. I told that I had some flight school friends up there including a close friend who was my buddy in flight school. He remarked it is better not to ask for names in this business. I worried about the coldness of the remark but figured *that three wars might do that to you.*

That evening, he and I and a recently arrived chaplain were sitting together listening to the Stilwell farewells. I had never seen Kelly so animated. He was by nature a quiet private man, but this night he was cheerful. He read between the lines of the speeches and his remarks were colorful and his language rather earthy. The chaplain winced on more than one occasion.

At their last meeting, Kelly presented Stilwell with a plaque decorated with five red crosses and the tail numbers of our aircraft. He told Stilwell, "General, you wanted my aircraft so bad, here they are." I have a picture of that encounter, and Stilwell is smiling. I don't think the Dust Off issue was settled by then, but Kelly had his antagonist at bay. For all their differences, I always felt there was something rather special between Kelly and Stilwell.

I took Kelly back to Soc Trang after Stilwell's farewell and once again bugged him about his promise to let me have Detachment A. I was shocked when he said I could take over on 1 July. I think he was concerned about the fight for Dust Off and had finally decided he should be in Saigon for that battle.

I can still remember the cold chill I felt in in my belly when we got word that Kelly was down. We all raced for our birds and headed for the Delta. On the way down we monitored the operation. A slick (troop-carrying helicopter) went in and got the Dust Off, and we heard they were safe at Vinh Long. We all breathed a sigh of relief, and I remember smiling to myself as I thought about Kelly's reaction to being picked up by a slick.

I saw a lone Dust Off on the ramp at Vinh Long and another parked behind it. One of our pilots was sitting in the door. I was in a cheerful mood until I noticed he was crying. Then I the saw the body bag behind him. Before I could say anything, he nodded at the bag and said it was Kelly. All the air went out of my body, and I sank down beside him. He had come through so many tight spots, so close so many times, that it never occurred to me that they could kill him. The reality just shook me.

He had gone into a supposedly secure area for some urgent wounded—one of them a U.S. soldier. Once on the ground, they began drawing fire. It was not unusual in those days to take fire out of friendly lines. The ground forces screamed at Kelly to get out. He replied in his quiet Georgia drawl, "When I have your wounded." His next words were "My God," and he curled up from a single bullet shot right through his heart. The ship curled with him, and the rotors beat it to pieces. The crew got out safely but would not leave until they dragged Kelly out. There was a U.S. physician on board, and he declared Kelly dead on the spot. Then they were rescued.

They had only been at Vinh Long a few minutes before I got there, and the same people were yelling for a Dust Off to come back for the urgent patients Kelly was killed trying to rescue. I recall Kelly's deputy, now our new commander, rushing over to us as we sat there in silent numbness. He began to shout and wave and give orders and question why we sat while there were patients in the field. I can remember rousing from my stupor and becoming outraged at his insensitivity to what had happened to

Kelly. They had been friends for years. He saw my anger and said simply and quietly, "it's over; it's done; and we've got work to do."

He was right. Kelly was probably smiling in the body bag behind us. We cranked up and went back for Kelly's patients. That area is so clear in my mind. Kelly's ship was still burning, the area still called secure and the patients still classified urgent. We were landing beside the burning Dust Off when our ship took several rounds, probably the same folks who shot Kelly. We jumped over a tree line, checked to ensure we were still flyable and went back.

This time we made a tactical approach, found some cover and retrieved the patients. The U.S. patient walked to the aircraft carrying a bag. All the patients were ambulatory. None was urgent. I was told that one was coming out of the field to go on R&R.

I stayed in Kelly's room that night and slept in his bed. I remember sitting at his desk writing up the missions of that day. It was 1 July, 1964, and I was finally the commander of Detachment A, just as Kelly had promised. He was the 149th American killed in Vietnam, and the outcry was overwhelming. I think it was then that we all realized how revered he was in the Delta.

You will read more about MG Brady in Mission 21 of this book.

This author highly recommends the book "Rescue Under Fire, The Story of Dust Off in Vietnam" by John L. Cook. It is a very definitive history of Dustoff and goes into much detail about Dustoff, Major Kelly and (now) MG Brady. Schiffer Military/Aviation History, Atglen, PA.

From very early in the Vietnam War, I offer this Mission, set in 1963:

Mission 2

All in a Day's Work

By: <u>Charlie Ostick</u>

"There are old pilots and there are bold pilots but there are no old, bold pilots."

Mr. Ketchum, my flight instructor at the helicopter primary flight course, Camp Wolters, Texas, often said these words when he was talking safety to us aviation students.

"All In a Day's Work"... a story about 22 July 1963.

0425 – Reveille
0500 – Chow
0530 – Flight Line
0600 – Start engines and line up for take off
0605 – Take off (from Tan Son Nhut – that's the main airport near Saigon in South Vietnam)
This day is about a mission for the Utility Tactical Transport Helicopter Company (UTT). The UTT was the Army's first armed helicopter unit. You can see that we started really early on mission days by getting up and hurrying to the flight line. When we

got to the flight line, we would perform our preflight inspections, load our weapons systems and brief our crews. Our flight crews at the UTT consisted of a pilot, a copilot, a crew chief and a door gunner. Often, when we went out on these gunship missions, we would have a strap hanger from headquarters or someone from a newspaper or a television station or a CBS reporter.

We started the mission just after we lined up for takeoff at 0600. The Hueys that we were flying were UH-1A's, which was an older model, and the UH-1B's, which we had brought in C-124's from CONUS much earlier in the spring. The B models had more power and could actually hover with a fully loaded helicopter with a full crew and a full load of fuel on board. Now the UH-1A's were a different story – they could hardly hover at all and we often struggled to get them off the ground. We would literally bounce along the ground because we could not hover without losing RPM. As we bounced and skidded along the hard runways we would get enough speed that we could go through translational lift.

Translational lift is when the rotor blades get additional lift because of the forward speed of the helicopter. When you would hit translational lift you could actually get about 200 feet per minute climb and you could gain altitude. Then, as you burned off fuel, things got better and better in the A models. The B models generally could take off fairly well and complete their mission. On this day I was flying a UH-1B armed with quad machine guns – that's four M-60C machine guns mounted on a flexible hydraulic/electric mount- and I had a load of eight 2.75 inch rockets on each side.

The mission was to support the ARVN (which stands for the Army of the Republic of Vietnam) at a little airstrip near Nui Ba Den. The H-21's had flown up with the ARVN. While they were on a sweep north of the city the ARVN had captured an arms factory. During a lull in the battle, a couple of us pilots had taken a jeep and had gone over to the factory to have a look around. In this arms factory was a small, roughed out, crude classroom. In the classroom on a string across the front was a cut-out of a UH-1 helicopter – looked just like our Hueys. Tied in front of the helicopters at two helicopter lengths was a bull's-eye on the same string. The instructor would pull the helicopter and the bull's-eye across the classroom and the students were taught to fire at the bull's-eye and not at the helicopter. This technique would thereby give them a two helicopter lead on a moving helicopter as they were firing at it. This is much like duck hunting, you don't fire directly at the duck in order to shoot it, you fire in front of the duck a couple of leads and you will probably hit it because the duck will fly into your buckshot. The same principle applies to shooting down helicopters. It works very well. You shoot a couple leads in front of them and guess what, at 60 -80 knots they will fly right into your bullets. This story about the classroom target practice will become more important later in this story.

We were still supporting the ARVN when they got into a firefight just west of the arms factory near Nui Ba Den. As we were supporting them with machine and rocket fire and had neutralized the target area. A bullet came into our chopper and shot off the anti-torque control pedals on my copilot's right foot. Needless to say his other foot went all the way out. We thought we had lost our tail rotor as the Huey swerved out of control. We had quite an exciting moment while we tried to figure out what had happened to our chopper and I regained control.

We had gone back to Nui Ba Den and refueled, rearmed, and repaired the pedal in preparation for another mission. In the meantime, a Vietnamese Ranger Battalion had been attacked just south of where we were at a little village called Ben Suc. I was serving as aircraft commander and flight leader of team of two helicopters. I had a copilot, door gunner, and crew chief on board. We had participated in several firing runs over this area against the Vietcong positions and we were doing a good job of suppressing their activities. Our platoon leader had been hit by hostile fire and he was forced to go back to Nui Ba Den. On his way back, he radioed and directed me to take over command of the platoon.

I led several more attacks against the VC. We were directing very effective machine gun and rocket fire and we had neutralized many enemy positions. When our ordinance was nearly expended and we couldn't make any more firing passes, I volunteered to evacuate critically wounded Vietnamese Army Rangers from the battle area. We were landing to load the wounded less than 100 meters from the enemy firing positions. Just as we were preparing to depart and I was to applying power, a Vietcong soldier pops up along the tree line. He had a long-barreled shotgun. He pointed the shotgun directly at the chopper – it looked to me like it was pointing straight at me – and then he took two leads. You could just see him counting in his mind. He pointed the shotgun at the chopper and then he took two leads – he just went bump, bump - then he fired his shotgun in front of our chopper. My door gunner on that side was very effective and that particular VC soldier never fired again. To this day, I thank that VC classroom instructor for drilling into those Vietcong soldiers how important it is to take two leads when you are going to shoot down a helicopter. It doesn't matter that it is sitting on the ground and not moving but thank goodness for the over trained Vietcong. I think I am here today because of that instructor who was teaching that class. We had pulled out of that landing zone with some difficulty because not only had they put wounded on, they had also loaded some dead soldiers on and we were probably overloaded. But we were able to struggle out of the little clearing near Ben Suc and head back to Tan Son Nhut and safety.

When we landed on the flight line at Tan Son Nhut, I was not surprised but I was a bit concerned because there were seventeen bullet holes in our chopper. Almost all of them were in the tail boom because the VC had not yet figured out how to shoot down choppers. Some of the holes were in the rotor blades too. We got home about sunset. That was a long twelve-hour day. Later, I was presented a Distinguished Flying Cross for this action.

Charlie Ostick. Note weapons system; 8 shot rockets and twin M60 machine guns on each side. The machine guns flex with a control hanging above the left pilot's seat and the fixed rockets are fired from the right seat.

Mission 3

We Had Survived the Fall

By Paul Harpole

Dustoff Crew Chief

We had survived the fall. The ship was badly damaged. We had heard the tearing of metal just as we lurched forward, while the motion of the crash sank us deep into the oozing mud of this water-filled rice paddy. That is when silence replaced the screams of our wounded passengers; they had imagined this was their last moment on earth.

They had heard the engine go silent and felt, deep in the pit of their stomachs, the initial fall. It was their first roll-a-coaster ride and to these native rice farmers of the Delta, it was uninvited. There was no preparation for them as they witnessed us scramble half way out on the skids leaning out into the darkness around the litter racks to close the doors, to secure loose items, to pray. They had seen our faces, as the medic and I moved about the ship, in the dim light of night to inadequately prepare for the final moments of flight. They looked with us, down, down toward the darkened landscape of shadows in the dark of night and they understood without words exchanged, we were going to crash. The fall is quick. They had come aboard this loud machine to ride away from a war. Their wounds gave them a ticket to presumed safety. Their screams accompanying the simultaneous sound of metal tearing confirmed there was no safety here.

Everything was dark now as we hit the rice paddy, no lights survived our fall. The Huey's battery is contained in the tail-boom inside the battery compartment. I hadn't yet realized that the entire tail-boom had stuck in the mud as we flared to increase rotor speed and then quickly convert the rotor speed into lift to cushion the fall from nineteen hundred feet. The boom had stuck so deep and hard that the mud wouldn't release our tail as we rocked forward. The boom had torn completely off the rest of the ship, the battery was gone, the lights were gone. Our new instant silence was enclosed in darkness.

We all climbed off each other. The medic and I struggled to slide the rear doors partially open. The mud and water of the rice paddy that had cushioned our fall, saving us, now began to encumber us. The mud was thick and dark and stunk of the rotting vegetation, a smell that permeated so much of our breathing here in the Delta. The oozing mess came to within a foot of the floor of the ship. Every time we moved the mud attached itself and immediately began to envelope every part of us and our equipment and our patients. We removed our helmets. These peasant rice farmers were in their environment now and were prepared for this. Now we were the unprepared. They instinctively didn't get out. They moved slightly for some semblance of comfort, but stayed put. We diagnosed one broken leg to add to our list of injuries. Not much price to exact for this fall.

The ship's floor began to get slippery with a film of mud and water. I found the only weapon we had, my M-16, tucked behind me. The medic's seat and mine consisted of a simple armor plate; about 18 inches square, lying loose on the ship's floor. The darkness and shuffling of the crash didn't change my instinctive reach for the primary survival tool we had, that M-16. Then I reached up to the cubbyholes on my left. I felt the two ammo clips I had stored there. One went quickly in the M-16, the other in the top pocket of my jungle fatigues. Our medic didn't bring an M-16 with him in the quick switch of medics back at the aid station pad earlier. We had successfully evacuated our patient's neighbors on two earlier missions this night. The more severely wounded had gone out on the first two loads. Now we, the crew were unprepared for this new mission, to survive in the delta until we are found. Who would find us first?

We had to get out in the mud to open the pilots' doors. The pilots are somewhat protected by armor plates that encompass their head, sides, and back. Each time we departed on a mission the medic and crew chief would slide one piece of armor forward on the side of the seat to protect the pilot's side, then we shut the ships front doors and latch them. Now that protective armor trapped them, keeping them from a quick exit from the pilot and copilots seats. The depth of water and thick grabbing mud shocked me as I slid, more than stepped, out of the ship. I felt it ooze inside my combat boots. I couldn't lift my foot out of the mud. I thought of the old Lassie TV show with the terror of quicksand and Jimmy being saved by Lassie. Stupid, the ship had stopped sinking, you aren't going to be sucked under, and Lassie wasn't here tonight to save us.

I finally got my foot loose and twisted my body back towards the ship. I announced it would take a minute to extract them, our slightly claustrophobic pilots. My other foot was now wedged deep in a mud's grip and the process of moving continued slowly as I moved painfully slowly to release my Pilot. The medic struggled similarly on his side. The water was cool, but not cold. The pilots door came open with a quick downward flip of the door handle and my now wet and muddy hands dripped and slipped as they struggled to release the pin that held the armor in place. It popped up and the armor slid to the rear. He was out of his seat belt.

I moved back through the mud to extract the ammo can from under the hellhole seats, which were behind the litter racks and face out towards the side of the ship.   These seats now held three small peasants with bandaged frag wounds. I slid the door the rest of the way open past these patients and struggled to move their feet, which blocked my access to the ammo-can under the seat. I grabbed it and yanked it out. It was very noisy, they always were, but now it echoed loudly in my mind and I wondered who else might hear it in the nearby tree lines as they moved toward this crash that had unexpectedly disturbed the night and the rest that they held dear. Who was investigating our crash? How far away were they? Were they in the nearby tree line or somewhere between that point and our base? We were just due back now. I hoped friendlies would win the midnight race to find us first and deal with us.

The co-pilot and medic were struggling through the mud to get around to Warrant Officer Nice and I.

The "book" said to evacuate the ship with all of the radios and patients and set up a defensive perimeter close by. How the hell were we supposed to move thirteen patients through the mud to high ground, which consisted of a dike that was six to twelve inches elevated, narrow, wide enough to walk on, but a crazy place to put twelve patients? Mr. Nice was reconnoitering our situation. He asked me what we had in the way of survival equipment on my ship. Not much, just three pen flares that fit in your pocket to signal aircraft at fairly close range. That and a couple of smoke grenades that would work fine if it were daylight. I hoped we would be out of here long before then.

It was about ten thirty in the evening. Mr. Nice asked me to get my pen flares ready to use in case we saw an aircraft in sight to signal. I fumbled around in the cubbyholes, grabbed them and put them in my other fatigue shirt chest pocket. It was the only part of my clothing not soaking wet. I had the M-16 in hand and the can of ammo, poised to move towards safety. Where was it?

Mr. Nice decided that we could see a dike about seventy-to-eighty feet to the east on my side of the ship. He told me to go over to the dike and set up the eastern perimeter. I said, "Fine" and started slogging through the mud. He, the pilot, and medic checked the patients and looked over the dilemma of the severed tail boom. As I trudged through the mud I began to wonder what the other perimeter would look like without a weapon. I reached the dike and lifted one leg high out of the mud to plant it on the dike. As I put my other foot ahead and felt for terra firma it slipped and slipped, down forward into another muddy embankment into a canal. The dark-looking dike-line had fooled us all. It was no dike.

It was a canal, which was now four feet deep and getting deeper as I slid further. To rescue the M-16 and ammo can I flung them over my head and behind me as I continued to slip down the mud embankment. The water went over my head and I released the ammo can and weapon even though they were my anchor, planted into the mud top of this natural "slip and slide". My feet scrambled under me as I pressed my back into the mud embankment. I got my head above water and turned over to face the bank. I scrambled out. My weapon was now coated with a natural camouflage of thick mud and slime. I yanked the ammo can out of the mud and got to my feet, stepped back into the rice paddy and moved back towards the ship, and the crew, who were concerned and stifling a laugh.

It was too serious a time to respond much to this utterly laughable experience. I was colder now, but not too cold. It was like when you get out of the swimming pool. My clothes clung to me. I had the weapon and the ammo can. I checked for the pen flares. They were in my pocket where I had deposited them before the canal incident. I cleared the breach of the M-16, attempted to get any water out of it and clear the mud from the firing mechanism with medical gauze. At this point everything was coated in mud and dripping it.

We reconnoitered again. We talked about the possibility of rescue. We talked about what to do if a ship came overhead. Mr. Nice told me to get the pen flare ready. We talked while I got it out. It consisted of a holder, the pen part, three cartridges held in a plastic magazine and attached by a cord to the pen. I took off a flare cartridge from the magazine. I looked the pen over. I had never really loaded one of these things. I thought for a minute; screw on the flair then cock the spring into the locked cam position, or cock it and then screw the flair in. I didn't like the idea of screwing the flair onto a cocked pen. It looked like it could go off and explode threw my hand. I screwed it on and began to slide the cocking knob back. We were standing near the pilot's door in a sort of triangle. The medic was in the ship looking at patients.

In the dark I was trying to see how far back the spring pulled before shifting it to the side into the cam lock. The mud and slim took a terrible toll. My finger slipped off the cam. It exploded and flew out horizontally between the two pilots, just past Mr. Nice's face and off into a tree line. The fire and noise could be seen and heard for eternity. I was happy I hadn't blown Mr. Nice's head off. But I figured I had killed us all. Anyone who had some curiosity about the earlier noise of crashing and had not carried the investigation too far, I figured was now up and on the move towards us. I apologized and hung my head. It was not like in the movies. Mr. Nice told me to forget it.

We moved out to the front of the ship. We could see another canal or dike on the western perimeter, about seventy or so feet away. The tree lines nearest us were over there too, north about five hundred meters and southwest about fifteen hundred meters. We had seen a village about one mile southwest. If we were going to be approached that was the direction it would come from. Mr. Nice told me to move over there with the weapon and ammo and one of them would follow. The other two would go to a clump of bush to the northeast about one hundred feet.

We all saw it at once, a light flashed out of the trees way southwest of our position near that village. We froze. It was a light and now it was gone. Mr. Nice said in a low tone, "Keep going and get set up and we'll see if there is any movement down there." I kept moving to the dike. When I got there I felt with my foot and again it was a canal. I lay down on my stomach and slipped into the canal. I was under water to mid-chest. This dike I was looking down in the direction of the light went straight south. It connected to other dikes and ran to the village. I patted and dried the dike in front of me. It was just thicker mud. I had a clip in the M-16. I took out the other from my pocket, laying it on top of the ammo can in a ready position.

Mr. Nice said they were going to stay put by the ship for a while, which was fine with me. I could be quiet there by myself. I had the only weapon and Mr. Nice had the final two flares. We knew how to load them now. There were some low bushes of some sort off the dike to the south, which gave me slight cover, I thought. Right in front of me was the ship. There were still thirteen very anxious Vietnamese sitting there talking to each other; we couldn't understand a thing they said. Fortunately they were not critically wounded. In fact, we had injured a couple of these patients on our prior trip into evacuate their neighbors.

The scene was surreal. Mortars were flashing in the village about 500 meters south of our pick up LZ. The noise had been deafening to them and we knew it had been going on for hours. This was our second trip into the LZ. The LZ was loaded with people and they were clamoring to get aboard. We succeeded by getting in and out quickly. The controller had followed us with our transponder and said, "Dust Off, you are getting very near the red line." In fact, the village was across the "red line." We had it plotted about one and a half miles into Cambodia. I didn't know what radio relay had given us the missions.

Typically a unit or a militia would radio in causalities to an American Military Assistance Command Vietnam, MACV, advisor. He would call in the Dust Off and we would go. When we got near the area of the pickup the MACV advisor would relay calls to the unit directing us in. Right down to the flashing of lights or ground or aerial flare to call us in. If it was a tight spot, lots of trees, or in the jungle we could also request the guys on the ground to call in artillery parachute flares. They exploded about 1000 to 1500 feet up and slowly parachuted down to illuminate the area so we could get in. All this I'm sure was pretty frightening to the average peasant rice farmer. We weren't known for our stealth either. Damn noisy describes us.

They all wanted out of this LZ and they shoved and fought to the door nearest them, which was mine, to get out of this madness. We had filled the ship with all we could lift on the first run. It may have been twenty. On the second trip I began to worry that the mortars could be easily redirected to the LZ. Speed was important. The ship was full. We lifted and they clung to the skids and we settled down, luckily not crushing anyone. The medic crawled across the wounded to help knock them off the skids so we could go. We had shed the proper number and we lifted. They clamored to grab on. I reached for my "gook getter", a sort of small baseball bat we had fashioned. I only had to raise it, in the past and they scattered. Now they wrapped their arms around the skids. I smacked their arms and hands; some fell three feet or so to the ground. Two persisted and we couldn't go. Finally I pried one off as I hung out and down to the skids. My medic held me in. Not meaning to, I struck the last one on his head as he wiggled and fought to stay attached. He fell away and we flew east, out of Cambodia. He was one of the first to load on the third and last trip in there, bandage on his head. I looked underneath his bandage; there was nothing too bad there.

He seemed not to remember me. He wanted out. He got part way out. He hadn't bargained for this shortened trip. He was in that ship as I looked over and alternately down the dike line, south.

Now I settled in. I slid down to see how far I could get into the water, up to my neck if I wanted or deeper. I thought I felt things crawling on me and I didn't care. I couldn't see the rest of the crew now. They had moved off to the northeast corner of the ship. Then there was another light. It went off quickly. I thought I'd never heard of VC or NVA with flashlights. This was a good sign. Then I checked the credentials of whoever had said that. Hell, I couldn't even remember who had said that. I sure wasn't going to stake my life on it. "Stay right where you are." I thought.

Then they came. I saw shadows moving, running and then running back. They were on an east-west dike-line moving out of the village towards my dike-line. They were very distant; still their voices carried. I could hear them chattering occasionally. They began to move out east, then up the long dike-line that I claimed as mine. They moved very, very slowly; tiny shadows, movements undistinguishable, but out there. They were all I had to look at. I tried in vain to count them, but couldn't. I looked at my situation again while I waited. There were only two clips out. Hell, I needed to open the ammo box. I needed to remain silent too. I struggled with the latch and the metal lid popped. It was partially open, the noise to me was deafening. Had they heard and had I given away my position? I finished opening the lid. It continued to make noise. I took out several magazines and laid them out on the dike, also arranging them in the ammo box. I looked at my weapon checking the operation, but I knew it.

We had shot at sharks in the South China Sea, diverting between Vung Tau and the Baria Mountains, then into Nui Dat. Hell, now this might be for real! We weren't versed in weapons; our tools were speed and bandages. We were unprepared to be on the ground. I didn't feel I had much chance, but I would damn sure try. I watched them move somewhere on my dike; others were on the east-west dike. There were about twenty to thirty of them. I saw weapons. They were still distant and the moonlight was medium. My night vision was now at it's best. There had been no lights for about three hours. They kept coming; slowly, talking, stopping, moving.

They were unsure. I thought very carefully, considering my options. I had plenty of ammo, surely enough; if they fired at me, I would not be out before they killed me. It was thirty or so to one. I had made a serious pact with myself not to be taken. I wouldn't. If they were friendlies I must be very careful. They had no idea who I was, hiding in the canal. Moving was out of the question. I would just draw unwanted attention. Besides, if there was a fight, the crew might get away to the north. I didn't know if they had gone far or not. I wanted them to be able to, though.

They moved straight towards me north up the dike. Many men and many weapons. They walked. We could not communicate. They were just shadows. The quiet murmur of speech in the ship was gone. There was silence. They were worried just as I was, who was coming. Now they were only about five hundred yards south. A couple of them retreated back south towards the village. Each carried a weapon. I saw silhouettes of the guns as they moved towards me. A couple looked like old carbines. I saw no AK-47 outlines, which were very distinctive, with their curved banana clip. I found no real comfort in any of this. I was committed to ride this out. I could not act first, but if there was any shooting I wasn't going to ask any questions.

I checked the automatic setting on my M-16. They continued up the dike, then, suddenly the leaders stepped off into the rice paddy. Each person followed, stepping in; they were about one hundred yards away. They began to stretch out across the rice paddy. They readied their weapons, and my heart sunk. They kept coming but no one was on the dike now, they trudged towards the ship. They heard the Vietnamese murmuring among themselves but the two groups weren't communicating with each other. I didn't think this was good. I readied my ammo. I had slipped deeper into the water, barely exposed now. I had a perfect field of fire. They hadn't detected me and I swept my weapon across the silhouettes in preparation.

While they were coming up the dike-line during that slow walk I had made my peace and said goodbye to everyone. I missed them again tonight. I counted them off; Mom, Kath, Tom, Jer, Marg, Bill, Maureen, John, and Phil. I thought of my grandparents. I had thought they might die while I was over here, hadn't considered beating them. Then Mary Ann, I hadn't written in a while. She had backed off writing a little too. Mom had written about every three days. She was faithful to us all. I knew everything that happened at home. There was plenty in our large family. I had said goodbye, but I prayed I'd see them again.

Suddenly the patients began to talk to the men in the rice paddy, who moved faster towards the ship. Don't do anything, I told myself again. If they were enemy, things would unfold quickly enough. If they were friendlies, I didn't want to be discovered by some nervous militia afraid of an ambush with a deadly reaction to me. They kept moving slowly, because of the mud, towards the ship. They were fifteen yards away when the shouting between the groups intensified. Then a woman sitting in the door on my side of the ship screamed something and pointed right at me.

Everyone turned towards me and started moving my direction. The mud became my friend. It slowed them. I could see them, weapons ready, slogging towards me. I held my breath and fire. I was dead if I reacted wrong. My finger alternately moved on and off the trigger, then it held. The back of my trigger finger was pressed against the front of the trigger guard; I couldn't afford to slip again like in the pen flare incident. They were still cautious as they came closer. They saw me now and didn't shoot. Thank God, but I was paranoid, now sunk down in this watery canal. I kept my weapon trained on them and they on me. They began to flank my position. I could no longer keep them all in my field of fire. Finally one was leaning over me. He reached out, and I sighed slightly. I would not give up my pose. One reached for my ammo can. I waved him off and hollered, "No, no." Then I was on my knees. I was saying, "You good, you good, you good?" Like they were going to throw down their arms and surrender to me. I was losing it. I was exhausted. I was wet. I was safe. One man helped me as he said, "Captain Tomarocki radioed MACV advisor." He struggled with the words. Captain Tomaroki's name sounded Japanese. I'm sure I misheard it. He was an angel by any name.

We made our way to the other side of the ship. The rest of the crew was coming out of the brush and across the rice paddy. We were reassured our position had been relayed back to our base. So now we waited. We stripped the radios from their compartment trays in the nose. The tail-boom held other radios and set them in the ship by the door. It was now about 2:30 AM Dec 9th. As I cleaned out the ship I came across our survival tool, which was a blunt machete type tool with a hook blade built in on one side and a knife blade on the other. The hook was designed for quickly tearing at brush. I offered the tool as a reward to one of our new friends. I wasn't sure he understood what the hell I was doing but he took it as we waited.

Then the distinctive wap, wap in the air, way off, a ship. They came in circled once and landed. We loaded patients. Carried them to a wide spot on the dike where the ship balanced as we weighted it down. We carried the patients from one ship to another. While they were muddy they had not set foot in the muck. The radios went. The patients, our crew and the crew that came to get us, there where twenty-one aboard. The ship shook, it sensed we wanted out, the aircraft commander balanced his tug on the collective with a forward nudge to the cyclic and we moved, bounced twice into transnational lift then flight. We were out, clear of the mud and brush, then tree lines, then into the night sky.

Back thirty miles in moments, we reflected and could not fathom our good fortune. We dropped our patients, now finished with their detour, they were at the aid station, not a hospital, but adequate and safe. They were excited, pleased. I was dropped where my ship would come tomorrow. I found a hutch, there was a bed. My gear, my mud, was piled outside. I flopped and slept. Five thirty, my eyes opened to dawn and sergeant stripes hollering in my face, "Was that my gear outside?" I thought nothing of what he said. I opened my eyes to wonder if I was in heaven or hell. I didn't know. Then I smiled, got up, and smiled all day. I began a new life.

Paul Harpole working the hoist. Photos courtesy Paul Harpole.

Hand in the hole in the door. I hollered, "Break hard left sir" when I saw an unexpected NVA in a pith helmet pick up his rifle and aim at us as he passed over, low level, leaving a supposed "cold LZ". We had disturbed his breakfast in his camp. Pilot broke hard left instantly and bullet meant for me, instead split the door open as we banked away from danger. Scared me but I was fine after thinking the shrapnel from the door and the bullet had hit me. Medic checked me out and we all laughed our way home shaken by a bit of a close call. Bullet missed and shrapnel bounced off my fatigues. No body damage.

THE WALL

By Paul Harpole

We didn't know their names....

I look at the wall to see their names,

The reflection is so clear—

we know their faces....

We rescued their bodies,

we didn't know their names.

We evacuated them—"Dust Off!"

--we didn't know their names.

their bodies were torn....

Their families heard their names....

after we did our job.

Too much noise to hear their names

 on our chopper.

We knew their faces—

surely not as their families did.

They were much older today.

Their families knew them,

we only saw them....

They had lived in the boonies—

no comfort there....

No comfort on our ship.

The red cross brought no real

comfort to them.

Yes, we brought relief and aid,

but pain came with it too—

to them....and to us.

I hope their pain is gone now....

but I know it is not—

until we are....

We see their faces lying on our ship,

which is covered with their blood....

and those from the prior days.

Thirty years have passed, and yet not a day.

We see the reflection of each face in the names.

THE WALL!

They begin to come together now.

Some day, that God knows of,

we will put the faces with the names....

<u>Then</u> we will rest...

.--Veterans day 1998--

Paul Harpole

Crew Chief

45th Dust Off Air Ambulance

Mission 4

Mission Nightmare

By Steve Vermillion

The story that you are about to read is completely true, although you may think it quite unbelievable. Some people say that we should have never attempted the mission, but under the circumstances, we could not have refused. Our primary mission was to rescue injured people and we felt compelled to make as many attempts as necessary to bring this mission to a successful end or before making a decision to not make any further attempts until the situation made a reasonable change in our favor. Read this story, put yourself in the cockpit and make your own decision. The crew makeup; both pilots were experienced aircraft commanders with an estimated 1200 hours of combined time as aircraft commanders. For this nighttime mission, one pilot who had other non-flying regular duties, would often join a crew in order to log flight time thereby bumping the "co-pilot" for the remainder of the night standby missions. Onboard were an experienced flight medic and crewchief. Aircraft type was a UH-1H.

We were asleep on this eventful night when the radio telephone operator [RTO] called and told us we had an urgent mission. Hurrying down to the alert shack, we discovered we had two US soldiers that had received one or more traumatic amputations due to a mortar round going off prematurely in the tube.

Their need for evacuation was classified as urgent.

As we proceeded east out of Long Binh, we plotted the landing zone [LZ] right on top of Giah Rey Mountain, just a mile or so Northeast of Xuan Loc. The mountain served as a robust communications site on top while the US Military also maintained a base camp at the foot of the mountain on its eastern side. Not known to us by fact but more by assumption was that the NVA occupied the vertical space in between for the same purposes. As we approached the mountain from the west in clear skies without lunar illumination, we could see that a stratus type cloud layer was forming around its top and extending a bit beyond its leeward side. Elsewhere, it was perfectly clear with unlimited visibility. Climbing to 4000' above Mean Sea Level, MSL, I ensured that all of our instruments were still functioning properly and set for IFR conditions.

As we arrived on station, our initial observations regarding the cloud formation were confirmed. The top of the mountain was not visible due to the cloud layer which was also enveloping its lateral sides as well. While in route, we had made contact with the ground unit. They advised we had two critically injured soldiers who needed immediate evacuation. Our landing point was an improved helipad with several communications towers to the east of the landing pad creating vertical obstacles to our approach. They reported zero visibility on the mountain due to the cloud layer and winds were out of the west.

After surveying our situation, we notified the ground unit that the chance of being able to land at their location was slim at best due to the enveloping cloud.   Before we got another word out about possible options, the ground unit's RTO became slightly incoherent. All he could say was for us 'to come in and land and pick up the wounded.' Also on the same push was an emotionally charged doctor from Xuan Loc who kept telling us that if we didn't make the pickup, the men were sure to die.

We were able to get the ground commander on the radio and talk the situation over with him. His solution was to have us hover generally over his location and he would talk us down through the clouds using the sound of the aircraft for reference. Pretty much a hovering vertical GCA approach without the use of radar and a highly skilled controller was not a favored choice of either of us sitting in the Huey cockpit that night. Our first option was to see if we could hover up the side of the mountain and hopefully slip under the cloud layer. We made several attempts at hovering up mountain side only to end up going inadvertent IFR and having to make a hovering IFR turn and climb to hopefully clear skies. Compounding the problem for these approaches was wind speed swirling and moving over the trees making it difficult to hover. We flew low along the slope of the mountain with our searchlight and landing lights on until we found what appeared to be a draw that may lead us to the top. Hovering up the semi-draw with our lights on, moving one tree to the next attempting to maintain a visual reference point, only led us to the end of the draw where we became enveloped in zero-zero conditions. From a hover over one tree as a reference point, we made a 180 degree turn to the south and then made an Instrument Take Off, ITO, until we once again hit clear skies.

Climbing clear and back to VFR on top, letting the adrenalin settle a bit, we asked the ground commander if he had any way of illuminating the landing spot at his location. They said they had found a limited number of "spooky flares". Not sure what "spooky flares" are, but this certainly looked like a reasonable option from our end. They put three flares into a triangular shape and ignited them. They were easily seen from our location on top of the clouds, so we advised the commander we would attempt the approach.

We decided that given the head winds from the west and the need for a quick steep approach, we would use 50 Knots Indicated Air Speed, KIAS, during our descent. As we started our first approach, the left seat pilot was making the approach, due to better external visibility, using the flares as his approach reference, while I stayed on the instruments in case IFR flight became necessary. Additionally, the left seat pilot was given verbal callouts of airspeed, vertical speed and altitude. Approximately half way through the approach, the flares went out, so we made a go-around climbing back to VFR on top for a second attempt. From that approach we determined the cloud layer was about 300 feet thick. The burn time on the illumination was around a minute and a half.

We just had to get our skids on the ground so that we could reach the wounded and from there we could make an instrument takeoff without any problem. The problem though was getting our skids on the ground.

Because of our low fuel state, we decided to refuel at either Xuan Loc or Blackhorse which was about ten minutes away depending on the weather. Since we had been on station over two hours, we found the cloud encompassing the mountain becoming thicker while expanding its mass in all directions. With the cooler night time air displacing the warmer surface air of the day, much of the area around Xuan Loc and Blackhorse was also fogged in with about a two hundred foot layer of cloud hanging on the deck. As we flew over the lower cloud layer, we were able to find a hole allowing visual contact with a road that was familiar to us. With our search light and landing light turned on, we slipped down through the hole and headed south along the dirt road towards Blackhorse. We were flying about 50 feet above the ground and 60 KIAS with all lights out except for our landing and search lights. We flew a rough time distance and heading calculation, picked up lights through the fog off to our west, and figuring this was Blackhorse, made a 90 degree turn to the west and headed there for fuel. It took a quick minute to orient ourselves coming through the low visibility and into the Blackhorse compound area to determine where we were and then make our way over to hot refuel. No doubt we pissed off some people by hovering around and over buildings and other structures as we headed to the refuel point.

While we were refueling, out hoist aircraft had been dispatched from Long Binh and was on station. After refueling, we made an instrument takeoff from Blackhorse, climbed to around 300 MSL heading back towards our mission location while continuing to climb to 4000 MSL,

circumnavigating the building cloud base around the mountain top. The hoist ship pilot couldn't complete the mission due to lack of hover reference point and in reality the lack of sufficient cable to reach the ground. What did happen though is they used up precious illumination flares in that attempt. The hoist ship departed and it was once again up to us to make this mission successful.

We decided to make another approach! The ground unit only had three flares remaining so this approach had to get us on the ground. On our previous approach, the flares went out about halfway through our descent, so our plan was to now hold a slower approach speed with a faster rate of descent in hope that we could reach the ground before the flares went out. The cloud layer was also thickening increasing the distance between us and the ground. Our only fiscal reference points were the burning flares, all other obstacles, towers, wires, etc. were hidden someplace within the cloud layer.

Beginning our descent into the top of the cloud layer, everything was going smoothly. As before, the left seat pilot was making the visual approach and I was on the instruments. Descending deeper into the cloud a radio tower passed by the right side of our aircraft, at first startling us but then giving us assurance we were probably within 75 feet of the ground. Seconds after passing the tower, the medic yelled out over the intercom that we moving backwards and towards the radio tower. The pilot reacted by lowering the nose and applying power. Our airspeed was around 40 KIAS and with an estimated 20 to 30 knot wind flowing over the mountain, we were good on speed and rate of descent.

What we were not good on was remaining burn time on the flares as shortly after making the power adjustments to avoid the communications tower, the flares went out leaving us in total darkness at 35 to 40 knots airspeed, 50 AGL or lower on top of a mountain top and close to one obstacle we knew about- the radio tower, and out of control.

As the pilot was struggling to gain control of the aircraft, and not wanting to relinquish control to me, I saw the instruments indicating the reality of the situation and wondering at the same time why we were still flying. The radio magnetic indicator [RMI] had rotated at least three times, the airspeed indicator was pegged on zero, and the low rpm audio was blaring in our headsets. Along with the attitude indicator alternating plus or minus 20 degrees in relation to the horizon, our altimeter read that we were 100 feet below the top of the mountain's highest point. The crewchief and medic were screaming that sand and leaves where swirling into the open cargo compartment. As quickly as we got ourselves into trouble, we popped out of one spot in the cloud and once again found ourselves in VFR conditions. We quickly got the aircraft back under control and took a few minutes moments to see if we were even still alive.

At some point in this ordeal, one of us got out a radio transmission of what was happening. We were brought back into reality by Dustoff Operations calling to see if we need any assistance. For a moment, we really weren't sure if it wasn't St. Peter heralding our arrival at the Golden Gates. After regaining our composure and our heart rates back in normal operating range, we orbited the mountain looking for another way to make the rescue. With no ground flares remaining to illuminate the landing zone and with the clouds getting thicker, we headed back to Long Binh after nearly five hours on station. Once on the ground, the crew chief realized that his complete toolbox had been thrown from the aircraft during our wild ride, along with some other miscellaneous items that had not been properly secured.

The next morning when the clouds over the mountain top began to break up, another aircraft from our unit was able to get in and lift the wounded soldiers out. To our joy, we found out that the two men were still alive. Our aircraft was gone over with a fine tooth comb and subsequently test flown to ensure we had not inflicted any structural or operational system damage to it. None was found, but the aircraft did experience an in-flight hydraulic failure within two days of that mission and it really never seemed to fly the same as it had before that night.

Since this mission occurred, I have frequently thought back and tried to analyze the decisions we made. How far beyond the 'envelope' had we extended ourselves where our 'experience' was more apt to have gotten us killed than providing a basis of success? Could we have gone further up the mountain side, hovering from tree to tree so to speak until we reached the top? Some say they could have done it while others say it was not possible. Without wind and a moving cloud layer, it might have been possible. But that night our collective experience said no. And the skeptic in me continues to ask the question, what was the true extent of the injuries of the two wounded soldiers? If they were that badly injured, someone on the ground did a superb job of keeping them alive for another eight hours until our sister ship was able to reach them the next morning.

To this date, I am sure it was only a miracle that we survived this experience. I really can't say how close we actually came to the mountain top or exactly what our aircraft was doing for those few long seconds between loss of control and breaking out in the clear. I suppose the only person who actually knows what happened is the Being who was flying as our "copilot."

Steve Vermillion. "Magnet Ass 11 II Dustoff 40" on the back of the helmet. Note weapon holster thrown over his shoulder.

Mission 5

REMEMBERING AUGUST 20, 1969, ON VETERANS DAY.

by Robert B. Robeson

When I first contacted Colonel Robeson for permission to use this story, he asked me when I served in Vietnam and what unit was I with. When I told him, he said "I met you in Da Nang." Quite frankly, I did not remember meeting him although I am certain that I did, and I was amazed that after 45 years, he remembered me! Hey, I have trouble remembering what I had for breakfast this morning, yet he remembered me, just another young Warrant Officer Dustoff pilot. I was impressed...thank you, Sir. So with great appreciation of his contributions to Dustoff as a pilot and also as a Commanding Officer, I offer you 3 missions that Col. Robeson so graciously allowed me to share with you. Phil

Here is his first story:

An intriguing chain of events began with a story titled "The Postcard," by Rocky Bleier (with David Eberhart) in the 2001 edition of Chicken Soup for the Veteran's Soul. It caught my attention as I was browsing through displays in a local bookstore in Lincoln, Nebraska. As I glanced at the first paragraph, the words "Hiep Duc, in the Que Son Valley," and "August 20, 1969," stopped me in my tracks. Instantly, these words brought back 31-year-old memories of danger, darkness and death.

On August 20, 1969, I was a U.S. Army Captain assigned to the 236th Medical Detachment (Helicopter Ambulance) in Da Nang, South Vietnam as operations officer and a medical evacuation pilot. Our mission entailed evacuating wounded (and dead) Americans, South Korean, South Vietnamese, Australian allies, Vietnamese civilians and often enemy soldiers to aid stations and hospitals in our 5,000-square-mile operational area.

From August 20-22, I had assigned myself as copilot to a field-site crew of four at Landing Zone (LZ) Baldy, approximately 25 miles south of Da Nang. Warrant Officer 1 William A. (Wild Bill) Statt was the aircraft commander, SP5 John N. Seebeth was our medic and SP5 Paul L. Sumrall was the crew chief. As a rookie pilot, I'd barely been in the unit and Vietnam a month.

What we weren't aware of was that we were about to be shoved into the middle of a major battle involving four regiments of the U.S. Army's 196th Light Infantry Brigade, two battalions of the U.S. 7th Marines and batteries of the U.S. 82nd Artillery that provided fire support from four firebases. These Americans were facing 1,500 Communist troops.*

In those 2½ days of devastating action, our crew evacuated 150 wounded Americans from the Que Son Valley on 42 missions, 15 of which were "insecure." This meant that our ground troops couldn't guarantee the safety of the LZ because the enemy was in contact and too close or friendlies were low on ammunition and couldn't provide appropriate covering fire. On a majority of these insecure missions, helicopter gunships were unavailable to cover our unarmed aircraft because there was too much action requiring their services in other parts of this battleground. So our only alternative was to take our chances and go in alone because most of the wounded wouldn't have survived if we'd have waited for gunships to arrive.

During late morning of August 21st, our UH-1H (Huey) was shot up by enemy AK-47 rifle fire while exiting another insecure LZ. One of our three patients was wounded for the second time. A burst of enemy fire ripped into a can of oil our crew chief kept under my armored seat, spraying this liquid over my Nomex, fire-retardant flight pants. Another round locked me in my shoulder harness when it clipped a wire on the unlocking device attached to the left side of my seat. After depositing our patients at the battalion aid station at LZ Baldy, a replacement bird and a different crew chief were flown down from Phu Bai (a medevac unit north of Da Nang) for our use.

Less than 24 hours later (August 22nd), we were shot up for the second time on another insecure mission. This one involved evacuating an African-American, infantry staff sergeant who'd been shot in the back. Seebeth was wounded in the throat as we made our hot-and-hairy tactical approach into the LZ. An AK-47 round tore out his larynx before we'd even landed. As we exited the landing zone with our original patient, who'd been literally thrown aboard by two of his comrades under heavy enemy fire, two of our three radios were also shot out.

In the aid station at LZ Baldy, Seebeth kept mouthing the words "I can't breathe" as he kicked his legs in frustration. I held his legs and attempted to calm him while Captain George Waters, M.D., performed a tracheotomy without anesthesia. The wound had swollen so fast that it was cutting off his oxygen. Time couldn't be wasted being concerned about alleviating his pain. Doc Waters immediately initiated an incision. Mercifully, Seebeth quickly lapsed from shock into unconsciousness.

John survived, but has endured twelve follow-up operations since then...one of which gave him back a voice. But it's not the same voice we'd known and grown to love as he provided emergency medical care to thousands of his patients. Today it's produced by a plastic Montgomery T-tube that's inserted into his tracheotomy opening. When he wants to talk, he must plug an opening on one end with a finger to force air through his mouth.

Since that first paragraph of Rocky Bleier's story in 2001 had caught my attention, I decided to do some research. I'd heard that Bleier had written an autobiography titled Fighting Back (with Terry O'Neil). In it, he'd written about his early life, the fact that he'd been drafted into the U.S. Army in 1968 and details concerning his subsequent service in Vietnam in 1969 where he was severely wounded in both legs. He also provided an inspiring story of how he overcame his wounds and a right foot that doctors thought, at one point, would have to be amputated. This ultimately led to Bleier being a part of four winning National Football League (NFL) Super Bowls as a starting running back with the Pittsburgh Steelers in 1974, 1975, 1978 and 1979.

Both the 1975 and revised/updated 1995 editions of Bleier's autobiography were out of print. So I contacted an out-of-print book dealer who was able to acquire a copy of the 1975 edition. I sat down to read the entire book as soon as it arrived in 2002. Before beginning the first chapter, I glanced at the "Contents" page. Chapter 7, titled "August 20, 1969," quickly caught my eye. This is when things became interesting and nearly unbelievable.

On August 20th, Bleier was an M-79 grenadier with the 196th Light Infantry Brigade of the Americal Division. He was wounded twice on this Wednesday near Million Dollar Hill (which gained its name and fame because a million dollar's worth of American helicopters were shot down there in one day) that was located east of the infamous village of Hiep Duc. His book described in detail how a "Dust Off" medevac helicopter had previously completed two missions to their location that night evacuating other wounded Company C members. Bleier was next to the last patient crammed into the cargo compartment on this third and final flight to be evacuated to LZ Baldy at 2:00 a.m. on Thursday the 21st. That's when it hit me.

I went to my military files and pulled out my combat flight records. Then I retrieved a citation for the Distinguished Flying Cross that our entire crew had been awarded for those traumatic 2½ days. Everything fit. Our unit's lone field-site was at LZ Baldy and I only assigned one flight crew there at a time. Hiep Duc and Million Dollar Hill were in our area of operations. That's when I recalled our crew landing on the same hilltop three times in one night during that period of time. We were obviously the crew that had evacuated Bleier and his other wounded infantry comrades from that ambush site during this chaotic night.

Ernest Hemingway wrote, "The world (and also combat) breaks everyone and afterward many are strong at the broken places." Perhaps this is what happened to Rocky Bleier, our flight crew and so many others in Vietnam. Adversity has a way of introducing you to yourself.

As soldiers (especially medevac crews, doctors, nurses and medics) we were all our brothers' and sisters' keepers...and still are to this day on different battle fronts. It was a fact that many of our brothers needed evacuation and immediate medical care during that horrific August 1969 night on Million Dollar Hill in Vietnam. I'll always be grateful that our crew was there and able to assist those courageous American warriors.

On this Veterans Day, I'm again reminded of how war changes veterans' lives forever in painful ways. Those who've experienced combat's physical and psychological pressure cooker know it can be like swimming with piranhas, great white sharks and moray eels in a sea of blood. Surviving in such an atmosphere is often as easy as attempting to perform disappearing magic tricks in front of a firing squad.

When we veterans returned home, and so many of our friends and comrades didn't, nagging doubts had the ability to creep into our minds about whether we really accomplished everything that we could have done. Survivor's guilt can overwhelm a combat veteran with an emotional tsunami just because he or she is still alive.

In my own case, I know how it feels to make a judgment error that cost a South Vietnamese lieutenant colonel (with seven children) his life. My crew could have saved him but, as aircraft commander, I failed to recognize the danger he was in quickly enough. Forget those other 987 missions that ended successfully. That particular incident continues to wend its way through my thoughts almost daily. I finally forgave myself for this personal blunder, many years later, but the survivor's guilt I internalized for so long etched this mistake deep into my conscience. How quick and easy war can destroy lives. Just the blink of an eye and their lights are extinguished forever.

A persistent voice in the back of my mind used to whisper a disturbing thought. "Why did you survive when so many others didn't?" I don't know the answer to that question and may never know in this lifetime. That's one of the reasons I became a writer. I've made it a personal goal to ensure that the legacies of courage, duty and dedicated service our military members have provided through over 234 years as a nation don't die and aren't swept into the dustbin of history.

I celebrate my combat survival, and over 27 years of military service on three continents that began at the age of 17 in La Grande, Oregon, by writing and publishing the truth about the heroism and sacrifices of military personnel that I've witnessed. That's because it's important to honor all veterans—dead and alive—who've served America in time of both war and peace.

Some of our fellow citizens, journalists, college professors and politicians apparently lack understanding about our warrior culture. They often fail to fully appreciate its deep loyalty to comrades, Ramboesque competitive nature, periodic paranoia (generated mostly by reality) and profound sense of service. I feel obligated to help educate them, whenever possible, about this magnificent "band of brothers and sisters."

A day seldom passes when I don't recall bloody scenes of young men sprawled on our cargo deck, most of whom were barely out of high school, and how they were cut down defending the freedoms of others before their own lives had barely begun. I think of all the milestones they never reached such as graduation from college, marriage, children...and old age with the rest of us. Remembering is a continuous act. I don't need Memorial Day or Veterans Day to remind me. Every day is Veterans Day in my world.

August 20, 1969 was merely another dangerous and dramatic day for so many in our country's history of sacrifice and service on behalf of others. But it taught me an important lesson. We never know who our actions might impact in this life or who might touch and influence us in return. And each time Memorial Day or Veterans Day rolls around, we can benefit ourselves and others by celebrating, acknowledging and never forgetting those who gave—and are still giving—their all in the fight for freedom around this planet. We forget their strength, courage and dedication at our nation's peril. Honoring their memories, missions and meritorious achievements is the least we can do for them, now and forever.

*Nolan, Keith, "Hiep Duc 'Death Valley,'" VFW,

(August 2008),p.39

ABOUT THE AUTHOR

Robert B. Robeson flew 987 combat medical evacuation missions in South Vietnam (1969-1970), helping to evacuate 2,533 patients. He had seven helicopters shot up by enemy fire and was twice shot down.

As a writer, he has been published over 725 times in 250 publications in 130 countries, which include the Reader's Digest, Positive Living, Vietnam Combat, Soldier of Fortune, Official Karate, Frontier Airline Magazine and Newsday, among others.

He's been awarded 15 George Washington Honor Medals for essays, articles and speeches on freedom by national award juries of the Freedoms Foundation at Valley Forge, Pa.

Robeson retired from the U.S. Army as a lieutenant colonel after 27½ years of military service on three continents. He's also been a newspaper managing editor and columnist and is now a full-time writer.

Mission 6

The Longest Night

By Robert Robeson

More than 29 years had elapsed since my 1969-1970 Viet-Nam combat tour of duty when I received a letter from Charles Harris. He was one of my former flight medics who had won two Silver Stars—America's third highest award for heroism—in less than 1½ months during that war. Harris provided new information and insight concerning a bizarre helicopter medical evacuation mission that could have claimed the lives of his crew, my crew and those of ten wounded Americans at dawn on May 1, 1970 near the edge of Hiep Duc. This was a notoriously dangerous settlement approximately 36 miles southwest of our unit that was located at Red Beach in Da Nang.

1. A medical evacuation helicopter preparing to land with a load of wounded at the LZ Hawk Hill aid station pad, approximately 32 miles south of Da Nang in 1970. (Photo by Robert B. Robeson)

On April 30, 1970, I was unit commander of the 236th Medical Detachment (Helicopter Ambulance). At 2100 hours, I was in Dust Off flight operations at Red Beach when the urgent call was broadcast over our FM radio.

"Da Nang Dust Off, this is Charger Dust Off. Dust Off 6-0-8 was just shot down at Hiep Duc with 10 U.S. wounded aboard. Request another crew be sent to cover their AO (area of operations) until they can be evacuated. Also, be advised that there are at least two reported enemy .51-caliber machine guns working out in that vicinity. Gunships are on station."

The longest night of my 27 years on Earth had just begun. An initial decision was easy for me to make. One of our six UH-1H (Huey) helicopters with 14

Americans aboard had been shot down. As unit commander, I wasn't about to ask others to do what I wasn't willing to do myself. So I asked for a volunteer crew to go with me to get them out.

For as long as I could remember, my father—a Protestant minister—had taught me to believe that God is my constant source of courage and strength. I'd learned as a small child that relying on Him for guidance and protection was never a sign of weakness. It was then that I had a premonition that a need for this "source" of power would be in great demand before the night was over.

2. (L-R) SP5 Tom Franks (medic on author's helicopter that rescued Yost and crew), SP5 Dave Farnum (crew chief), Capt. Robert Robeson (author and aircraft commander) and CW2 Tim Yost (aircraft commander of downed helicopter at Hiep Duc) pose for a group photo on the Red Beach flight line in early 1970. (Photo courtesy of Bild am Sonntag, a West German newspaper)

This wasn't a new experience for me. In the previous nine months, I'd had seven of my helicopters shot up by enemy fire and had been shot down twice. I'd flown over 900 missions for more than 2,300 patients. In the previous 30 days, alone, our thirteen pilots and flight crews had 16 helicopters either shot up or shot down due to heavy action in our area of operation. We'd gone through our authorized inventory of six helicopters nearly three times.

Dust Off flying was a profession precariously balanced between joy and sorrow, pain and pleasure. It was intense and meaningful. As supposed noncombatant medical personnel, we pilots often talked among ourselves about the daily danger and death faced on nearly every mission. That was the nature of this beast called "war." Sometimes you were able to evade and outrun that bear. Sometimes the bear would lay in wait and attack you before you had time to react and attain safety for yourself and your patients.

Unit pilots referred to the Hiep Duc Valley, where Hiep Duc was located, as "Ulcer Alley" and "Death Valley" because it was a main North Vietnamese Army infiltration route. We had more aircraft shot up in this stretch of dangerous real estate than anywhere else in our 5,000-square-mile AO. As we took off and flew over the U.S. Marine base on Freedom Hill, located toward the southern edge of Da Nang and adjacent to Da Nang Air Force Base, I invoked my usual prayer for our safety and that of those we sought to evacuate.

3. Capt. Robert Robeson stands outside the entrance to the Dust Off underground hootch and bunker at LZ Hawk Hill a few months before the mission to rescue the downed crew at Hiep Duc. (Photo courtesy of Robert B. Robeson)

Charger Dust Off, our field-site battalion aid station, was located at Landing Zone Hawk Hill 32 miles south of Da Nang and 19 miles northeast of Hiep Duc. We received an update on what had happened from Charger's radio-telephone operator (RTO).

"6-0-8 took a bunch of hits on takeoff, lost their engine and had to autorotate (descending on just the energy in their main rotor blades alone) from about 100 feet. I don't know how they got it down in one piece with all that weight aboard."

"Are they in a secure area?" I asked.

"Firebird gunships (Huey helicopters also stationed at

Hawk Hill) have been relaying information to me," Charger replied. "They somehow landed on a bunker without tipping over, are in an ARVN (South Vietnamese Army) outpost and have taken over one of the ARVN FM field radios. They're up our primary frequency and are directing gunship fire because the compound is currently under ground attack. So give them a call when you get in range."

"Roger that," I replied. "In the meantime, we'll be taking all of their missions until we can get them out." *(Author's note- So what this means is, the crew has been shot down, They made an incredibly difficult safe landing, they are under attack, and "when we get your butts out of there, here's another helicopter, get back to work!")*

In the distance, we could see the intense firefight enveloping the northern outskirts of Hiep Duc. Tracers from helicopter mini-guns formed red streams of fire earthward while green enemy tracers arced skyward or ricocheted off the ground into the air. Some of the green tracers looked as big as basketballs as they stalked their aerial targets.

"Well, Bill, they weren't kidding when they reported that .51-cals were out there," I told my copilot, WO1 Bill Payne, over the intercom. He'd only been in-country 1½ months. For a moment, I fought an urge to politely complain to God.

"Dust Off 6-0-8, this is 6-0-5. How do you read me?" I broadcast over our FM radio.

"Got you loud and clear," CW2 Tim Yost, the aircraft commander replied.

"Is everyone okay, what's the tactical situation and what kind of an area do you have for me to land to?" I asked.

"Negative on the landing," Yost replied. "It's too hot to get us out at this time. We got hosed-down pretty good, but everyone's okay. Doc (SP4 Harris, their medic) says all of our patients should be able to make it to first light."

"I don't want to leave you there overnight," I said.

"You can't risk it," Yost replied forcefully. "We're taking mortars, small arms and .51-cals down here and there's barbed wire and concertina wire all over the place. I'm not even sure there'll be enough room to land near our bird in the daylight," he added. "It's just too hot and we can't get 18 on your bird, anyway. I recommend that you come back at first light to give it a shot. The gunnies should be able to keep their heads down until then."

"Okay," I grudgingly agreed, "but if things quiet down, have the Firebirds relay a request for us at Hawk Hill. We'll be back there covering your area until we can get you out. Over."

"Roger that."

I'd wanted to get them out of there as soon as possible, even if we were forced to make two trips. It was often better to attempt an evacuation sooner than later. Now, if something happened to them, I'd feel even more responsible. But Yost knew the ground situation better than me and I had to rely on his judgment. For the first time, intense anxiety crept over me as I banked toward Hawk Hill and darkness closed around us like a jackal smelling fresh meat.

4. (L-R) Capt. Robert Robeson and CW2 Tim Yost shut down their UH-1H (Huey) helicopter at Red Beach in Da Nang after a medical evacuation mission in early 1970. (Photo courtesy of Bild am Sonntag)

At our underground Dust Off hootch and bunker at Hawk Hill, across from the aid station, the rest of my crew didn't seem worried. SP5 Tom Franks, medic, SP4 Walt Tominaga, crew chief, and Payne kidded around under our two, bare, 100-watt-lightbulbs dangling on cords from the ceiling. They fashioned a bull's-eye on heavy timber beams that served as walls and had a knife-throwing contest using their survival knives. But I think it was just a way to lessen their own anxiety, knowing that their friends were still in jeopardy at Hiep Duc.

Not long after this, the lights were turned off and they fell asleep on their cots. I lay fully awake on mine. My boots and flight suit were still on and my mind was going over the Hiep Duc terrain and approach I'd have to make early the next morning. Thinking about those waiting .51-caliber machine guns didn't make it any easier. A .51-cal is so big and bad enough there is little that can protect you if someone is firing one of these weapons in your direction. Its projectiles simply go through everything in sight.

In the blackness of that underground bunker, I wrestled with a premonition of imminent death unlike anything I'd experienced before. I prayed that we would be able to get all of them out alive and that I wouldn't make any stupid decisions or pilot errors. All of us experienced fear and apprehension nearly every day in combat. But this was different. It seemed to permeate my entire being. My final request was that this heavy burden of foreboding and anxiety would be lifted.

It is often in the dark hours of trouble, self-doubt and fear that many take refuge in Biblical teaching and guidance. I remembered Psalm 46:1 (NAS). "God is our refuge and strength, a very present help in trouble." But I still felt extreme anxiety over my responsibility for the safety of that crew and their patients...and then insomnia set in.

Realizing that sleep was out of the question, I quietly got up, walked outside and climbed into our helicopter. I mentally went over my tactical plan to get into that confined outpost. At first light, we'd fly out to LZ Karen at 2,000 feet, parallel the Song Thu Bon River between Karen and LZ Siberia (both American artillery bases), then drop down on the deck low-level and come in over the rooftops of Hiep Duc into the landing zone.

Taking my flashlight, I then performed a thorough preflight inspection, wondering if another mission would be called in to take my mind off what was going to happen in a few hours.

Around what some referred to as the Hour of the Wolf, the night became quiet.

Outgoing artillery from the other side of the hill had ceased. Troops manning the bunkers spaced around the base had settled in for their continuous watch. That was the moment, usually between 0100-0200 hours, when you stare at the ceiling or sky, stone cold awake, listening to

5. Red Beach in Da Nang looking south above Da Nang Harbor over the 236th Medical Detachment's airfield toward the unit area and Freedom Hill in the distant upper-left corner of the photo. (Photo courtesy of Robert B. Robeson)

the throbbing of your own heart and wondering *What in the world have I gotten myself into now?* The rest of my crew didn't appear to have any illusions about their life expectancy. They obviously had faith in my ability to complete the mission because Tominaga had even "pulled rank" on another crew chief to go along in an attempt to rescue his friends. I appeared to be the one having difficulty dealing with my personal insecurities.

I stood on the medevac landing pad for a while looking at the stars and scanning the floodlit bunker line stretching around the base that was surrounded by eerie-looking rice paddies. I also observed a number of Viet Cong POWs sleeping under a series of lights in a guarded enclosure behind the aid station.

Then I went inside the aid station to check on the downed crew's current status and talk with our night shift RTO. It still felt like the Empire State Building was propped on my chest. The long weary wait was working overtime on my mind.

About 0400 hours, I returned to our aircraft. I probably looked as wired as if I'd spent the night inside the guitar of a heavy-metal band. I sat quietly in my armored cockpit seat and prayed for peace in my spirit. That's when I recalled the words of Psalm 91:5 (NAS). "You will not be afraid of the terror by night; or of the arrow that flies by day." After a few minutes, I took a deep breath, inhaled the night air and felt myself slowly starting to relax. My tension began to subside. In that special moment, I felt a rare sensitivity to life.

The sun began to faintly smear the eastern sky red, orange and yellow as it slowly poked its head above the South China Sea on the horizon. Past, present and future were in the process of merging. It was time to get out of Dodge. My crew was rousted from bed and we were soon airborne. It was our turn in the barrel, now.

Halfway to Hiep Duc, I made contact with 6-0-8 again. Everyone was fine and their patients had survived the night. Things had quieted down, the enemy had slunk away and the gunships had gone home. Yost later noted that there were enemy bodies still slung over the perimeter wire, but, because of the gunship cover and their ability to communicate directly by radio to the pilots and direct their fire, the outpost had not been overrun.

As we talked, the pilot of another aircraft broke into our conversation. It was a Dust Off helicopter from Chu Lai, a unit farther southeast, bringing in a load of wounded to Hawk Hill. He'd monitored our conversation and asked if we needed assistance. The first of my prayers was answered before we even approached Hiep Duc. Now we wouldn't have to make two trips. Payne gave him the coordinates and told him there would be four of the least seriously wounded for them to evacuate.

The downed crew had already removed all three radios from their downed bird to keep them from falling into enemy hands, so I requested that Yost get his crew of four and six of the most seriously wounded ready for us. I hadn't topped off our fuel at Hawk Hill in an effort to reduce weight so I figured we could take their crew, six patients, three radios and our crew of four without bleeding off too much engine rpm on takeoff. The other helicopter would only be about 15 minutes behind, to evacuate the other ambulatory patients.

"Okay, 6-0-8, we're about a minute out," I broadcast. "Get ready to pop a smoke and have everyone available to move quickly if we take any fire."

"Good copy."

It was now 0500 hours and dawn was just beginning to touch the mountaintops around Hiep Duc. I banked right around LZ Karen at 2,000 feet and pointed the nose of our bird toward the Vietnamese settlement, as we paralleled the river on our left.

That was the moment when we all heard the distinctive belch of AK-47 rifle fire. In the early morning light, Payne and I witnessed something I'd never seen before in nearly 900 combat missions. I believe God allowed it to happen as a graphic reminder to me of His protecting grace and power. We could actually *see* the enemy's non-tracer rounds slicing through the air in front of our aircraft. They were silvery reflections in the rising sun's rays.

I immediately banked hard right into a tight spiral and dove for the deck. Then I keyed my mike. "Go ahead and pop smoke, 6-0-8. Be advised we're taking fire from across the river at the base of Siberia, so don't expose yourselves until we're down."

"Smoke's out."

"Got your purple smoke at our twelve o'clock," Payne said.

7. WO1 Bill Payne, copilot of author's aircraft on the Hiep Duc missions. (Photo courtesy of Robert Terrell, now deceased)

"Good color. That's us."

"Keep your heads down," I added. "Here we come."

I tore along dragging our skids a few feet above the sheet metal rooftops of Hiep Duc. If these Vietnamese civilians weren't awake before, our 1,200 horses pounding overhead probably did the trick.

As we bore down on the purple smoke at 120 knots, Yost scrambled out of a trench—raising his arms like Moses must have done prior to parting the Red Sea—and served as a ground guide. I sideslipped the aircraft, performed a hairy flare to reduce our airspeed and then skidded to a high hover above a tiny enclosure jammed with concertina wire. I could see a huge smile spread across Yost's mustached face.

As soon as our skids touched down, tail rotor dangerously close to the heavily-coiled concertina wire, a bevy of shouts rang out as his crew charged out of their trenches.

They assisted six wounded comrades into our aircraft. PFC Gary Hagen, their crew chief, tossed the radios aboard as they packed themselves into every available niche and cranny of the cargo compartment. Then laughing and slapping us on our backs, they yelled above our Lycoming jet engine's roar, "Go! Go! Go!"

I'd had a host of athletic thrills in high school, college and the military, but I'd never experienced the excitement and emotion of anything that compared to that moment. Using my collective control to pull in all of the available power our engine had, I hovered up until we were clear of the wire, then eased the nose over to gain translational lift and hunkered off toward the relative safety of LZ Karen, to the southeast. I climbed to 2,000 feet while circling Karen in case we needed a safe landing area in an emergency. While we flew toward Hawk Hill, Payne briefed the Chu Lai crew who followed us in to evacuate the remaining four Americans.

We unloaded our wounded at the aid station pad, shut down the aircraft next to our bunker and then walked with their weary crew to our mess hall. I spoke to each of them briefly before coming to Harris. He'd just been promoted to specialist four on February 17, 1970 and had only been in-country approximately three months. He was a short, soft-spoken 20-year-old from Falkland, North Carolina. His white T-shirt was covered with dirt and blood from treating his patients all night in a slit trench under fire.

"Chuck," I said, "I'm really proud of the job you did out there last night...taking care of those guys." He'd helped to keep the lights lit in their lives throughout that chaotic and dangerous night in the dark.

He looked up, grinned self-consciously, and replied, "Sir, I wasn't worried at all. I knew you'd get us out."

I suddenly felt very old and disgusted with myself. Here was a gutsy young medic who'd had complete faith in our ability to get to them. Yet I'd spent that interminable night primarily preoccupied with my own anxieties about how I was going to extract them, rather than on how I believed God would help me to make the right decisions and prepare the way for us. His faith in me made my faith in God look suspect as my thoughts had wavered on the proper course of action to take. It was a humbling and illuminating experience.

War is dirty and ugly. It is killing and maiming, suffering and hardship. Yet, in a perverse sort of way, it is also the springboard for acts of human courage, self-sacrifice and nobility of spirit. The crew of 6-0-8 demonstrated all of that and more. They'd tried to lighten the dark moments of the night with comradely caring of the sort that helps soldiers survive wounds, shot up aircraft and enemy action. And they all proved to me that love and determination can be forces stronger than chaotic and dangerous circumstances.

I would have missed an opportunity to see what God could do with bad news, if we hadn't gone through that testing time. It became apparent to me, once again, that if you never go, you never get. Obstacles are mere hurdles to be leaped. Setbacks are opportunities to learn. And when we descended into that treacherous valley for our fellow crew members and their patients, I believe God was with us, pushing back my anxieties.

It embarrasses me now to recall my trial of faith and the initial fear I experienced during those missions, after all I'd previously been through. Over 43 years later, it's a fact and lesson I've never forgotten. I'm sure I never will.

Harris' letter provided additional background information I hadn't been aware of and ended with a memory that still appeared vivid to him over 29 years later.

"I can remember thinking how beautiful the red cross on (the nose of) that chopper was when it popped-up over the crest of that hill the next morning," Harris wrote. "You were the one who came in and got us."

Coincidentally, on May 25, 2000, my wife received an e-mail from Gary Hagen. It said, "Tell Bob 'hello' for me...I was the crew chief on that crew that he came in and picked up that morning after we were shot down in Hiep Duc on May 1, 1970. Tell him 'thanks' again for me."

Yost, WO1 Ed De La Vergne (copilot), Harris and Hagen all were awarded Silver Stars for that night's action. And these two enlisted men were thanking *me*? That's the kind of true American heroes I was surrounded by in combat.

The author today. (Photo courtesy of Robert B. Robeson)

Postscript

The downed helicopter at Hiep Duc was so riddled with hundreds of additional bullet holes, from being exposed to that night-long firefight, that my superiors gave me authorization to call in a U.S. Air Force jet to blow it in place so it wouldn't fall into enemy hands.

"Dust Off" was the radio call sign used by U.S. Army Medical Service Corps evacuation crews who flew unarmed helicopters to evacuate wounded and dead civilians and soldiers on both sides of the action. This term originated because their rotor blades continually blew sand, dirt and debris over ground troops when they landed or hovered in dry and sandy areas.

All scripture verses are taken from the New American Standard Bible®, Copyright © 1960, 1962, 1963, 1968, 1971, 1972, 1973, 1975 by The Lockman Foundation. Used by permission.

Mission 7

Combat Medics Badge

Since the end of the Vietnam War, there has been a "push" to have Dustoff Medics awarded the Combat Medic's Badge, CMB, a very highly regarded award to recognize the achievements and sacrifices of the Combat Medic. Sometimes that push to include Dustoff and Medevac medics has been concentrated and included some high-powered individuals. As you will read here, there has been a lot of opposition to expanding the criteria to include our flight medics. Included was a hearing with a Senate Committee in 2003. The following 3 presentations, all a matter of public record, are reprinted for you to judge for yourself...to award or not to award, that is the question.

Statement of Fred Castleberry

before the Committee on Veterans Affairs United States Senate on the U.S. Army's policy of the award of the Combat Medic Badge

July 29, 2003

Good afternoon Sen. Specter and all the members of the committee:

Please know that I am extremely honored to be here. In 1965, while stationed at Fort Lee Virginia, I visited our Nation's Capitol. At that time, I never dreamed I would someday visit here on Capitol Hill. However, once I heard the details about this hearing, I knew I had to be here. I thank you for the privilege to testify before a committee as important as this one.

The Fred Castleberry that went to Vietnam was much different from the one that came home. The injuries that my body suffered are plain to see. I lost my right arm and left leg and the partial use of my other arm and leg. However, I am not here to talk about Fred Castleberry any more than I have to; what I am here to talk about is the fact that I am here at all, and how I got out of a very bloody jungle on the day I turned 21.

Prior to going to Vietnam, I was a drill sergeant. I tried to prepare the recruits for what they would face in war. But like anyone else who has never been in combat, I truly did not have a clue. There is no manual that can prepare you for the paralyzing fear that grips you when bullets go whizzing by your head. There is no veteran's account that can accurately describe what it is like to watch the life drain from someone who just moments before was so young and full of life. In combat, everywhere you look, there is death and destruction. Unfortunately, it was my job to be part of that strange world.

One day during a firefight, I went into a tunnel after an enemy soldier. When I came out of the tunnel, I noticed this helicopter coming in. For some reason, I knelt on the ground and watched this Dustoff crew come in and pick up the wounded and fly off. I remember thinking, "Why bother?"

Like I said, I was wounded on my 21st birthday, hit by a rocket propelled grenade that left pieces of me, literally, all over the battlefield. I fully accepted the fact that my life was going to end that predawn morning. As I was telling my loved ones goodbye, the ground medics told me I was being medevac'd. I told them that they were crazy, the site was too hot.

For the rest of my life, I will never forget the whopping sound of the Huey's blades, and the sight of that spotlight clearing the tree line. As the helicopter got closer, I could see sparks flying everywhere as countless small arms rounds hit the helicopter. I remember thinking, there is no way any of those guys will make it. I honestly thought the helicopter would be shot down and we would all die. But somehow through all the gunfire, they got in. I remember seeing those beautiful angels pick me up and take me aboard. I remember the pinging of bullets ripping through the skin of the Huey and hearing the crew excitedly, yet calmly, talking to one another and I saw this face above me. The face had blood all over it and it was saying to me "Buddy, stay with me. Hey buddy, you're going to be all right". Over and over again, I would drift in and out of consciousness, and all I can recall is this bloody face telling me I was going to make it.

When I came to, a nurse asked me if I felt like company. Something happened that will live with me the rest of my life...the Dustoff crew was in the hospital with me. The guys that saved my life, the young boys that rescued me, themselves had been wounded. The blood on the air medic's face was not mine; it was his. A bullet had gone through his cheek, but rather than attend to his own wounds, he kept me alive.

There are no words to tell you how I feel about Dustoff. You can hear and read all the stories you want, but nothing replaces having gone through what I did.

These young fellows went into the paths of all those bullets to save my life, someone they didn't even know. I cannot think of one reason why a Dustoff crew would put their lives on the line time and time again, other than what one of the crewmembers told me when I asked: "That's our job."

We in the infantry, when we come under fire, we could hug the ground a little closer. A Dustoff crew, when they come under fire, has nothing but air to hug. You want to know what heroes look like, look at a Dustoff crew.

I visited the Wall today for the first time. The only reason my name is not on that sacred site is a Dustoff crew risked all their lives to save mine. Think of the thousands of lives that have been saved over the years because Dustoff crews were, "Doing their job." I will probably never know the names of the Dustoff crew that saved my life, but I can honor them today by joining my voice with Mike Novosel and John Travers, and ask this Committee to make sure the Dustoff Medics are awarded the Combat Medic Badge. Thank you for your time.

At the Hearing, two Senators, Senator Arlen Specter, PA, and Senator Patty Murray, WA, sat at a table facing those testifying. Off to the side of the Senators, their Aides were positioned along the wall. At the conclusion of Fred Castleberry's testimony, some of the aides were seen to be crying and many at least had tears in their eyes.

Statement of Chief Warrant Officer

Michael J Novosel (USA, Retired)

Medal of Honor Recipient and former Dustoff pilot before the Committee on Veterans Affairs United States Senate on the U.S. Army's policy on the award of the Combat Medic Badge

July 29, 2003

Good afternoon Sen. Specter, members of the committee, and honored guests:

My name is Michael J Novosel; I am a retired Air Force and Army aviator. I was a military aviator in three wars, and saw combat in two. 32 years ago the parent body of this committee, the Congress of the United States, bestowed upon me the honor that has defined so much of my life: the Congressional Medal of Honor.

One cannot be exposed to years of war in combat without being aware of the dedication, selflessness, and bravery of those who do the fighting and dying. Without a doubt, some of the most heroic people were the Dustoff crewmen and medics who rode with me in my medevac helicopters in Vietnam. I was honored for my efforts while commanding one of the air ambulances, but those young men behind me, caring for the wounded, and saving lives, were the real heroes.

To appreciate the sacrifices they made, one has to understand the magnitude and intensity of the task. These medics, armed with stethoscopes, blood, and IVs rather than guns and ammunition, managed to save hundreds of thousands of lives. Their operating table was the litter; sometimes the flight deck awash in blood. They kept men with traumatic amputations, sucking chest wounds, and bullet-riddled bodies alive; finding the collapsed vein to give them the sorely needed transfusions. Mouth-to-mouth resuscitation was often administered regardless of race or nationality. They knew their responsibilities: giving life-saving medical treatment to the men in their care, until they were delivered to hospitals for more advanced treatment. They were under intense physical and mental pressure.

When they flew, they put their lives on the line to save others, and 55 of them did not return. Many were killed while tending to the wounded; others died in crashes caused by attempts at rescue under impossible weather conditions. They are memorialized on the black marble Wall down by the Reflecting Pool, along with 58,000 others. But what sets them apart, at least to those who served with, and knew them, is the singular sense of mission that they displayed. Yet their efforts have not been recognized; they have not received the honor they so richly deserve.

For years, American soldiers who carried a gun into battle were authorized to wear the Combat Infantryman's Badge. Eventually, it was decided that those equally heroic men who went into battle without a gun, but with the medical bag, would be authorized to wear the Combat Medic Badge. However, the Medic's Badge award criteria is written in language which precludes Dustoff medics from being eligible for the award. Overly strict interpretation of the regulation produces this dichotomy. The regulation requires the medic to be "assigned to an infantry" unit. Had the regulation read "assigned to or supporting an infantry" unit there would be no problem with the award of the CMB. Dustoff regularly works with infantry units, but its personnel are assigned to aviation units, not infantry units.

The regulation covering the award of the Combat Medics Badge was written at a time when Dustoff did not exist. Those who administer the regulation have not adjusted their interpretation of it, to coincide with the realities of the changing nature of war. Dustoff is a product of that change. Its personnel pioneered and developed the concept of aeromedical evacuation. In Vietnam they regularly went into the thick of battle to rescue wounded soldiers. Dustoff crews did this, knowing they would be subjected to enemy fire, yet the medic jumped off the helicopter, got to the wounded, and proceeded to load the casualties. It was not uncommon to see bullets hitting the rice paddies while the Medic tended to the wounded, but he did not waver.

I witnessed the heroism of my medics, as they performed their duties. I cannot recall a single instance of a Dustoff Medic seeking refuge from enemy fire, shirking his duty, or ignoring the plight of his brothers. I do recall, however, a continued commitment to the mission: easing the pain of the wounded, relieving them of the trauma of battle, rescuing people, and saving lives.

My Dustoff crew and I flew the mission of 2 October 1969 expecting no reward, but the Army, and the Congress, presented me with the Medal of Honor. I am aware that the Army writes the regulations; that Congress does not. Therefore I ask this Committee, and this Congress, to honor the Dustoff Medics, and direct the Department of the Army to change that regulation, and make them eligible for the CMB. No group of individuals can be more worthy of that badge. I further ask that the Army expedite the matter, and plan to present the awards by November 11th, Veterans Day. It would be a magnanimous gesture for the Department of Army representative to posthumously award the first Combat Medic Badge to those 55 brave men who are memorialized on the Wall, and lost their lives saving others. I thank you for your time and attention. I will make myself available to any questions the committee might have for me.

Michael J Novosel, Medal Of Honor,

CW4, US Army, (Retired).

Statement of Chief Warrant Officer

John Travers, (US Army, Retired),

former Dustoff pilot, before the

Committee on Veterans Affairs United States Senate on the U.S. Army's policy on the award

of the Combat Medic Badge

July 29, 2003

Good afternoon, Sen. Specter, and members of the committee.

It is an honor to come before you today to speak on behalf of not only all those who served in Dustoff, but also the literally hundreds of thousands of men who are alive today because of Dustoff Medics. It is also an honor to lead such a righteous fight with the support and assistance of some of the most sincere people a person can ever know: the people who are here with us today - and I take this brief moment to thank them publicly, on behalf of every Dustoff medic that ever was. Thank you very much, all of you.

I had the very great privilege to serve as a Dustoff pilot during the Vietnam War, with the bravest group of men I have ever known. Typical of them was Kevin Donoghue, a medic who I personally watched jump from my aircraft, under extremely intense fire, and run through a mine field to retrieve a wounded soldier and bring him back to our aircraft, all while AK-47 rounds exploded around him. That picture still plays in my mind over 30 years later, and will never diminish. No rational man would have done what Kevin did that day; I witnessed what love of your fellow soldier can inspire a man to do. You must understand this was not a singular occurrence, but rather a daily ritual that gained the admiration of him and love of those on the ground for the call sign "Dustoff".

It is those experiences that drove me to start this campaign to right the injustice that has gone on too long. I believe, as God is my judge, that if the authors of the Combat Medic regulation had known that in the future there would be wars with non-linear battle lines, where helicopters would become the means to rescue wounded soldiers from the battlefield, they would have put Dustoff medics at the top of the list of defined recipients. I am constantly frustrated by the irony of our army allowing a 58-year-old regulation to remain intact when all of this battle doctrine has been upgraded to reflect the modern waging of war. I suggest that when one reduces this fight to that - its simplest level - it just doesn't make any sense, does it?

Those of us who served our country as Dustoff crew members in Vietnam did so to the best of our ability. When we came home to an unaccepting America, there were no parades and few words of appreciation, but we learned to accept that, because we knew we had made a difference to our fellow soldiers, and that it was the ultimate difference, the difference between life and death. We went on with our lives, and asked for very little, if anything. And the experience made us a very close-knit family.

Ironically, as the years have passed, we have seen what can only be described as a slap in the face by the Army we served so loyally. After the Desert Storm War, the Chief of Staff of the Army waived the requirement for the Combat Medic Badge, and awarded it to medics in Armor and ground Cavalry units; in fact, over 3000 CMB's were awarded for a 100 hour war. Now let me be perfectly clear on this: I am glad the medics of Desert Storm received these awards, but cannot help but question why the

Dustoff medics of Vietnam, who did their duty for a year, day in and day out, under fire - are not qualified? The numbers speak for themselves, and the Gulf War pales by comparison: in Vietnam, Dustoff flew thousands and thousands of missions, and saved hundreds of thousands of lives. Is it any wonder so many Vietnam Vets feel abandoned and forgotten by the very institutions they pledged to defend with their lives?

On a black piece of granite, just a few short blocks from here, appear the names of 55 of our brother Dustoff medics and over 200 Dustoff crew members, pilots and crew chiefs included. Perhaps those within the Army who oppose this award should take a walk some lunch hour along that Wall, and then tell me Dustoff medics did not earn the combat medic badge; I would be happy to meet them there - face to face - and discuss, and, if necessary, to debate that notion. I suspect those who oppose this award have never been to that Wall, which is one of the reasons we brought it here today, in the form of the etchings of those 55 names.

We who are before you today ask no favors, nor anything for ourselves. But we have earned the right to demand the Army do what is morally correct. Every day my medics grow older; indeed, some have already died, unrecognized and unrewarded by a bureaucracy that has all the inertia of the coffins they have been buried in. I humbly, respectfully, and fervently beg this committee to do whatever has to be done to correct this, since the Army seems unable to, itself. Thank you for your time and patience.

Warrant Officer John Travers. Note he is wearing an ammunition bandolier for his personal weapon and there is an open reel tape recorder in the background. A "must have" by helicopter crewmen in Vietnam, the bigger the tape recorder and the higher the wattage of the amplifier, the bigger one's status.

Now that you, the reader, have seen the testimony, I will add this...it is this author's understanding that the Senate Committee recommended awarding of the CMB to Dustoff and Medevac medics. However, a 3-Star (unnamed) General apparently bent to the "wishes of Higher-Ups" and testified against the change. To this day, the regulation remains the same.

There *are* a few Dustoff medics who wear the CMB today, legally, but they are an extremely small percentage. I know that a few of our 237th Medical Detachment Medics, the unit that I flew with, did receive orders from the Commander of the 5th

Mechanized Division for the award of the Combat Medics Badge. This was in recognition of their continuous support and contributions to the men of the "5th Mech", men that we supported on a virtually daily basis. Whether other air medics have been officially awarded the CMB, I do not know.

Should Dustoff and Medevac medics receive the CMB? This author thinks so, as I, too, saw them earn it on every combat mission we flew. I have said many, many times that as pilots, we were just "bus drivers" up front. Highly trained and highly skilled bus drivers, yes. But the *real* heroes were the guys in the back, the medics and the crew chiefs. They were the ones who did the dirty work while keeping their patients breathing and stopping the bleeding.

Finally, a huge *Thank You* to Bernie "Goldy" Goldenzweig, a Vietnam Dustoff pilot (Dustoff 84) and my newest friend, for sharing these documents with you and me.

Researching this Mission, Goldy told me the story of how he almost crashed at night on a mountain top during a rescue of a soldier with a chest wound. And why did he almost crash? He was trying to land to a guy holding a blinking flashlight, but because the enemy was nearby, whenever 8-4 would get relatively close to landing, he would turn off the flashlight, afraid that he himself would become a target.

So Goldy would pull in power and climb to altitude while telling the ground guide not to turn off his light. A second attempt was made, and the light went out again, and again he had to regain altitude for another attempt. Finally, he told the guy on the ground something like "I'm almost out of fuel, if you want your buddy picked up tonight, you've gotta keep the light blinking."

The message got through, and the pick-up was successful. By the time he got to the nearest place that he could refuel, a Special Forces Camp, (the refueling point was two barrels with a hose), he had flown 16 minutes on the 20 minute fuel remaining warning light. It is known that the 20 minute light is not all that accurate; a friend of mine ran out of fuel 12 minutes into a 20 minute light.

Or...Goldy told me about the time he had 28 Vietnamese soldiers on his Huey, plus his crew of 4 Americans, for 32 souls on board, and was barely able to take off, nursing the aircraft to stay in the air all the way from takeoff to landing. It all started when he picked up 3 KIAs as a favor to the ground unit. Then, he got a radio call for a Dustoff. Casualties kept popping up in the same area, so he kept picking them, until there was no more room on the aircraft. After the last pickup, he had 3 KIAs, 7 WIAs on litters, 18 ambulatory WIAs, and his 4 man crew. The only reason he was able to pick up so many was because he was low on fuel on this mission, too. As he jokingly said, "There are 4 *unofficial* weights for Army aircraft: Max Gross, Over Gross, Combat Gross, and Combat Over Gross." But such was the norm for many of our missions. Very few dull moments flying Dustoff and Medevac in Vietnam.

Goldy also emphasized that every Dustoff and Medevac pilot flew these types of missions in Vietnam. Bad weather, mountainous terrain, pitch black nights, and enemy bullets were all considered occupational hazards by everyone. It was a testament to the dedication to the mission of not only the pilots, but also the crew chiefs and medics, who through their vigilance, actions, and advice, helped guide the pilots in tight situations, and <u>kept the patients alive.</u> Without their exceptional performance, which often went "Above and Beyond the Call of Duty", the number of names on the Vietnam Memorial Wall would be several times greater than it is. It was also a fitting tribute to Major Charles Kelly, whose final words, "When I have your wounded", set the standard for Dustoff operations, that prevail to this day.

Goldy's helmet, a rendition of Snoopy and his doghouse taking fire. "Routine Dustoff My Ass!!!" Photo courtesy of Goldy Goldenzweig, taken by one of his medics.

Warrant Officer Bernard Goldy Goldenzweig in his office, the front seat of a Huey.

Sp4 Simmons, medic and Sp4 Aydelotte, crew chief, with aircraft 569 at Can Tho POL.   82nd Dustoff

Mission 8

Covering MEDEVAC Maniacs

by <u>Ronald L. Huber</u>

(Author's note: When Ron Huber first gave permission to use this Mission, he wanted to "clean it up" and correct the English that he used many, many years ago when he first wrote this, shortly after returning from Vietnam. He didn't want his students to see this writing style, if one can call it that! Regardless, I begged and pleaded with him to leave it just the way it was because it so beautifully demonstrates the enthusiasm that we young pilots exuded in the primes of our lives...flying helicopters in combat in Vietnam. He relented, so please forgive his grammar and enjoy!

I was an Aircraft Commander, AC, though not a flight lead yet. Among the myriad things I don't recall, I'm uncertain who flew lead, though I think it was Don Wallace, Mad Dog 38. As I recall, we took off from Bearcat with the intent to head south toward Rack Kien for a day of supporting the 9th Infantry Division in Combat Assaults, CA's. We weren't too far when a MEDEVAC called for any gun cover for a cable extraction of three Wounded In Action, WIA, for a unit working north northeast of Bearcat about 15 clicks.

The call had that disciplined urgency of dedicated warriors, in this case those special Gods of mercy who'd do what had to be done, gun cover or not. We had an assignment, yet, as we slowed our airspeed and listened, nobody responded to the call. The MEDEVAC pilot repeated his call several times, finally saying that he was going to pick up the WIA's, but he figured, due to the heavy ground fire (The unit was in a run 'n' gun.) that he'd fail to get them out and end up with them.

Lead cracked the send key. "21?" "Go, 38." "You monitoring this?" Click, click. "What d'ya say?" "Somebody's gotta do it." Lead advised the slicks and in route of the situation, and "6" (the Commanding Officer, Maj. Bill Overholser) released us to tend the need. 38 rogered with assurance that we'd advise when we were clear and in route to join the flight at Rack Kien. We turned north as 38 answered the MEDEVAC. Particulars exchanged regarding location and distance with ETA, and we rolled the cyclics as far forward as those ol' C Model's would tolerate. Shit-far! I betcha we wuz lickin' out 95 knots, sorta straight 'n' level! Har! When we arrived on station, 38 and the MEDEVAC AC, Aircraft Commander, talked up the situation. He'd been hit already having tried solo. A moment here. Note that I wrote SOLO! This over-endowed toter of watermelon gonads had been workin' solo while taking lots of heat and hits. How on earth, one might wonder (this one did), where the hell did he place the cyclic in a cyclic climb?!?! "Where do we get men such as these?"

We worked up a plan to provide cover, but it was a potential pisser. I'd never covered or seen cable extractions, but I figured it would be slow work in a hot oven. I was right. I remember our separate conversation between and within aircraft. Odd, sorta. We didn't fly in a democracy, but, on this mission, 38 advised that we ALL agree to do the mission. In fact, I recall this vividly, we talked on my aircraft and between aircraft. Fast talk, of course, but this was done with all eight crew committed to the chore to a man. 38 advised that this MEDEVAC driver was certifiably insane, and we didn't HAVE to die with him in his madness.

Ron Huber at left, next to pilot door of a 240ᵗʰ Assault Helicopter Company, Charlie Model gunship, call sign "Greyhounds". Crew chief and door gunner standing with him. Note pilot doors removed to save weight. Cyclic stick can be seen just beside Ron's right elbow. Seven tube, 7.25 inch rocket pods and flexible mini-guns installed, XM-21 system. In addition, the door gunners had M60 machine guns, which also fired 7.62 caliber ammo...they were just called "60s". The 60s and the 6000 round per minute miniguns fired the same ammo.

Unanimously, we agreed that we did if that was demanded of the event. An impromptu strategy was arranged requiring the friendlies to pop lots of different smokes as we worked. The idea was to prodigiously conserve ammo while making as many passes as we could while the MEDEVAC held high treetop hover working the cable. The area was forested, reminding me of my time with Charlie Troop, 1/9th when we worked the Parrot's Beak, Fishhook and points east in that phoucin' intimidating triple canopy chit near Cambodia. I shudder at the recall! I digress. We figured/hoped that our passes would leave enough doubt combined with intimidation that Mr. Charles' concentration on the MEDEVAC bird would be distracted enough to give him a chance to string up his ambulatories. This brilliant strategy was conceived by men under twenty-one with little to no strategical IQ. Wingin' it? Youbetcherass! Hope springs eternal. We laid back while the MEDEVAC approached, waiting for him to call taking fire. Amazingly, he got the first stringer on and nearly all the way to the bird before the ground fire rose to him. I s'spect those glorious bastards in whatever the grunt unit was were doing titanic and heroic deeds to protect the flying hospital that offered their Mates the chance to survive. "Where do we get such men as these?" The MED pilot held till the first PAC was grasped.

Then, he hauled all the collective he could muster in that steroid (Compared to a C) H model, and he didi'd. We made two passes, I think, lobbing a pair of rockets from each bird with a shitpot of mini and lotsa .60. We impressed them lightly, at best. The MED pilot chattered with 38 about his next route in while the grunt 6 *(Author's note: "grunt 6" is the Commanding Officer, CO, of the ground unit. CO's were normally given the call sign number "6" so one would know who they were talking with, the CO.)* advised that he'd be moving and popping new smoke. He didn't move too far. The MED pilot headed in to purple smoke. As soon as he came to his high hover the popcorn started. He, simply, stated, "Mad Dogs? Charley is makin' a racket. I could use your noise for a bit." 38 rogered, and advised me to go left of the MED AC as he went right when we got "close." We hosed the area with a couple pairs each and lotsa 7.62. One of my minis locked, so we had a little less noise to make. Sumbitch! Each of us broke to our respective sides and Wally had an idea on the fly. "21?" Click, click. "Do a 180 from your current heading, and make a run facing me. I'll do likewise." GULP! "38? We'll be firing in the direction of each other!" "Roger, 12. You make it as wide as you can and, still, hit the area. I'll do likewise." (Sheeeeeeeeeeeet!!!!)

We rolled out, facing each other at a distance, and he went left of me as I went right of him. I pooped of a couple pair, one mini and lotsa .60. I hoped he'd be considerate enough to, just, make faces and curses at them, so's to not shoot in my direction. ;-) As we completed the opposing pass, the MED pilot yelped, "Way to go! We got another one!" He pulled pitch, and flew to a distance. One more to pick.

We had a check-up conversation. All three aircraft had taken hits. The MED ship had taken the most. What a F'n' surprise! We agreed that we were flat outta unique strategies. The best we could muster was for the MED ship to take a new route, and we'd make a bigger noise with what we had left. Both our ships were set up with seven shot tubes and minis. Wally's mini's worked; one of mine did. By now, we were way low on 2.75's, 25% light on mini's and had our .60's, which were good on my aircraft since the crew could link the dead mini's feed, or so I thought. It gave me courage. Har!!!! Al three aircraft had gauges in the green, so away we went. By this time, Mr. Charles was raggin.' He got more aggressive, if that were possible; we got more aggressive in response. They were on the MED ship now. He was chattering, "Taking fire!" as fast as a fat lady sweats at a polka. We returned to what we knew. Two ships running the same direction, hard break to a 180 and give 'em what we had. It got a bit radical with relation to angle of attack for the blades 'n' all dat. I'm sure we were banked 110 degrees or more to make a quick git' round, so we could return as fast as possible. I dunno how we made it, particularly the MED ship, but the third WIA was up, and the MED Aircraft Commander transmitted a "Thank you, kindly," and he didi'd, I presume to Hotel 3. WTH do I know? I know this...

Our last pass(es) were on empty. It was one of those rare times I unholstered my sidearm, popping it off to "make an impression". Har!!! Also. I shouted all the virulent curses I could muster. That'll teach 'em!

I took the time to write this novel for a couple reasons. One? Frank? You provoked me. Two? In all the forgotten memories of flying guns in Nam, I, never, witnessed greater courage, dedication or commitment to one's Mates than I witnessed when that MEDEVAC crew refused to be denied. I have no freakin' idea what the end of this adventure was. I hope all three survived, healed and returned to the land of the big PX, unfettered tits and merriment. Finally, I scribe to advise you and all medical crew how much reverence respect and awe I own for you, all of you. Most of us, I surmise, me, certainly, were bent on killing as many and as often as possible. You and yours dedicated your whole being to nursing our broken long enough to recover, hopefully, and return, either to battle or home. "Where do we get such men as these?" Thank you, medics and MEDEVAC crew. Thanks over and again! Finally, I certify that this TINS *(Author: This Is No Shit)* is, at least, 5%, no, 10% true. I hope it's more, but WTH do I know? My memory's length is as long as . . .. Well, you know how it is. This I know.

It's worth what you paid to read it.

Mission 9

Thanks For The Ride

LZ English

Bong Son, Viet Nam

November 1968

By Dany Pennington

The typhoon was somewhere in the South China Sea moving closer. The rain started during the night and was coming in waves now that it was morning. All the flying for today was cancelled due to the low ceiling and poor visibility. LZ English was eerily quiet and the 61st Assault Helicopter Company, which normally created most of the noise and commotion here, was equally still and inactive. The large helicopter parking area, known as the Crap Table, strewn with its many revetments was still and lifeless. Most of the pilots were lounging around in their tents while the crew chiefs and gunners were securing their helicopters for the expected high winds and torrential rains.

Meanwhile, 20 miles to the north on the western slopes of the An Lo Valley, Team F, 74th Infantry Detachment (LRRP, Long Range Reconnaissance Patrol) of the 173rd Airborne Brigade was being pursued by a platoon of North Vietnamese Regulars

(NVA) using tracker dogs. The "Lurp" team had been out several days in search of three enemy base camps reported to be in that area. The team killed the NVA point man leading the platoon size unit and began a hasty retreat away from the area. Their location now known by the enemy and their security compromised, the Lurps called for helicopter extraction.

After Team F, a six-man reconnaissance unit, made contact with the NVA they moved away from that area. Their many attempts to make radio contact with their TOC (Tactical Operations Center) were unsuccessful. Knowing the dogs would track them down and that they would be overrun and ultimately killed, they tried the radio frequencies of several adjoining units. After several long minutes at a dead run through the dense jungle and steep terrain, they made radio contact with the Americal Division some 50 miles to their north.

When the Lurps situation was relayed to the 61st Operations, the helicopter unit that supported the Brigade's special operations, it came as a mission assignment to extract the team.

A typical Long Range Reconnaissance Patrol Team extraction consists of a four-helicopter element; Two UH-1H Huey aircraft, known as slicks, and two UH-1C armed helicopter gunships. One slick is used as the Command and Control (C&C) flying overhead directing the mission while the other slick is used to fly into the Landing Zone (LZ) to extract the Lurps. The gunships are used to cover the extraction ship as it approaches, lands, and departs from the LZ.

Inside the 61st Operations bunker at LZ English

the operations officer, Capt. Easterwood, assembled two crews from the first platoon and two crews from the gun platoon. The pilots from the first platoon were on standby for any immediate emergency missions including Lurp extractions that might arise. They were also the same pilots that had inserted this Lurp team several days ago. Their leader was Warrant Officer Sam Kyle.

LRRP team headed out on a mission. Note that they are sitting on the floor of the helicopter, feet hanging out a couple thousand feet in the air. It's a guarantee that they are NOT wearing seat belts. Hey, John Wayne never wore seat belts!

Minutes later the Lurp detachment commander, a first lieutenant, accompanied by the unit's first sergeant carrying a PRC-25 FM radio, arrived in the helicopter company's operations bunker.

"OK boys lets go get my team out", the Lurp lieutenant said.

"We've got a problem here, lieutenant. We are grounded because of this weather" came the response from the Ops officer, Capt. Easterwood.

"That's not gonna get it. We got men out there in Indian Country being tracked by goddamn dogs. There's an entire NVA platoon chasing my <u>six</u> men – now we've gotta go out there and pull them out. Do you understand that, Captain?" Military decorum clearly ignored by the lieutenant over his concern for the survival of his men.

"I understand your situation lieutenant but <u>you</u> have to realize that we have rules and we can't risk the lives of four helicopter crews to fly in this kind of weather" came his reply almost apologetically.

Captain Easterwood, sensing the building tension, motioned for one of the ops specialist. "Go get the C.O." he ordered the man and off he went.

The Lurp lieutenant nods his head slightly toward WO Sam Kyle in recognition from so many previous Lurp insertions and extractions. The unsettling calm and quiet of the tension-filled room was suddenly shattered as Major Wade came busting into this damp, cramped space with a loud and overbearing presence.

"What seems to be the problem here?", Major Wade blurted to no one in particular.

Captain Easterwood briefed the major on the Lurp situation and gave him an update on the weather. As soon as that was finished the major looked up and turned toward the group. Sam Kyle spoke.

"Sir, I would like to go get them out."

"Sam, you know I can't order you or anyone else to go out there in this kind of weather."

"I know, sir, but I would really like to give it a try. I'm the one that put them out there."

The major turned toward the other slick platoon

pilot and asked, "What do you think Dan."

"I'm with Sam, sir."

The major then turns to the gun team lead and before he could get the question out the team lead said, "If the slicks want to try it, we'll cover'em."

"You know I can't order you to do this. This is strictly a volunteer mission."–a smug little smile appears on the major's face–"if you idiots want to go check the weather I'm not going to stop you". Before the sentence was completed, Sam grabbed his helmet and headed for the door. The rest of the group followed him out.

Walking toward the helicopters the pilots discuss the details of the mission. They decide that Dan would fly the C&C (Command and Control) ship, often referred to as the "high bird", and Sam would be the extraction ship. The Lurp lieutenant and first sergeant loaded their guns, ammo and radio on the C&C ship while across the Crap Table the rotor blades on the light fire team of gun ships slowly started to turn.

After cranking up and making a radio check, the two slicks hover out followed a short distance back by the two gun ships. Easing forward the aircraft shutters as an invisible windshield wiper of air from the rotor blades shake and vibrate the water droplets from the windshield. Four minutes after leaving operations all four ships were airborne off LZ English.

The rain had stopped for the moment and the flight visibility was about three miles. The clouds would only allow the departing helicopters to reach an altitude of 500 feet. Any higher than that and the ground would disappear.

The most direct route to the Lurp's location was not possible. Clouds obscured the ridges west of English. The flight of four would need to travel south to enter the mouth of the An Lo Valley before proceeding north up the river. As the four helicopters followed the river north up the valley, the weather continually deteriorated. There was a light misty rain and as the terrain of the valley floor kept getting higher, the clouds kept getting lower.

Midway between the entrance to the valley and the Lurp team's location the lieutenant in the C&C ship finally heard from his team leader.

"Wisdom Crown, Wisdom Crown, this is Overlord Delta, over."

"Overlord Delta, Wisdom Crown, hear you loud and clear. What's the status of our extraction, over," the team leader said his voice half yelling half gasping over the radio. His voice contained the urgent sounds of expectancy and hope.

"Wisdom Crown what is your situation, over" the lieutenant in the C&C helicopter asked.

The Lurp team was on a dead run. They were trying to put some distance between themselves and the pursuing NVA. The jungle was dense and the going was painfully slow. The only good thing in their favor was that they were traveling downhill.

As the four helicopters travelled further north in the river valley the cloud base continued lower. The forward visibility made worse by a thick misty swirling fog that was slowly encasing the helicopters.

"Lucky Star lead, Starblazer One Five" came the call from the gunship leader to the leader of the two slick helicopters.

"Starblazer One Five go ahead.

"This cloud base is too low for us to give you any gun cover for your extraction. What are your intensions?"

Sam keyed the mic and said, "We are in radio contact with the Lurp team now and we are going ahead with the extraction, over."

The Starblazer fire team leader replied, "Lead, we don't have enough altitude or forward visibility to cover you. We are turning around and RTB (returning to base). Sorry Sam, you are on your own."

"Roger One Five, understood", was the only reply.

The situation, as bad as it was, just got worse. The weather was making flight on the valley floor nearly impossible, the extraction site was in the obscured ridges above, there was a Lurp team in enemy contact with shots fired and now the gunships turn around and go home. It was expressly forbidden to make a hot extraction, such as this one, without gunship support. The prudent decision for the remaining helicopters would be to turn around and RTB with the gunships. That's not what they did.

When asked later, after the mission, why he continued when it was obvious that the mission should have been aborted, WO Kyle simply said, "If I were out there on the ground I wouldn't want the helicopters to leave me, so I didn't leave them."

So the mission continued.

The forward progress up the valley floor, however, did not continue. The two helicopters, out of necessity, had formed into a trail formation and were flying only 100 feet apart. Even at that distance it was difficult to see the aircraft ahead. Both helicopters slowed to only a fast hover when suddenly the FM radio erupted.

"Overlord Delta, Wisdom Crown, we hear the helicopters, over."

"Wisdom Crown, what is your position, over?"

"We left our last RP 10 minutes ago moving east toward the blue line. Estimated platoon size NVA unit is pursuing us. They're tracking us with dogs, sir."

"Wisdom Crown, can you prepare an LZ (landing zone) for extraction? Extraction birds are on station."

"Negative, Overlord Delta, we are on the move, over."

As the Lurp lieutenant and sergeant are discussing how best to proceed with the mission, another radio call from Wisdom Crown interrupts them.

"The helicopters are louder now. They sound below us. We are in fog and can see nothing, over."

Lucky Lead, sensing that time is running out and with very few options available, decides to split the helicopters up sending the empty extraction ship after the Lurp team while the C&C ship lands on a sand bar in the middle of the An Lo river. The weather conditions would not allow the C&C ship to orbit over the LZ as is the usual practice. In fact, continued flight by the C&C ship anywhere in the valley was too risky. Team Foxtrot's luck turns from bad to worse. The NVA troops caught up to the team and a firefight begins. The Lurps set up a defensive perimeter to return the enemy's fire while constantly pulling back from the NVA toward the valley in pairs. This action continues until the team reaches a bluff over the valley. It is a rock ledge with a 100 feet shear drop. On a clear day it would offer a spectacular view of the An Lo Valley. Today it is shrouded in dense fog. Further retreat is no longer possible. This is where Lurp Team Foxtrot will make their stand until they are overrun or extracted.

Sam Kyle, piloting the extraction ship, hears the radio chatter of the Lurp team and decides that he must make an attempt to locate them and pluck them off the ridge. Time is not on their side. Their location is 500 feet above the valley floor. The cloud height being a mere 100 feet above the valley presents the pilot with only one option. Sam turns his helicopter sideways to the ridge and, while looking out the left side window, starts hovering up the side of the hill. With the crew chief helping keep the tail rotor clear of rocks and trees, the helicopter disappears into the clouds climbing slowly up the hillside.

The Lurp team announces that the sound of the helicopter is getting closer. To maintain sight of the trees covering the hill Sam maneuvers the helicopter as close as possible to the trees and rocks. Normally the sound of the main rotor blades striking tree limbs is unwelcomed but in this case it is somewhat reassuring.

"Lucky Star, I hear you. You are below us and to our south. Move farther north, over."

Sam starts the helicopter moving forward while still climbing upward slowly. After several minutes, which seemed like hours to all those involved, the radio crackled, "I hear you louder now. You are directly below us. Please hurry. We can't hold on much longer. Ammo almost depleted, over." The sound of small arms fire can be heard in the background.

"I see you. I see you. You are about 50 feet below us. You need to move forward 100 feet. We are popping smoke, over."

Looking upward through the rotor blades Sam sees purple smoke mixed with the fog.

"Wisdom Crown, I have your smoke in sight."

He slowly moves upward and forward until he can place the left landing skid against the rock ledge. The rotor blades clicking away as they hit the trees above while the remainder of the helicopter dangles over the foggy valley. Beads of sweat travel down the pilot's nose and drip into his lap. With the helicopter perched delicately on the rocky ledge, the Lurps move two at a time toward the helicopter, step on the skid, and jump into the cargo bay. Once the last Lurp is in sight the rest of the team along with the crew chief start firing their weapons at the advancing NVA. Upon hearing the helicopter the NVA charge the Lurp teams position. Knowing that this would happen the Lurps earlier placed their remaining Claymore mines with trip wires around the LZ. The advancing NVA tripping the Claymores created sufficient chaos and distraction to allow the team to move toward the helicopter and escape. Amid the exploding Claymores and small arms fire, Sam moved away from the edge and descended into the fog. All six Lurp team members are onboard, safe and sound. The helicopter makes its approach to the Crap Table at LZ English. It hovers into the revetment and lands. As the Lurps are gathering their gear and leaving the helicopter, the team leader walks up to the open door where WO Kyle is sitting, taps him on the shoulder and says, "Thanks for the ride, sir."

No greater thanks was ever accepted or expected.

L to R, Dany Pennington, Sam Kyle and Michael O'Connor. Taken on the day they were all promoted to Chief Warrant Officer 2, CW2. Note that all have grown mustaches.

Kyle and Pennington's 4-Star accommodations.

Dany Pennington

Dany Pennington notes: The main character, Warrant Officer Sam Kyle, flight school class 67 – 19 and 67 – 21, served with the 61st Assault Helicopter Company in Vietnam from January 1968 to January 1969. Upon returning from Vietnam he served as a Standards Instructor Pilot at Fort Rucker, Alabama in Instrument Method Of Instruction and Rotary Wing Qualification Courses. After release from active duty in 1978 he served in the Tennessee National Guard as a full-time Technician Instrument Pilot. He was killed 8 July 1984 when his OH-6 helicopter hit a wire in remote Tennessee while searching for escaped convicts.

The author, Dany Pennington, attended flight school class 67 – 19 and 67 – 21 also. Along with Sam Kyle, he served with the 61st assault helicopter company in Vietnam from January 1968 to January 1969. He is a freelance copywriter and lives with his wife of 45 years in Monticello, Florida.

Mission 9

Epilogue

Pilot Braves Typhoon To Save LRRP Team

By Sp4 Adrian Acevedo

173rd Airborne Brigade Web Site

173rdairborne.com

BONG SON- A Helicopter Pilot from the 61st Assault Helicopter Company recently braved typhoon winds and rain to make a dramatic rescue of a 173d Airborne Brigade Long Range Patrol which was being tracked with dogs by a North Vietnamese Platoon.

Team F of the 74th Infantry Detachment (LRP) had been, searching for three reported NVA base camps in the northern An Lo Valley, an enemy stronghold 20 miles north of Bong Son when they detected enemy movement to their rear.

"We set up in a hasty ambush," said Sergeant Peter G. Mossman of Stamford Conn, leader of the six-man combined American Vietnamese team. "My rear security man Specialist 4 Chase Riley of Wayne NJ, killed their point man and two others fled. We searched the body, captured a Chinese bolt-action rifle and moved out about 150 meters." "We stopped again and heard movement behind us, talking, and dogs barking," continued Mossman. "They must have been trying to track us with dogs and we couldn't get anyone on the radio, so we tried to break contact by moving as fast as possible."

Getting Closer

During the next three hours, the NVA force kept closing with the team. The Paratroopers however finally made radio contact with elements of the Americal Division and told them their situation. The Americal passed the word on to the 173d. But, the team was told, that no helicopters could fly in the typhoon which had been building up for a week, and to continue on their escape and evasion course.

Meanwhile, the decision was made to send four helicopters anyway in case the weather let up. A team ship piloted by Warrant Officer Sam M. Kyle of Castalion Springs, TN, a command and control ship piloted by Warrant Officer Dany Pennington of Crossett, AR, and two gunships were sent to the rescue. The LRRP's were notified and headed for the closest suitable pick up zone about 500 meters away while the weather and visibility got progressively worse.

"When we got to the pick-up zone, the NVA were practically breathing down our necks," said Mossman. "They couldn't see us though because the visibility was down to about 25 meters. We couldn't see the choppers either, but we could hear them, so we just kept signaling with a strobe light and just hoped."

No Sign of Team

Pennington reconned the area but couldn't locate the team, so he moved out to make room for Kyle. By this time, the team had made contact with the choppers, and were told that the gunships were leaving because the ceiling was so low they couldn't bring suppressive ground fire."I made the decision to stay and try to get them out," said Kyle, "because I'd sure hate to be in their position and have the choppers leave me. I figured this was their only chance because the weather probably wouldn't clear up for a couple of days, so I just kept circling lower and lower until I finally spotted their light."

Shocked Me

"I thought all the choppers had left," recalled Mossman, "so I was really shocked when I saw that beautiful ship loom up suddenly out of the rain. It took about two seconds for us to pile onto the helicopter in spite the trees, clumps of bushes, eight-foot elephant grass and the bouncing of the ship as it tried to keep steady in the storm." "They sure looked happy when they got on," remembered Kyle. "Afterwards, one of the Vietnamese who couldn't speak too much English, came up to me with a big smile on his face and motioned for me to come and have a beer with him. That sort of made it all worthwhile."

For more stories from the 173rd Fire Base go to http://hometown.aol.com/e46piodet/fb173a.htm

Mission 10

The Loss of Warrant Officer Arvie Silverberg and Crew

There are times in one's life when the occasional coincidence is just too bizarre or too incredible to be happening merely by chance. For me, this was one of those times.

I have been to The Wall a few times over the years, the Vietnam Memorial Wall, in Washington D.C. Some of my friends are there. Notice I didn't say their names are there...I said *they* are there; not just their names. For the most part, whenever I am in town there are a few names I look for specifically. My best friend from High School, John W. Stahl, a Marine Forward Observer killed by friendly fire. An artillery round fell short, killing him instantly. The 101st Screaming Eagle warrior that died of a sucking chest wound on my helicopter the night I was wounded, Allen Grotzke...the only patient I ever lost in the air. But I also walk the distance of the Wall back and forth a few times while there to do my best at honoring those 50,000+ men and 8 women whose names are engraved in black granite.

On this particular day, many, many years ago, it was during one of those such back and forth walks that I heard a man say "Go ahead, ask him." Within a few seconds, a woman about my age stepped up to me. She was with a man our age also and a young girl of about 10. She asked "Did you know Arvie Silverberg? He was a Dustoff pilot. His name is on the Wall." I had on my Army flight jacket, and she had recognized the 44th Medical Brigade patch on my right shoulder, the unit patch that most Vietnam Dustoff crewmembers wore. I did not know the name and told her so, but I also asked her when he was killed and with what unit did he fly? "283rd Medical Detachment, January 23, 1969" was her answer.

"One of my best friends in flight school flew for the 283rd" I replied "but January of 69 was a few months before we got there, so I'm afraid my buddy would not have known him. Sorry." And she thanked me as she and her family walked away. I literally just stood there for a few minutes, thinking about our short conversation while looking at the Wall but not really registering anything. Then it hit me..."You dumb (butt)!" I thought. "Here you are, a member of the Vietnam Helicopter Pilots Association with tons of resources available, and you let her walk away without trying to help her find someone who knew her brother!"

Hurriedly, I stepped off in the direction they had gone, but did not see them. I went all the way out to the street, scanning people and inside cars as they drove by, but they were gone. Almost as if they didn't exist, perhaps ghosts that the guys on the Wall had sent to see if I would help a fallen pilot's sister and I failed miserably. How could I redeem myself? I wrote down what little bit she had told me so that I would not forget and at the first opportunity, I looked him up...Arvie (Arvid) Sliverberg; he was from Massachusetts. The internet was very young in those days, but with the information I had, I found his obituary. A little more digging, I found a relative of hers and explaining who I was and why I was asking, they provided me with her phone number. As it turned out, she did not live that far away.

At our earliest mutual convenience, I drove to her house and was introduced to her daughter, the little girl that was with her at the Wall. The gentleman she was with was a friend who lived in D.C. She gave me more details of her brother's death which allowed me to do some research with the materials that I brought with me and before too long, I found someone who was in the 283rd about the same time as Arvie. A call to 411 information gave me a phone number in Florida; I called.

The phone rang but no one picked up, however, I got a voice recorder. "Hello, my name is Phil Marshall, I was a Dustoff pilot with the 237th and I am with Arvie Silverberg's sister, we are looking for someone who knew her brother..." when the phone was picked up. He had been monitoring the message as I was recording it and with a soft voice that was strained, the man on the other end of the phone said "Yes, I knew Arvie, he was flying my mission the night he was killed."

"Oh, no", I thought, "what have we done?"

As it turned out, Arvie had asked this fellow pilot if he would trade flights with him. There was something pressing that Arvie wanted to do but he was scheduled to fly that night, would this guy trade with him? Not unusual at all to trade assignments, it happened all the time. No problem. Well, at least that eased my mind a little bit, Arvie was the one that wanted to switch, not this guy. He and I chatted for a few minutes and then I asked him, would he mind speaking to Silverberg's sister? He agreed.

After a few minutes of pretty much just listening, she covered the mouthpiece and whispered to me "He's crying!" I simply told her "Make sure he knows you don't blame him for your brother's death." They talked for several more minutes, exchanged addresses and phone numbers before ending the call. Everyone, including the other pilot especially, I'm sure, was emotionally drained.

Several days later, she received a lengthy letter from the pilot in Florida which she shared with me. He went into much more detail about the events surrounding his death and, of course, apologized several more times for what happened. Years later, I met this pilot and will assure the reader that he is a wonderful example of a Vietnam Dustoff Helicopter Crewman and I consider him a friend today.

Here is what happened the night that one more Dustoff Huey and her crew were lost...

From the records of the Vietnam Helicopter Pilots Association, VHPA, this information came from U. S. Air Force records of (most) all aircraft accidents and incidents that occurred for all services in Southeast Asia during the Vietnam War. This document, known as the "Gold Book" was graciously donated to the VHPA by the Air Force. Information regarding the deceased that is not pertinent has been deleted by the author.

Information on U.S. Army helicopter UH-1H tail number 66-16217
The Army purchased this helicopter 0367
Total flight hours at this point: 00000485
Date: 01/23/69 MIA-POW file reference number: 1365
Incident number: 69012310.KIA
Unit: 283 MED DET
This was a Combat incident. This helicopter was LOSS TO INVENTORY
This was a Rescue and Recovery mission for Medical Evacuation
While in PickUp Zone this helicopter was at Hover at 0050 feet and 000 knots.
South Vietnam
UTM grid coordinates: YA940681
Helicopter took 1 hits from:
Explosive Weapon; Non-Artillery launched or static weapons containing explosive charges.
causing a Blast.
Systems damaged were: PERSONNEL
Casualties = 07 DOI, 01 INJ . .
The helicopter Crashed. Aircraft Destroyed.
Both mission and flight capability were terminated.
Burned
Original source(s) and document(s) from which the incident was created or updated: Defense Intelligence Agency Reference Notes. Defense Intelligence Agency Helicopter Loss database. Survivability/Vulnerability Information Analysis Center Helicopter database. Also: 1365, LNNF, CASRP, JSIDR (Lindenmuth New Format Data Base. Joint Services Incident Damage Report. Casualty Report.)
Loss to Inventory

Crew: HENDERSON, WILLIAM R; LUSTER RL MOORMAN
FD Crew Members:

CE PFC SLOPPYE ROBERT ROYCE KIA
MD SFC HENDERSON WILLIAM ROY RR
P WO1 DAVIS SYLVESTER KIA
AC WO1 SILVERBERG ARVID OSCAR JR KIA

Passengers:
SP4 SMITH EDWARD JR, AR, PX, KIA;

REFNO Synopsis:
HENDERSON, WILLIAM ROY Remains Returned 27 January 1969, ID'd 23 February 1976 Name: William Roy Henderson Rank/Branch: E5/US Army Unit: Date of Birth: 18 February 1943 Home City of Record: Cincinnati OH Date of Loss: 23 January 1969 Country of Loss: South Vietnam Loss Coordinates: 141911N 1074330E (YA940681) Status (in 1973): Missing in Action Category: 3 Acft/Vehicle/Ground: UH1H Other Personnel in Incident: Robert L. Luster, Frank D. Moorman (both missing) Source: Compiled by Homecoming II Project (919/527-8079) 01 April 1991 from one or more of the following: raw data from U.S. Government agency sources, correspondence with POW/MIA families, published sources, interviews. Copyright 1991 Homecoming II Project. REMARKS: REMS REC 690127, IDD 760223 SYNOPSIS: MACV-SOG (Military Assistance Command, Vietnam Studies and Observation Group) was a joint-service unconventional warfare task force engaged in highly classified operations throughout Southeast Asia. The 5th Special Forces channeled personnel into MACV-SOG (although it was not a Special Forces group) through Special Operations Augmentation (SOA), which provided their "cover" while under secret orders to MACV-SOG. The teams performed deep penetration missions of strategic reconnaissance and interdiction into Laos and Cambodia which were called, depending on the time frame, "Shining Brass" or "Prairie Fire" missions. On December 19, 1968, PFC Robert F. Scherdin was the assistant team leader of a MACV-SOG reconnaissance patrol in Rotanokiri Province, Cambodia, near the border of Laos, Cambodia and Vietnam. The team leader, suspecting enemy activity, had taken four members of the team to check out the area. The rear element, with Scherdin in charge,

came under heavy automatic weapon fire as they were moving up to the leader's position. Montagnard soldier Nguang in this element, saw Scherdin fall on his right side and tried to help him stand up, but Scherdin only groaned and would not get up. Nguang was then wounded himself and realized that he had been left by the other three Vietnamese of the rear element, whereupon he left Scherdin and joined the rest of the unit. The team leader and his element were extracted a short time later, then the rear element was extracted, except for Scherdin. The team leader had been informed that Scherdin had been wounded and because of the tactical situation, had to be left behind. Scherdin was not seen again. On December 30, a platoon was inserted into the area to search for Scherdin, but had to be extracted because of heavy enemy activity. In January, 1969, the rear element of the original team was also reinserted and remained four days. They died in a helicopter crash shortly after their extraction. They had not been questioned by the investigation board, and it is not known if they located information concerning Scherdin. There are only three Americans missing who are associated with the loss of a helicopter in January 1969. Lost January 23, 1969, in the general vicinity of the Scherdin loss, they are SGT. William R. Henderson, SP4 Frank D. Moorman and PFC Robert L. Luster. These three were lost in the Tri-border area in South Vietnam. Their remains were recovered on January 27, 1969 and positive identifications confirmed February 23, 1976. According to Luster's wife, the remains were subsequently buried in a mass grave. She does not accept the identification of her husband. Further, Mrs. Luster states that one of the team "walked off the plane in 1973" (was a released POW). According to all available public records, only Luster, Moorman and Henderson were classified missing from this incident, and no released POW went missing that day. It is believed that these three may have comprised the flight crew of the helicopter extracting the Special Forces search party. [As the remainder of the rear element was probably completely indigenous, U.S. records would not contain reference to them. The individual released may have been an indigenous.]

This record was last updated on 05/25/98

The following is crew member information for this incident:

Name: WO1 Sylvester Davis
Status: Killed In Action from an incident on 01/23/69 while performing the duty of Pilot.
Age at death: 28.7
Date of Birth: 05/30/40
Home City: Akron, OH
Service: AV branch of the reserve component of the U.S. Army.
Unit: 283 MED DET
Major organization: other
Flight class: 68-7
Service: AV branch of the U.S. Army.
The Wall location: 34W-064
Aircraft: UH-1H tail number 66-16217
Country: South Vietnam
MOS: 062B = Helicopter Pilot, Utility and Light Cargo Single Rotor
Primary cause: Hostile Fire
Major attributing cause: aircraft connected not at sea
Compliment cause: fire or burns
Vehicle involved: helicopter
Position in vehicle: pilot
Started Tour: 08/23/68
"Official" listing: helicopter air casualty - pilot
Length of service: 08
Location: Pleiku Province II Corps.
Military grid coordinates of event: YA940681
Reason: aircraft lost or crashed
Casualty type: Hostile - killed
The following information is secondary, but may help in explaining this incident.
Category of casualty as defined by the Army: battle dead Category of personnel: active duty Army Military class: warrant officer
This record was last updated on 08/20/95

Name: SFC William Roy Henderson
Status: Remains were returned on 01/27/69 from an incident on
01/23/69 while performing the duty of Medic crew member.
Declared dead on 03/10/76.
Age at death: 25.9
Date of Birth: 02/18/43
Home City: Cincinnati, OH
Service: regular component of the U.S. Army.

Unit: 283 MED DET
Major organization: USARV
Service: U.S. Army.
The Wall location: 34W-065
Aircraft: UH-1H tail number 66-16217
Call sign: Dustoff
Country: South Vietnam
MOS: 91B2F = Medical NCO
Primary cause: Remains 1/27/69
Major attributing cause: aircraft connected not at sea
Compliment cause: stroke
Vehicle involved: helicopter
Position in vehicle: unknown or not reported
Vehicle ownership: government
Started Tour: 12/02/68
"Official" listing: ground casualty
The initial status of this person was: missing in action - bonified
Length of service: *
Location: Pleiku Province II Corps.
Military grid coordinates of event: YA940681
Reason: aircraft lost or crashed
Casualty type: Hostile - died while missing
The following information is secondary, but may help in explaining this
incident.
Category of casualty as defined by the Army: battle dead Category of
personnel: active duty Army Military class: enlisted personnel
This record was last updated on 07/30/95

Name: SSG Robert Lee Luster
Status: Remains were returned on 01/27/69 from an incident on 01/23/69 while performing the duty of Passenger.
Declared dead on 04/08/76.
Age at death: 19.1
Date of Birth: 12/30/49
Home City: Tiffin, OH
Service: regular component of the U.S. Army.
Unit: 4 INF
Major organization: 4th Infantry Division
Service: U.S. Army.
The Wall location: 34W-065
Aircraft: UH-1H tail number 66-16217
Country: South Vietnam
MOS: 11B40 = Infantryman
Primary cause: Remains 1/69
Major attributing cause: aircraft connected not at sea
Compliment cause: small arms fire
Vehicle involved: helicopter
Position in vehicle: passenger
Vehicle ownership: government
Started Tour: 12/02/68
"Official" listing: helicopter air casualty - non-aircrew

The initial status of this person was: missing in action - bonified
Length of service: *
Location: Pleiku Province II Corps.
Military grid coordinates of event: YA940681
Reason: aircraft lost or crashed
Casualty type: Hostile - died while missing
The following information is secondary, but may help in explaining this incident.
Category of casualty as defined by the Army: battle dead Category of personnel: active duty Army Military class: enlisted personnel
This record was last updated on 07/30/95

Name: SSG Frank David Moorman
Status: Remains were returned on 01/27/69 from an incident on 01/23/69 while performing the duty of Passenger.
Declared dead on 04/08/76.
Age at death: 20.4
Date of Birth: 09/08/48
Home City: Clifton, NJ
Service: regular component of the U.S. Army.
Unit: 4 INF
Major organization: 4th Infantry Division
Service: U.S. Army.
The Wall location: 34W-066
Aircraft: UH-1H tail number 66-16217
Country: South Vietnam
MOS: 11B40 = Infantryman
Primary cause: Remains 1/27/69
Major attributing cause: aircraft connected not at sea
Compliment cause: small arms fire
Vehicle involved: helicopter
Position in vehicle: unknown or not reported
Vehicle ownership: government
Started Tour: 12/02/68
"Official" listing: helicopter air casualty - non-aircrew
The initial status of this person was: missing in action - bonified
Length of service: *
Location: Pleiku Province II Corps.
Military grid coordinates of event: YA940681
Reason: aircraft lost or crashed
Casualty type: Hostile - died while missing
The following information is secondary, but may help in explaining this incident.
Category of casualty as defined by the Army: battle dead Category of personnel: active duty Army Military class: enlisted personnel
This record was last updated on 07/30/95

Name: WO1 Arvid Oscar Silverberg, Jr.
Status: Killed In Action from an incident on 01/23/69 while performing the duty ofAircraft Commander.
Age at death: 22.5
Date of Birth: 08/01/46
Home City: West Brookfield, MA
Service: AV branch of the reserve component of the U.S. Army.
Unit: 283 MED DET
Major organization: other
Flight class: 68-1/67-25
Service: AV branch of the U.S. Army.
The Wall location: 34W-068
Short Summary: Hit by B-40 rocket while performing MEDEVAC hoist mission out of Pleiku, RVN.
Aircraft: UH-1H tail number 66-16217
Call sign: Medevac
Country: South Vietnam
MOS: 062B = Helicopter Pilot, Utility and Light Cargo Single Rotor
Primary cause: B-40 at hover
Major attributing cause: aircraft connected not at sea
Compliment cause: fire or burns
Vehicle involved: helicopter
Position in vehicle: co-pilot
Started Tour: 06/04/68
"Official" listing: helicopter air casualty - other aircrew
Location: Pleiku Province II Corps.
Military grid coordinates of event: YA940681
Reason: aircraft lost or crashed
Casualty type: Hostile - killed
The following information is secondary, but may help in explaining this incident.
Category of casualty as defined by the Army: battle dead Category of personnel: active duty Army Military class: warrant officer
This record was last updated on 08/20/95

Name: PFC Robert Royce Sloppye
Status: Killed In Action from an incident on 01/23/69 while performing the duty of Crew Chief.
Age at death: 20.9
Date of Birth: 03/15/48
Home City: Sacramento, CA
Service: component of the U.S. Army.
Unit: 283 MED DET
Major organization: other
Service: U.S. Army.
The Wall location: 34W-068
Aircraft: UH-1H tail number 66-16217
Call sign: Dustoff
Country: South Vietnam
MOS: 67N20 = UH-1 Helicopter Repairer
Major attributing cause: aircraft connected not at sea
Compliment cause: weapons
Vehicle involved: helicopter
Position in vehicle: crew chief
Started Tour: 12/10/68
"Official" listing: helicopter air casualty - other aircrew
Location: Pleiku Province II Corps.
Military grid coordinates of event: YA940681
Reason: aircraft lost or crashed
Casualty type: Hostile - killed
The following information is secondary, but may help in explaining this incident.
Category of casualty as defined by the Army: battle dead Category of personnel: active duty Army Military class: enlisted personnel
This record was last updated on 07/30/95

Name: SP4 Edward Smith, Jr.
Status: Killed In Action from an incident on 01/23/69 while performing
the duty of Passenger.
Date of Birth: 01/03/43
Home City: Steele, MO
Service: component of the U.S. Army.
Major organization: 4th Infantry Division
Service: U.S. Army.
The Wall location: 34W-068
Aircraft: UH-1H tail number 66-16217
Country: South Vietnam
MOS: 11B20 = Infantryman
Major attributing cause: aircraft connected not at sea
Compliment cause: fire or burns
Vehicle involved: helicopter
Position in vehicle: passenger
Started Tour: 04/25/68
"Official" listing: helicopter air casualty - non-aircrew
Length of service: 01
Location: Pleiku Province II Corps.
Military grid coordinates of event: YA940681
Reason: aircraft lost or crashed
Casualty type: Hostile - killed
The following information is secondary, but may help in explaining this
incident.
Category of casualty as defined by the Army: battle dead Category of
personnel: active duty Army Military class: enlisted personnel
This record was last updated on 07/31/96

Please provide any additional information on this helicopter to the
VHPA.

Warrant Officer Arvie Silverberg

Update:

Since including this mission in this series of Helicopter Rescues Vietnam, I have wanted to give Arvie's sister Alison a copy of this book. But where to find her? It had been over 20 years. Again, the Internet came to the rescue and I found one of her daughters on Facebook.

A phone call later and we were re-acquainted, to include her 96 year old Mother who was living with her for a few months during the Winter. Mrs.

Silverberg even told me she remembered my phone call to her when I was searching for her daughter. Her voice had the strength of a much younger woman. Mrs. Silverberg also mentioned something to me that tugged at my heart. "One day at the cemetery, there was a small flag laying on top of Arvie's grave stone. It had a note on the back 'We will never forget you' and it was only signed 'Paul'". I told her that it had to be a friend who knew him from Vietnam.

While still on the phone with her, I again pulled out my Helicopter Pilots Directory, just as I had done 20+ years ago. Looking at the list of pilots in Arvie's unit, it showed only last names and first initials, so I looked for the first initial "P". There was only one name with that initial and as I looked at the last name, I couldn't believe it. Paul Mercandetti, a friend from the 1970's, and he is on my cell phone list.

I didn't say anything to Alison or her Mother, but as soon as I hung up with the Silverbergs, I hit my speed dial for Paul. He answered the phone and after I made sure he knew it was me, I said to him "Two words; Arvie Silverberg." His answer was yes, he knew him, he had flown with him in Vietnam. So I asked him "Did you leave a flag on his gravestone?"

"Yes, it was me."

Amazing...again!

Mission 11
174th Assault Helicopter Company, ASC
The "Sharks" and "Dolphins"
By Wally Nunn

A Participant's View of
The Battle of Dai Do/Nhi Ha
April 29 - May 15, 1968

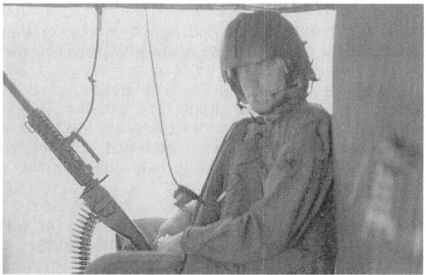

This photo was taken of SP4 Wally Nunn in the Summer of 1968 in his gunner's position on the right side of a UH-1C Shark gunship. This photo provides a good view of the modified M-60 7.62mm machinegun and the bungee cord attached to the top of the aircraft's cargo area and to the handle on top of the gun. The cord to the right is the microphone cord for his helmet. Also note the flak jacket Wally is wearing, and the sew-on subdued SP4 stripes on his fatigue uniform.

Photo taken in a Charlie Model Huey Gunship, before she was a gunner on an H Model slick. (Photo property of Wally Nunn)

SP4 Wally Nunn's story is reprinted here with his permission and with the 174th webmaster. It also appears on the 174th Assault Helicopter Company's web site; notes from the webmasters on Wally's web site posting are also reprinted in this mission.

On 29 April 1968, the 2/4 Marine Battalion Landing Team of the 3rd Marine Division, locked horns with an NVA Division (304th) in the 'ville" of Dai Do on the Cau Viet River 'horseshoe' just south of the Demilitarized Zone, DMZ (I Corp, Republic of Viet Nam, RVN). Intelligence had tipped our Forces that an entire North Vietnamese Army, NVA, Division was in the first stage of a major march to seize and destroy the 3rd Marine Division Headquarters at Dong Ha. The Army's grunt rifle battalion 3/21st Infantry, 196th Light Infantry Battalion, LIB, (out of the Americal Division) was attached to the 3rd Marine Division on May 1st to help quell the NVA's intentions.

The stubbornness of the NVA was stunning (as was always the case), though they out-numbered the US troops three to one. And though the loss of American lives was staggering (one is too many), the courage and the stamina of the Marines and Army was valorous. The campaign was marked by constant bombing and shelling (aerial, land based and Naval Cruiser USS Newport News). At several points the US Military powers used experimental 2000 pound bombs, when the village areas (Dai Do, Dinh To,

Dong Huan, An Lac, Thuong Do and Nhi Ha) turned into a NVA hornet nest. The 3rd Marines officially list the series of actions as ended on May 15 1968 and labeled it (during Operation Night Owl) as the Battle of Dai Do. The Americal classified it as a continuance of Operation Napoleon.

List of Casualties:

(KIA, Killed In Action, WIA, Wounded In Action, MIA, Missing In Action)

3d Marines Division- 233 KIA 821 WIA 1 MIA

3/21 Infantry 196th LIB- 29 KIA 130 WIA 1 MIA

Navy TF Clearwater- 15 KIA 22 WIA

ARVN- 42 KIA 124 MIA

NVA- 2945 KIA 47 POW

From the start of the battle, the Commanding Officer of the Marines 2/24 BLT 3rd Regiment, LTC. Hull, had great concern about air mobility. He requested that the Army provide helicopter support for resupply, extraction, insertion and medevac. The 174th AHC provided that air mobility for the entire battle. There were three Dolphin Slicks and Crews that accomplished this.

* Assistant Webmaster note: This Battle has been more than historically captured in our friend Keith William Nolan's fine book, The Magnificent Bastards. Dell Publishing: 1994. I highly recommend this reading. This is as good as it gets folks! Nolan's writing is chronological to the hour!

One of the 174th AHC aircraft (UH-1D 65-00910) was crewed by A/C WO1 Ken Johnson, Pilot WO1 Marty Wifholm, Crew Chief SP4 Frank Dailey and Door Gunner SP4 Wally Nunn. Out of the chaos of this Battle, Wally Nunn provided us here with his own personal collection of photos, and he and Ken Johnson tell us some "colorful" stories (factual). Dolphin #910 (the only camouflaged helicopter ever in the unit) is pictured below. That is Door Gunner SP4 Wally Nunn's "office" on the right side of the aircraft.

Stories from the Battlefield:

During a rare lull in their support missions, the 174th AHC Dolphin crew of #910 (WO1 Johnson, WO1 Wifholm, SP4 Dailey and SP4 Nunn) landed aside a clearing by the Cau Viet River to conserve fuel. They shut down the aircraft and two of the bored crew members (Nunn and Dailey) conspired to throw Pilot WO1 Henry "Marty" Wifholm in the River. "He kept bitchin' about how hot it was, and that he'd jump in that River for two cents. With my back to Marty, I gave them the nod for the go ahead."- Ken Johnson Upon coming out of the water, Wifholm took his clothes off to dry. As the hysterical bunch (with a half- naked- wet Wifholm), neared the aircraft, a call came over the radio for needed helicopter support for the Marines. Johnson says, "It seemed that they had a Unit which had taken a short burst from an Air Force fighter. They had some badly wounded, so we did what we were there to do and went after it." They all boarded the aircraft immediately and were airborne, with Wifholm 'sans' his clothing except for his shorts, boots and helmet. After they had dropped off the wounded, they got a priority call that The Commander for the 3rd Marines, COL Milton A. Hull, needed a lift.

Ken Johnson tells us, "We had to refuel first. We landed nose to nose with a Marine CH-46 at the POL point. We got to laughing at the look on their Pilots faces. Wifholm said he wanted to get dressed, but we were in a hurry. I tried to make 'delay' excuses, but you don't keep the 'O-6' waiting." Upon picking up Hull (in fresh fully starched fatigues), the Colonel spied Wifholm's lack of clothing and stated (with his trademark cigar between his teeth), "I always knew you Army Aviators were a bunch of queers." Upon reaching their destination, Hull told them to land 'angled' away from "his soldiers" and remain in the aircraft and get the hell out ASAP, to avoid his fellow Marines and counterparts from seeing them. Johnson also adds, "We laughed so hard, because we knew if we 'went down' and the NVA came upon us, they would see Marty and run!"

On Friday, 3 May 1968, a Marine Crusader that was making a bombing run on the Village of Nhi Ha was hit by enemy fire and did not 'pull up'. No one saw a parachute either. However, US Personnel with a nearby ARVN unit spotted (with binoculars) a lone figure walking around east of the battlefield. A FAC, in the air above, then confirmed the sighting. Ken Johnson and his crew chimed in on the radio saying, "We're coming in low and hot, so direct us up." The FAC Birddog guided the 174th AHC slick from their fifteen-foot altitude and then a hop over some trees. They immediately spotted an olive drab figure wandering aimlessly in a rice paddy. He appeared unarmed. When the Aircraft approached, the man just stopped and looked up. Johnson reported on the radio "We got the Pilot insight. We're going in to pick him up." Approaching very fast, Johnson saw the man's black hair and the misfit fatigues. He yelled, "It's a dink, that's a goddamned dink!" As he pulled up and out, he yelled, "It's not the Pilot! It's a hard- core NVA, and we are going to engage him!" The Marines (monitoring the Army net) said, "Don't shoot him. We're want to take him prisoner." Johnson replied, "What the hell do you guys expect us to do out here? We've got our butts hanging out! We're going to kill him." The Marines then responded with a direct order not to shoot and to take him prisoner.

Wally Nunn tells us, "We just circled around. I thought for sure it was a trap. I called over the intercom to Johnson, telling him that the Marines were crazy. I can have an 'accident' here you know. Ken told me again to hold fire. An ARVN unit was about 20 minutes away. We thought about letting them come get him, but that would give the enemy time to surround us. Johnson told me to look the NVA over real good, because we were 'going in'. I said this is f.....g nuts! No sh..t!

We landed, and I jumped out with an M16 and screamed, Get the F...k On! I assumed I was probably going to have to shoot him anyway, but he was real scared and jumped right in. I held my .38 to his head the whole way back to the 3/21st Command Post, CP, but he was noticeably trembling from the helicopter ride and hanging on for dear life When we got to the CP, he was still 'gripped', so I jerked him hard and threw him out. A Marine Captain pulled some identification off of him out of one of his pockets. In another pouch pocket was a Chicom Grenade! Johnson just lifted his helmet visor and dropped his jaw. I, in the meantime, had almost had my 'accident' I spoke about earlier.

Earlier in the same day (in same area- Nhi Ha), we were called to extract wounded Alpha Company 3/21 GIs. Practically the whole Company had been either killed or wounded. They were annihilated! However, 'fast- movers' (jets) were dropping 'drag bombs' just over the casualties to destroy the NVA that had them flanked. As we approached, Johnson and Wifholm were on the fire control net. They were getting trajectory reports from the artillery, tactical air and Naval counter battery from the USS Newport News. Johnson (who deserved a Medal of Honor) flew in under the onslaught of 'incoming'! The only thing is, that Ken orders me out on the skids to look up to see how low we were below the bombing!" Ken Johnson adds, "Actually, we advised the Forward Air Controller, FAC, and the Pilots that we were coming in under them and it was not a mistake. We didn't want them to pull up if they saw us passing under them. I think they thought I was crazy, but it was a tactic that worked, because the 'bad-guys' were either ducking for cover or shooting at the jets instead of us!" Ken was determined to get the WIAs out, thank God he came up with the tactics to get in and get out. We not only saved the men, we survived where two other helicopters and several attack aircraft did not.

Nunn continues, "Then about seventy-five meters out from the flank, I spied a bunker and I could see the faces of NVA through an opening. I yelled at the pilots; There they are! I'm going to take them under fire! Johnson called back; Don't shoot. For some reason they ain't shooting at us. Let's do our job and go get the wounded." Wally recalled "It was amazing, I could see their eyes but they didn't shoot at us, I think they knew we were coming in to pick up wounded. They had to be professional NVA soldiers, not new recruits or anything like that. We were able to safely land, pick up our wounded and depart without taking any fire, and believe me, there was plenty of that going both directions!

I remember one trip, we picked up some wounded Marines and once we got them on the aircraft, this one guy had his leg blown off and he is doing the best he can to help his buddy with a sucking chest wound stay alive. Amazing what we did for each other sometimes. For those who have never experienced combat, they cannot imagine the camaraderie and caring for each other like that." No wonder combat warriors are so close, then and even yet today.

The battle continued for several days, and Wally Nunn with his crewmates was there the whole time.

When two sister ships were shot down, the 174th sent a fourth ship to rotate. "Johnson, the Aircraft Commander, told the new ship to stay at Camp Evans as we already knew the AO and it would be difficult for a new ship to insert itself into the battle" Nunn recalled. "The crew sarcastically thanked Ken for volunteering us though we were actually glad he did, the men of the 3rd/21st had become family and you don't leave family when they need you. Artillery was firing all the time. Offshore batteries from the Navy, Marine artillery, tactical air support; even enemy NVA 152mm artillery, crew served weapons and tracked vehicles. It was crazy, aircraft were getting shot down all the time! We evacuated 90 wounded during that battle, and 2 Marines were awarded the Medal of Honor for their actions at this time." It was a constant battle for the air crews just trying to keep track of where all the ordinance was coming from and where it was impacting. Nothing like an artillery shell through the cargo compartment to ruin your day!

Years after the action the battalion commander of the 3rd/21st and the CO of one the line companies, Dennis Leach, decided that Ken should be recognized for his actions during this battle. In 2012, he was awarded the Silver Star, he deserved nothing less. Marty Wifholm, the pilot, has been put in for a Distinguished Flying Cross which is still working its way through the Army Awards Branch.

Assistant Webmaster note: We've already mentioned the helicopter and crew of UH-1D 65-00910. The other two 174th AHC helicopters and crew members were: UH-1D 66-00864- A/C WO1 Hank Tews, Pilot Unknown, Crew Chief SP4 Sam Davis and Door Gunner PFC Allen Weamer. UH-1D

67-17281- A/C Unknown, Pilot Unknown, Crew Chief SP5 Carl McCoy and Door Gunner Unknown. It should also be noted that these brave men all volunteered for these support missions! "Both #864 and #281 were shot all to hell- no injuries."-Nunn

This mission also appears on the 174th ASC, Assault Helicopter Company, website. Reprinted with permission from Wally Nunn.

Mission 12

The Rescue

By Charlotte A. Powell
In collaboration with Jeff Bounds and Fred Jackson

Memorial Day, May 30th, 1969

B Troop (Dutchmasters)
7th Armored Squadron, 1st Air Cavalry
Vinh Long Air Base, Republic of Vietnam

Author's note: We had to fight the Vietnam War with one hand tied behind our collective backs. This mission shows the absurd conditions under which we had to conduct the war. Imagine this; You are having a backyard Bar-B-Que with your family and friends, when the neighbors next door start throwing rocks at you over the fence. Not good...but you can't go over there because someone has drawn a line on a map and says "You can't go over there. It's their property." Yet they continue to throw stones at you. You might try to sneak over there later at night and retaliate, but in the meantime, during your get-together, they continue to throw rocks at you and you can't throw them back, You're not allowed! Is that stupid or not? Your hands are tied and they are killing your friends and family with their rock throwing. No way to fight a war, but that was what we had to do. Here is what happened to these helicopter crews in the 1st Cav:

Most combat units were in a Memorial Day stand-down. B Troop scheduled one visual recon along the Vietnam/Cambodia border. The preflight briefing included an intelligence report suggesting minimal enemy activity because they were in observance of Ho Chi Minh's birthday.

Scout and weapons platoons, commonly called a Hunter/Killer team, would conduct the recon. The team consisted of 2 OH-6A Light Observation Helicopters (Loaches), and 2 AH-1 gunships (Cobras) and 1 UH1 Huey, Command & Control. The Scout's normal mission was to fly low and slow, draw enemy fire, and then mark the contact with red smoke. Cobra Gunships would then roll in with high-speed dives, saturating the target area with lethal fire both covering the rapid exit of the Loaches and hopefully killing the enemy.

Loaches were lightly armed with a port (left) side mounted six-barrel 7.62mm minigun, which was capable of a cyclic rate of fire of either 2,000 or 4,000 rounds per minute, as well as various grenades, and the observer's CAR-15, a modified M-16.

Cobras carried a full weapons array, including chin turret mounted 7.62 mini-gun, or a 40mm grenade launcher, and a mix of aerial rockets, that could include fleshettes, HE (high explosive), or willi-peet (white phosphorous) with either PD (point detonating) or VT (proximity detonating) fuses.

The team's mission that day was to report any enemy movement or buildup, after which they would return to base for an afternoon of R&R, a time to kick back and enjoy a few beers with the rest of the guys. Warrant Officer Fred Jackson, whom everyone called Jack, readied his Loach, doing his pre-flight check. Though only in country 4 months, Jack had earned respect as a proficient scout pilot whose diligence was appreciated by others who flew missions with him. His observer that day was SP4 Craig Myers.

They often paired together because not only was Craig an excellent observer, but he was also the OH-6's crewchief, and he cared for the Loach as though it were his own. In the other Loach, 1LT. Jeff Bounds, the Scout fire team leader, and SP4 Vinnie Costello* as his observer, readied their aircraft. Along with their observers, Jeff and Jack had developed firm friendships, and respect for each other's abilities. Their mutual admiration was further honed as they frequently worked combat missions together.

On the Weapons half of the team was 1LT. Roy Sudeck, the Cobra fire team's leader. Sudeck's "front seat" was handling map reading duties and guiding the scouts from above. The border recon included, among other areas, the "Parrot's Beak" (an area of Cambodia that juts into South Vietnam west of Saigon and north of the Mekong River). This area was always difficult to work because the irregular border had few distinguishing landmarks.

The mission began with the Loaches dropping 'down on the deck,' flying low and slow, looking for anything that would suggest suspicious ground activity. The Cobras stationed themselves at altitude, out of range of any small arms fire, while directing the scout ships in their search. Unknowingly, the scouts crossed over the border into Cambodia by about 2 clicks (kilometers). Unaware of the misdirection they had taken, they came upon a small village adjacent to a dense wood line. As they overflew its southern perimeter, both Scouts noted that there were a number of young, military aged men, and it was the largest concentration either had ever seen. Their movements were not so unusual as to draw immediate alarm, but their presence suggested further investigation.

After receiving confirmation (later discovered to be inaccurate) that they were on the Vietnam side of the border, the scouts were given permission to overfly it again. This time there was more activity within the village. Jack called over the radio, reporting that he had seen something - possibly a weapon. A C&C (Command and Control) Huey had the immediate responsibility of the Hunter/Killer team, but it was on the ground at Bac Chien. The questionable ground activity and possible weapon sighting were relayed by having Roy's wingman climb to altitude to the 7/1 Squadron TOC (Tactical Operations Center), who passed it up to the 164th Group HQ. Shortly thereafter, the Scouts were instructed to do a third go around and verify the sighting.

Jeff Bounds later said that this was a major mistake and was probably one of the worst orders he had ever been given. They had followed the pre-flight briefing orders, had observed and reported, and had not made any engagements.

A Hunter/Killer team, although a formidable force, couldn't carry a fight very far with no backup and only four aircraft. Both Scout pilots had that uneasy feeling learned from hours of scouting; their instincts told them this was a mistake. They both radioed their concerns, and then reluctantly went ahead with the go around. Despite their apprehensions, orders were orders.

The third and final pass began. With Jeff as the lead ship, and Jack on his wing, they picked up ground speed, flying fast and low, as speed was always the best ally in this sort of situation. On returning, they found the village and surrounding area eerily quiet, and still. Jeff spotted a man who was crouched close to the ground, facing down, as though praying. Requesting cover from his wing ship, Jeff slowed down in front of the man to see what was going on. The man suddenly looked up in the direction of the approaching Loach and drew an AK 47 from under his body. Jeff decelerated, hit the pedal, and turned Vinnie, who was an excellent shot, toward the man. Vinnie, armed with a CAR-15, let out a few quick and accurate rounds, neutralizing the enemy soldier.

All hell broke loose. The village, and nearby wood line, exploded with enemy troops firing 50's, 30's, and all the small arms they had. None of the scouts had even been under such intense fire. It was the largest group of enemy military personnel that any of them had ever seen. Later intelligence report revealed that this concentration of enemy troops was part of a 9th Division, NVA [North Vietnamese Army] buildup, massing for cross-border infiltration.

Both pilots called in receiving hits to their aircraft as they pulled all the collective they could get, slammed the cyclic to the forward stop, and tried to build airspeed. Jack triggered his mini gun with streams of suppressive fire as he provided cover for Jeff's escape. With no shortage of targets, he was firing at anything that moved. On the way out Jeff heard the words a pilot never wants to hear. "Jack's down, Jack's down," Vinnie shouted. Jack had been hit. A round had entered his left thigh, shattering his hip, and then taking out much of his left buttock. Craig attempted to take control of the aircraft, but the ship took more hits and headed into the ground, bouncing several times after the initial impact, finally coming to rest on it's left side with the blades digging in and disintegrated with ground contact.

Meanwhile, Jeff wasted no time positioning himself to rescue the downed crew, it was what a pilot did, and it required no second thoughts, just action. Get his buddies out no matter what the risk. Vinnie pointed out that enemy troops were moving toward the downed helicopter. The gunships sealed off the downed aircraft in a ring of mini-gun and rocket fire to keep the enemy troops at bay. Jeff asked for a brief cease-fire so he could get in close to Jack's Loach. Roy Sudeck's fire team gave him the window he needed, and he settled into a hover near Jack's aircraft; firing on the converging NVA troops with his mini gun, spitting out 4000 rounds a minute.

Just as Jeff's mini gun jammed, an enemy soldier popped up out of a spider hole a few meters in front of them and opened fire with an AK 47. Jeff's only option was to drop down rapidly, try to avoid the bullets, and get Jack and Craig out of there. Just as the enemy solder fired a full AK clip above Jeff and Vinnie's heads and through the doghouse, control assemblies, and upper bubbles, Jeff's Loach took a hard bounce, sending the frag grenades that they kept between the seats into the air, almost to eye level. Jeff's struggle to keep his six foot, one inch frame behind his chicken plate resulted in a permanent back injury that was to flare up later and stay with him through the rest of his life. At the time, though, his back injury, like the small splintering shrapnel wounds he sustained, went unnoticed.

The enemy soldier who had been shooting at Jeff and Vinnie disappeared in a hail of fire from the gunships above. In the downed aircraft, which had rolled hard to the left, Craig figured that he'd never be able to pull Jack up and out of the right doorway, which was now above him. Craig took his CAR-15 and blew out the bubble, scaring the hell out of Jeff and Vinnie, who had landed close by.

Precious seconds passed as Craig, covered with blood and debris, fumbled to locate Jack's seat belt. Finding it, he pulled the release, and Jack fell into his arms. Vinnie didn't hesitate. He leapt from the Loach and ran to help Craig pull Jack through the blown bubble. Together the men carried and dragged Jack to Jeff's aircraft. Despite protests to hurry and get on board, Craig returned to the downed Loach and retrieved the radio and assorted personal equipment, keeping it from falling into enemy hands. Throwing what he had retrieved in the back seat of the Loach, Craig climbed into the aircraft and put his arm around his pilot to secure him for the escape.

Jeff prepared to lift off. Between the numbers of hits his Loach sustained, added to the hard landing, and the additional weight of two passengers, he had good reasons to worry that it might not fly. With gunships providing cover, by a miracle, the Loach lifted off. Jeff's objective now was to return to base with everyone still intact. Flying no higher than 100 feet above the ground, he milked as much speed as possible from the aircraft by holding the TOT [turbine outlet temperature] up to the redline and then dropping it back for a few seconds as per the operating limitations of the aircraft, nailing the air speed at nearly 130 knots for the 45 minutes return trip to Vinh Long.

Jack was in excruciating pain and bleeding profusely. Vinnie got both Craig and Jack's helmet jacks plugged into the intercom system, and Craig told Vinnie that they needed to find something to stop Jack's bleeding. Vinnie struggled to release the First Aid kit. When he finally got it open, he frantically dug through it. Finally, at the bottom of the box, he found a gauze pad that was big enough to apply pressure to the wound. Jack's left leg, attached only by muscle and tissue, bounced and was twisted by his position in the aircraft. Craig worried that his friend might die. Stopping the bleeding was almost impossible, Jack's face was ghostly pale, and he kept losing consciousness.

The forty-five-minute flight seemed infinitely longer. Jeff radioed Vinh Long Tower (Air Traffic Control) that they had a medical emergency and needed clearance for a straight-in approach. ATC cleared all air and runway traffic and vectored the surviving Loach to the medical pad. When they set down, Craig stayed with Jack as the medics transferred him to a waiting Medevac to be airlifted to the nearest MASH unit in Binh Thuy. Jeff and Vinnie took their damaged aircraft to the Loach revetments, threw all their gear in, did a quick preflight on another aircraft, and returned to the crash site. In the area adjacent to the village, a large number of solders were picking through the remains of the Loach, while many more were scattered throughout the area, apparently tending to their casualties. The Cobras were orbiting several clicks from the crash site and Jeff queried Roy as to why they weren't firing on the enemy troops when word came over the radio that they had inadvertently crossed the border into Cambodia.

There would be no recovery of the downed Loach and Jeff was ordered to remain clear. They couldn't even blow the aircraft in place! Jeff prayed that the mini-gun on Fred's aircraft had been rendered inoperable in the crash. He didn't want it shooting at him, or anyone else, some day in the future. Returning to base, Jeff and Vinnie learned that Jack was out of surgery, stabilized, but in critical condition. The OH-6A that had brought all four back safely was signed off as unsalvageable with over 130 bullet holes in it – virtually every critical component other than the engine and the transmissions had sustained such damage that any of them alone would have rendered it unflyable! A crew chief gave Jeff one of the bell cranks that had a bullet hole completely through it. He still has it today.

WO1 Fred Jackson was to spend the next 3 years in various hospitals, ending up at Walson Army Hospital at Ft. Dix, NJ. For the first year he was in a full body cast. Over the next two years he had multiple surgeries to enable him to walk again. He was awarded the Air Medal for Heroism. Observers, Craig Myers and Vinnie Costello* were also awarded the Air Medal With "V" For Heroism. Jeff Bounds and Roy

Sudeck received the Distinguished Flying Cross for their part in this rescue.

A day that was to have been uneventful would forever impact the lives of those who participated in the rescue mission. Fred Jackson, (Jack) was medically retired from the Army. He now owns an organic citrus grove in Florida, where he lives with his wife and children. Jeff Bounds is a retired FAA Air Traffic Controller, and resides in Salisbury, Maryland with his wife. Both men are grandfathers. This article has been written for the children and grandchildren of all these men so they will know of their father's, or grandfather's, contributions that day when bravery and loyalty saved two lives.

*Note: The name "Costello" is fictitious, as Vinnie's real last name is unknown. The authors would welcome information about Vinnie, Craig, or any of the other participants.

Copyright © May 30, 2001, Charlotte A. Powell

Mission 13

Destiny Joins Fate

By J. Bruce Huffman

The sun pushed its way over the horizon of the South China Sea that September morning in 1968 as I wandered down to the Tactical Operations Center, TOC, with my map under my arm, to get the final briefing for the first light mission that morning. WO Ernie Burns was my Red Bird and would drive his UH-1B to always be in a position to rain hell on any foolish NVA unfortunate to find his way into his gun sight reticle and threaten my low bird. Ernie and I reviewed the final details of the mission and covered the tactical frequencies we'd be operating on, who would monitor the emergency radio channel, and what frequency we'd communicate in VHF to stay out of each other's way.

The mission was a simple one: Check in with a D Troop platoon that had been in a night defensive position, monitoring trail activity between the "Street Without Joy" and the distant NVA base camps in the mountains west of Camp Evans. I was to be on the alert for military-age males without proper ARVN identification, and we would 'snatch' them for detailed interrogation at the base camp. Our Blues (infantry platoon) were standing by, in a lager at Evans, with the lifts (assault helicopters) monitoring the operation from the TOC. We finished the rest of the coordination briefing and made our way to the revetments to preflight and get cranked up and begin the hunt.

My crew already was there and loading up OH-6A Zero Seven Niner with the tools of the trade (e.g. fragmentation grenades, white phosphorous, a few thermite and concussion grenades, ammo for the chunker (M-79), clips for the M-16 (1 tracer, 3 ball), a half load for the mini-gun, and enough M-60 ammo for Doug Gossage's free gun to give him plenty to work with. We weren't going on a bear hunt, but if we saw a bear it would be in some serious trouble. I loved my crew and was proud of the way we'd come together to fly safe, fight hard, and come back home at the end of the day to yet another cold Ballantine beer.

My crew chief and gunner was Specialist 4 Douglas Gossage. Doug came from Missouri and could throw a grenade, from any combination of bank and airspeed, through the opening of a bunker with predictable consistency. When his M-60 would talk, six rounds later the target would be down. Doug had just turned 19 years old. Our observer was Staff Sgt. John States, who had been trained in armor reconnaissance at Fort Knox. John was from Baltimore, got airsick frequently and had trouble reading the map early on. States had the heart of a lion, though, and on those days when we would find 'em, he was skilled at sending the bad guys on a very long dirt nap.

As we began the mission, we flew east over the featureless terrain of the coastal plain toward Quang Tri. The crews had checked their guns and our Pink Team was in the hunt. The mission was a success.

We bagged no less than six guys who later turned out to be NVA, which had been in the villages the night before and failed to get home before we turned them into prisoner pumpkins the following morning. We had refueled and armed at LZ Jane earlier and had completed our last refueling at Camp Evans. All in all, it had been a good morning and I was looking forward to shutting down and pulling out my lawn chair to work on my R&R tan.

I landed to a hover on the nasty, oiled dirt strip we shared with Bravo Troop and saw WO Wallace running toward my bird. John Wallace was relatively new, but had shown skill and aggressiveness. I sat the bird down and Wallace leaned in and said: "Get out! I need your bird and crew. Lobes Echo is in contact and the snake is cranking." I said, "We've already been up for 3.8 hours. Give me the damn brief or get your own bird up!" John replied, "We don't have time, it looks like it could be a Prairie Fire!" I stepped out of the LOH, picked up my chicken plate as John flew over the concertina wire and turned west, headed for the foothills leading to the A Shau Valley.

Less than 30 minutes later Cavalier White — 1LT. James G. Ungaro — walked into my hooch to tell me, "Wallace is down and they are all dead!"

Charlie Troop's tribute to our missing warriors:

"WO1 John C. Wallace, Spec. 4 Douglas E. Gossage, and Staff Sgt. John Wayne States. KIA, 26 September 1968. Wallace had checked in with Lobes Echo and learned they were engaged with at least a battalion of NVA troops. Echo was under canopy on the high ground that overlooked a depression held on three sides by the ground and the great equalizer: Firepower.

Wallace made the initial pass and discovered a 12.7 mm heavy machine gun in a doughnut bunker and had Gossage mark it as they blazed by. The AC of the snake refused to shoot due to the proximity of the friendly positions. He recently had been involved in a short round incident that had wounded U.S. troops and had been badly reprimanded and humiliated by an officer who should have known better.

While the high bird was fooling around trying to get some artillery cranked up, Wallace decided to take out the gun. He flew in and, with a combination of M-60 fire and fragmentation grenades, got the 12.7 mm. Unfortunately, the other two positions protecting the NVA regimental command post got him. The aircraft landed in the wrecked position of the first gun. States stepped over what once had been the front console and canopy, and went head to head with an NVA who got in the first shot.

Wallace unstrapped and went out the right door and began a run for his life toward Lobes Echo, which was laying down an intense base of fire to cover him as he ran uphill. It was less than 100 meters from the downed bird to the ARVN position. Wallace was hit in the legs 40 meters from relative safety. He went down hard and before he could get up, an NVA officer, in full view of the U.S. adviser working with the ARVN troops, shot him in the neck with a pistol.

Gossage had everything he needed: Lots of ammo

and plenty of targets. The ARVN Rangers said the sound of the M-60 rattled on until finally the NVA fired an RPG-7 into the downed bird and the gun went silent. When our recovery was completed, the bodies of 12 NVA were found in and around the remains of Zero Seven Niner. Gossage had done his duty!" A plaque given to Charlie Troop by Company E, 1st ARVN Ranger Division commemorating the heroism of WO1 John C. Wallace, Spec. 4 Douglas E. Gossage, and Staff Sgt. John Wayne States. KIA, 26 September 1968.

I often reflect on "what if?" about their loss, but realize that on that day their fate intersected their destiny, with terrible consequences. It was an honor to have served with them; warriors to the end!

Author's note: In an interview with Mr. Huffman, he informed me that Wallace had recently received a "Dear John" letter. (How ironic, his name really was John!) "I think that the letter depressed him so much that he didn't care whether he lived or died" Bruce said.

The "Dear John" letter reminds me of a supposed event which happened in Vietnam. Apparently a guy received such a letter from his girlfriend, which, of course, devastated him. Here we were, fighting for our country half a world away while our girlfriends and wives were...shall we say...NOT fighting half a world away for their country. Of course most waited for their men to come home but not all did.

Even though this warrior was devastated, he asked all his buddies for photos of their wives or girlfriends. He then composed a letter to go with all the photos he had accumulated which said something like " I am sorry that you will no longer be waiting for me, however, I am having trouble putting your name with your face. Please indicate on the enclosed photos which one is you and then send them back so I will know who you are."

Don't know if it really happened or not but if it did, THAT guy deserves a medal for thinking outside the box!

A further interview with Bruce Huffman revealed some more memorable missions. Bruce told me that he realized he was the oldest Scout pilot in the unit, and because the Scout's job was very risky, it was determined that for his last two months in country he would start flying lift birds, Huey Slicks. The Slicks were the "do everything" Huey…troop insertions/extractions, "ash and trash" missions and even medevac missions when necessary. One of those medevac missions occurred at the infamous Khe Sanh landing strip. "We had a call to pick up a wounded Marine there under less than ideal weather conditions and the Marines were under fire. We landed at the designated spot, next to a bunker, and when we touched down, I saw two Marines kinda point the wounded guy towards our aircraft and then duck down back into the bunker! My crewman grabbed him and put him in the helicopter.

It seems that most of his newfound Huey missions involved LRRPs, Long Range Reconnaissance Patrols. Commanders wanted a prisoner for intelligence interrogations and the LRRPs provided. However, when they found and surprised their "person of opportunity", he refused to "Chu Hoi", the

Vietnamese phrase for "surrender and come to our side". He apparently tried to shoot his way out of his situation but received gunshots to the stomach instead of escaping.

With their prisoner now obtained, the gunfire alerted other enemy troops and the LRRP team was now in a race for their lives. Calling Huffman and his crew to pick them up, the LRRPs were running and shooting as they were trying to make their way to the river for their pickup...fire and fall back. Locating the pickup point, Bruce Huffman had to dip the aircraft's skids down into the river. "The trees went right up to the river's edge and there was no place to land, so I had to put the helicopter into the river. The good guys were trying to get their prisoner up into the aircraft but the water was so deep they could not get him up high enough over their heads. So I let the Huey sink deeper into the water, to the point that there was water flowing through the cargo compartment. I was concerned about the tail rotor getting in the water and the crew told me we were throwing a rooster tail off the rotor, so I figured I was as low as I could go." Of course, a couple of the LRRPs are now at the water's edge holding off the bad guys, shooting while we finally got everyone on board."

Returning to "Charlie Med", the closest medical facility, "We were still pumped from the excitement of the pickup. When we landed, everyone in the back of the aircraft was soaking wet and emotionally drained but still on that adrenaline high. Strangely, no one came out to meet us when finally this nurse shows up. She gave all her attention to the LRRPs until finally she looked at our wounded POW. The nurse then said something like 'Ah, does the little man want a drink?' as he pointed to his mouth while holding his stomach. As soon as he took a drink, he coughed up a big black blood clot and died!

At this point, I am still in my seat as the crew chief lost it. He tackled the nurse, taking her to the ground in a choke hold yelling 'Do you have any idea what we just went through to get this guy and you just killed him!' as she is screaming for him to let her up. She's yelling 'I'm gonna court martial you!'" Bruce's first thought was that his career was now over. " I jumped out of the aircraft and ran around the nose as a Major comes out the door and seeing the commotion, unholsters his gun and points it at my crew chief on the ground. All this time, the door gunner was apparently half asleep and now becomes alert. Seeing the Major pointing his weapon at the crew chief, the gunner swung his M60 machine gun around and points it at the Major!

Seeing the door gunner, the Major lowered his 45 while the Second Lieutenant with the LRRPs grabbed the crew chief and pulled him off the nurse, yelling "Let her go, let her go!" With the Major threatening Court Martial, everyone boarded the aircraft and Huffman flew them back to base.

Immediately upon landing, Huffman went to his Commanding Officer and told him what happened. The CO asked Bruce "Do you think what your crewman did caused any lasting damage?" Bruce said "No. I think she just got a red face and was crying." The CO's reply surprised Huffman, "F%&$ 'em, sounds like she deserved it. I'm standing by you guys, don't worry about it, this is over right now." And Bruce Huffman never did hear anymore about it. Months later, Huffman heard that the crew chief was killed in a crash; ironically, there is now a ball field in his home town named after him.

Such was one day in the "unshortened" career of Bruce Huffman, Vietnam Huey pilot.

Mission 14

Two Down

"I just wanted to be a part of the D Troop team."

By Mike Vaughn

HOME OF THE NOTORIOUS CU CHI TUNNELS.....

No more free ride for me...I'm the man now. I was barely nineteen years old, with all the headaches and responsibilities of a Crew Chief (CE): my very own helicopter. I was the proud owner of 65-09660 (old six-six-zero). A Huey UH-1D (slick): one-each, olive Drab, OD, in color. For those who may not understand, the CE actually believes he owns his helicopter, it's his baby. However, out of the goodness of our hearts, we would allow the pilots to fly our ships from time to time.

I had been a CE for only a few days before this mission, and I had been in country just a couple of months. I was still thought of as one of the new guys. Before getting my own ship, I had been lucky enough to get some very valuable experience from Specialist 4 (SP4) Laura, an incredibly skilled crew chief. I believe he was from Texas. During this period, I had been assigned to him as his gunner. I had flown with him for several weeks; but I was still pretty green. He was very patient with me during my training. After each flight, CE Laura would take the time to explain every part of the last mission. He would first explain what I had done right and then he would describe what I had done wrong. He told me what I needed to do to get it right. I learned a lot from him. One of the many things he taught me was to have pride in my helicopter and in my job as CE. I think of him often, even after all these years.

Our mission that day would be to make a pickup of a six man infantry ambush team; they had been out in the boonies all night. We were going to make the extraction just after first light, from a place called "The Devil's Playground." The Devil's Playground was only a short distance outside of the perimeter of our Cu Chi base camp, so we were going to low level out to the Landing Zone (LZ). I realize that everyone was not fortunate enough to experience what our pilots considered low level flight. Just to clarify, low level flight, or contour flight, means just what the name implies. It means on the deck, sometimes flying as low as 24 inches or less above the contour of the landscape. Just to illustrate, when we left base camp on that mission; we were flying so low we had to actually had to climb a few feet just to clear the barbed wire strung around the perimeter of the camp. I can only imagine how my Aircraft Commander (AC) Warrant Officer 1 F.L. Anderson must have felt on this particular mission. Mr. Anderson was hardcore all the way through, a very good pilot with many rough missions already included on his resume. On this mission, however, he was stuck with a brand new crew chief, a new gunner (SP4 Wilcox) and a second pilot that was still pissing stateside beer.

The sun is almost fully above the horizon, and the air still feels quite cool as I sat in the open door of the chopper. We are not expecting any trouble on this one, just a routine pickup. The chopper is cruising along at around 110 knots, just a couple of feet above the ground. We approach the LZ and start a gentle right turn; we are coming in very low and very fast. The new pilot is at the controls; he must have seen he was going to overshoot the LZ. He pulls back hard on the cyclic as he tries to dump his airspeed. Old six-six-zero's nose is pointed toward the sky and she is almost standing on her tail.

Unfortunately, we are too low and the maneuver too radical. There is the sound of a huge explosion, as the tail-boon of the helicopter comes into contact with a rice dike. I feel a tremendous jolt run through the whole helicopter. The tail rotor and the complete gearbox assembly are immediately ripped away from the tail of the helicopter. It's as though everything is moving in slow motion. I feel myself holding onto my machine gun with all the force I can muster -- like that's going to help me. We hit the ground the first time with a glancing blow. All I can think of is the fuel tanks are going to explode. We briefly become airborne again while managing to miss several more rice dikes in the process. As we become airborne, the helicopter goes into a very violent spin. By this time, I knew Mr. Anderson (AC) had taken over the flight controls, and I feel him instantly floor the collective pitch; the helicopter and crew proceed to hit the ground extremely hard.

God! This has to be a dream; it can't be really happening to me. My head is a kind of fuzzy, I'm a little shaken, but I soon realize that the chopper has come to a complete stop. Thank God, there is no fire. The entire crash lasted only a matter of seconds, but it seemed to me as though the helicopter would never stop bouncing and banging around that rice paddy.

The crew is momentarily dazed, but somehow I manage to quickly exit the crippled chopper. I run to the front of the chopper to open the pilot's doors, and I help both of the pilots out of their armored seat enclosures. I hear the main rotor blades as they are still spinning above my head. As the rpm's of the blades slow, they start to dip lower, and the blades begin to make contact with the ground. Here we go, I thought. I managed to live through this extremely frightening crash, only to be crushed by those spinning rotor blades. I just try not to think about that and continue to help the pilots out of their seats. I turn to see if my gunner needs help. He gives me the thumbs up sign as he starts to unhook his monkey harness (a long harness attached to the gunners to keep them from falling out of the chopper before they has finish their tour duty)... he's ok.

Most of the final impact is on my gunner's side of the chopper. During the crash several small trees ripped completely through the bottom of the chopper, under the gunner's seat. A few more inches and the trees would have punched through his flimsy canvas seat and impaled him.

After everyone is safely out of the chopper, we franticly rush around the chopper, quickly removing all the radio equipment, the guns and ammo. Our gun ships have heard our "May Day", and in only minutes they are overhead providing cover for us.

Our other slicks quickly land. The legs (our infantry), in full battle gear, unload from the choppers and start to set up a perimeter around our downed helicopter. We hastily load ourselves and what we have salvaged from our wounded bird onto one of the other slicks and we head back to good old base camp. As they say "any landing you can walk away from, is a good landing." We have a few cuts and bruises, but everyone is ok.

My reward for that very eventful ride on six-six-zero was a couple of days off. Much appreciated time I assure you. I got time to just rest, to catch up on sleep and write some letters home. Well, to be brutally honest, it wasn't really a reward. The much needed time off was only because Uncle Sam didn't have another helicopter for me. It would only last until we could get a replacement helicopter, then it was back to work.

A few days after our last ride on poor old six-six-zero, Mr. Anderson came to talk to me. He approached me as I was on the flight line working on my replacement chopper. He said he "liked the way I had handled myself during the situation in The Playground. He said he "thought I had remained cool under pressure." Man, did I ever have him fooled. The only reason I got out of that chopper so fast was because I thought it was going to explode into flames at any time. For a moment, I considered running off in absolute panic, but it was a long walk back to base camp, and, besides, I didn't really know the way. I quickly decided it would probably be a lot healthier to just stick around and help the others out of the chopper.

Mr. Anderson said he wanted me to join his crew, to be his gunner for a big Long Range Reconnaissance Patrol (LRRP) mission that was coming up soon. He explained that he needed me for just this one mission and then I could return to my own chopper. This man was a very experienced pilot, and, as I said before, he was hardcore; all business. For him to have that kind of confidence in me, to ask me to join his crew on such an important mission, I felt very honored.

That was the first time since I arrived at D Troop that I felt like I belonged, and I was being considered a part of the team. At the same time, the thought of going on my first LRRP mission made me, well, let's just say I was a little nervous. I had heard many stories about those missions from some of the older, slick crews. I remember them saying, "You don't usually have to worry much about the insertion (putting the team on the ground). Likely that part will be a piece of cake. It's the extractions (getting the team out) that can end up being the real entertaining part." As I would soon learn, more fun than a trip to Disney World.

Nice day for a helicopter ride...

The much anticipated LRRP mission was now a reality. We had landed at a small fire support base named "Go Dau Ha" just a few miles north of Cu Chi, our base camp. As we sit around and hurry up and wait, the morning sun was completely up, the air had already started to get thick with the heat and the humidity. This would be a daylight insertion. We gathered around the helicopter, the LRRP team and our chopper crew, waiting on the Brass to give the order to go. Nervously, we all try to make small talk with each other. Everyone handles the pressure of this kind of combat mission differently. Some men get very quiet, some seem to talk constantly, and others may laugh a lot or joke-around. One of the members of the LRRP team told us, "We are going to a place in War Zone C where no American Soldier has ever set foot." Two of the men on the LRRP team are new guys. One of the new guys said that he had just completed his training and was fresh out of RECONDO School. I remember one of the new men was named Rose, a real nice guy. The other new guy, man he was a real talker. I had never met him before this mission. Sorry I didn't know him long enough to remember his name. He was full of piss and vinegar and tried his best to convince us that he was a real bad ass. He told us he, "had been out on only a few training missions and a couple of ambushes so far." He boasts, "I want to get into some real shit this time out. I want to kill a few gooks." The old timers on the LRRP team just looked at him like he was nuts. I think we all understood that he was only talking like that to mask the fear he was trying very hard to hide. I knew exactly how he felt; he wasn't the only one who was trying to hide fear that day. We were all dealing with that same emotion, in our own ways.

Finally, we get the call to "saddle up" (remember this is a Calvary Troop). The mission is a "go". We load up and start our climb into the bright morning sky. We fly to a heavily wooded area northeast of Tay Ninh. My eyes scan the jungle below, even from 2500 feet, it's obvious to this old country boy...this is not a good neighborhood. This is Indian country, nothing but triple canopy jungle everywhere. I can just make out a small speck in the jungle below. We start to make a very steep approach toward that speck; it feels more like a zero pitch autorotation, actually. We are approaching the ground at a high rate of speed. That speck in the jungle is our LZ. We are on short final; the AC starts to slow our descent. Now maybe my stomach can return to normal; it feels like it is somewhere around the roof of the chopper. The LZ is nothing more than a freshly made bomb crater, probably made just for us. The LZ is littered with fallen trees and other debris, it is impossible for the pilots to land the helicopter.

The bomb crater is about 20 feet deep, , we hover about five feet above the rim of the crater as my eyes scan the jungle for any sign of movement. My M-60 is locked and loaded. The CE tells the LRRP team to get off his helicopter...jump, jump. I had never seen the kind of damage that those bombs can do, not this close anyway. I see enormous trees splintered and snapped like twigs.

The LRRP team got off the helicopter safely and we make a nearly vertical climb out of the LZ. I may be new to this game, but as I scoped out our LZ, it seemed a little on the small side. Oh, well, everything went well on this one, and I took some comfort in knowing that we would surely have a more accommodating LZ when we made the extraction...Ha, little did I know.

We have two down...come and get us; now !!!

We flew to Tay Ninh base camp, where we made our temporary home on the edge of the airfield. We started a very long wait. Since we were the main extraction ship on this mission, the CE and I were required to remain with the helicopter at all times. A call for an immediate extraction could come from the LRRP team at any moment; we had to be in position and ready to go. The waiting was the hardest part of all. It was so boring, continually listening to the radios for a call from the LRRP team. The CE and I even eat our meals (C-Rations) and sleep on the helicopter. We would sleep on the stretchers we carried for the wounded and actually found they were pretty comfortable. Well, at least they were better than the hard floor of the chopper. We would get a break once in a while to go get some real chow (the Army's version of food) or to try and find some clean water to shave and brush our teeth. That is if you could find someone to stand in for you.

We continue to just wait. After a while we had all told our life stories to one another. At first the extra sleep and rest was kind of nice, but after a day or two it gets very boring. I just wanted to be flying. I would have taken just about any mission to end the boredom. But we must endure many more hours of waiting and constant monitoring of the radios.

The LRRP team has been out for about two days, maybe three. We received a radio message that they had made contact with two Viet Cong, VC. They reported that they had killed one VC but the other one had gotten away. This detail would prove later on to be a problem for the LRRP team. The Chuck (VC) that got away must have wasted no time in rounding up every VC in the province. They were busy planning a nice welcoming party for us, and I don't mean "Welcome Wagon."

While we continued waiting for a call from the LRRP team, a flight of about 10 or 12 helicopters from the 196th Light Infantry Division landed just in front of our choppers. Those poor bastards had been through hell; many of their slicks had been shot to pieces. One of the slicks had holes in the cabin floor and tail section the size of softballs. The CE on that chopper told me what happened. VC mortars had been trained on their LZ and they had to leave three of their helicopters burning in the LZ. The site of those damaged helicopters made me think, what the #$%%XX am I doing in this place!

Finally, in the wink of an eye, our waiting is over. A frantic call comes over the radio. One of the LRRP team members shouts "We have two down...come and get us, now!!!" It was not a particularly good time for this to be happening, as the other chopper crews have just gone to chow. The CE and I are right where we are supposed to be, and we hastily start to get the chopper ready to go. Mr. Anderson arrives within two or three minutes. He quickly puts his chest plate and helmet on, but we can't find the pilot who is assigned to fly the second seat. A pilot from one of the other slicks arrives on scene and without any hesitation, jumps into the seat of the chopper. By this time, the AC has the helicopter's turbine engine running up to speed. The CE and I load up, and our helicopter is immediately cleared for takeoff. We are now leaving absolute boredom behind for the possibility of a great adventure.

I listen intently to the radio conversations over my helmet headset. The LRRP team is in a hell of a mess; they're definitely in real trouble. I hear them say "We have one KIA" (killed in action). Later I would learn that it was one of the young guys...the talker. They also had one WIA (wounded in action). The wounded man had been hit in the chest and he was having a lot of trouble breathing. I'm sure glad we have a medic with us on this one. We are a few minutes out of Tay Ninh when we hear the call from our gunships. They are just taking off from Tay Ninh and will not be able to catch up in time for the extraction. Oh dear God, this can't be!! I hear my AC inform Centaur 6 (troop commander) "we're going in without the guns" (words that still strike fear in my heart). Centaur 6 replies "Rodger...Continue the mission."

To quote a source that's unknown to me "Be careful what you wish for, you may just get it." I had wanted to be a part of all this and now it looked like I was going to get my wish. The LRRP team is telling us over the radio, "A very large force of VC has us surrounded three hundred and sixty degrees" also they are currently taking very heavy enemy fire. The AC calls to the LRRP team, "We're coming in to get you...you'd better be ready." They reply, "We are going to try and break through the enemy position and make a break for the predetermined emergency LZ."

We are on a very steep approach to the LZ. In the distance I hear the sounds of the LRRP's M-16s as they start to break through the enemy encirclement. The VC answered with a massive volume of AK-47 fire. We are on final approach; I hear the loud echoes of the exploding LRRP claymores and the sounds of exploding grenades. The AC gives the command for the CE and me to start firing. With only our two M-60 machine guns for support fire, it's important that we concentrate our fire very carefully. I start to hose down the area to the front and below the chopper. My face is stinging from the hot powder as it is blown back into my face. Anything that moves within my target range, even a leaf blowing in the wind, will be met with a hail of bullets from my M-60. Man, I sure miss those heavy hitters (the gun ships).

The air is filled with the sounds of heavy automatic weapons fire and the thud of more claymores and grenades. The AC starts to flare out just above the LZ; he gives the command to "hold your fire." It is a very tough order to obey. Right now the last thing I want to do is stop firing my machine gun.

Our chopper finally hits the LZ. All the members of the LRRP team are on my side of the helicopter. Just before the AC sat the helicopter down, the team had made a break for it and fought their way to the edge of the LZ. They start their run through a gauntlet of small arms fire and try to fight their way through the thick under brush. I can't see the VC, but I know they can see us. The air is full of their tracers and I can see a lot of muzzle flashes at the edge of the LZ.

I watch helplessly as the wounded LRRP struggles toward the chopper. He can't make it without some help from one of the others; he's hurt awfully bad. His team members stop to help him, but then they are unable to return fire on the enemy positions. I hear myself screaming "Come on, move it, move it, we're a sitting duck here!!" It's obvious that we can't stay here a minute longer; the VC will be all over us any second. #%XXX#%!!! Man, I can't hold my fire much longer!!!

After what seems like an eternity, the LRRPs finally fight their way aboard the chopper and at last the AC yells, "Full suppression". We open up with all we have; I start to return fire on those commie bastards. Before, I was gripped by intense fear, but now I'm pissed. Everyone on board the helicopter, that is, everyone who is able to pull a trigger, is firing some kind of weapon...M-16s, M-79. The CE and I keep blazing away with our M-60s. It is total madness. The AC has our big green bird powered up and ready to roll, we start our take off run. There's not a lot room to work with...would you believe another very small LZ. The VC are not our only problem at the moment. Our helicopter is dangerously over loaded, we have the extra man on board, the medic. Some good news, the helicopter is starting to pick up airspeed. The bad news, we are also running out of prime real estate and we are approaching the end of the LZ. A wall of very large trees awaits us if we can't gain enough airspeed for our climb.

Man, these trees must be at least a hundred feet tall. The AC is trying to get everything out of his ship he can. He waits until the very last possible moment to pull pitch. He must gain more airspeed or the helicopter will stall when he starts his climb. Without enough airspeed, the Laws of Gravity become quite undeniable. The chopper will fall out of the sky with all the aerodynamics of a giant brick. Mr. Anderson will get us out of here if anyone can. Hell, he's already saved my ass once.

My fingers are locked onto the triggers of my M60; I'm squeezing so hard I actually feel the trigger cutting into my fingers. All the fear has disappeared, I'm in a zone, right this minute I'm locked in my own little world. All my training, the lessons learned from the older guys...it has taken over. My M60 is on rock-n-roll, and I keep on firing a relentless stream of tracers. My gun is beginning to overheat; starts to slow down it's rate of fire, then speed up again. One thing is for sure, I am not going to let up until we are out of this place or my damn gun burns up.

One of the LRRP team leaders starts to throw ropes and any other nonessential, non-lethal gear out of the helicopter franticly trying to reduce weight. It is now do or die time...the AC starts to pull pitch. He has only one shot and he had to get it right.

The chopper starts a rapid climb; the g-force pushes me down against my seat. We all continue firing out both sides of the helicopter. One of the LRRPs tosses smoke grenades out to mark the enemy positions. I watch the "Low RPM" light on the dash of the helicopter...the red warning light is flashing like crazy. The helicopter made a quick climb to just about treetop level, then just seems to float there for a second. Man, this turn of events is not good. This is not turning out to be one of my better days. The AC instantly drops the nose of the chopper, it's his only hope to get back some of his airspeed.

The chopper begins slipping through the tops of the trees; the branches are hitting my M-60. The impact of the tree limbs against my gun almost knocks it from my hands. The tree limbs are like giant fingers, reaching up from the jungle floor, trying to rip us from the sky. For a while, the bottom of the chopper is actually flying through the tops of these huge trees. This is definitely not what the UH-1D helicopter was designed to do.

By the grace of God and the phenomenal ability and courage of our pilots, we begin to gain some valuable airspeed and altitude. In only a few short seconds we are finally out of the tops of the trees and clear of the LZ. We are cruising at max airspeed just above the jungle canopy. At last we can stop firing our guns.

Silence, it seems so quiet, all I hear is the sound of the turbine engine, the slap of the rotor blades, and the ringing in my ears. All guns are silent for the first time since we began our approach to the LZ."

A forward air control aircraft (FAC) soon arrives over the area. Over the radio, I hear him directing the incoming jets onto that little piece of real-estate we had left behind. He tells them to unload their lethal cargo of napalm and high explosive (HE) on the smoke. I hoped all those little bastards down there are blown to hell. They will receive no pity and absolutely no mercy from us today.

I began to relax a little...for the first time, I tell myself... we made it. I sat quietly thinking, how in the hell did we ever get out of there. For the first time, I understand what this outfit, D Troop, is all about. Through baptism by fire, I am now an important part of it. It also dawned on me that the next several months were more than likely going to be very interesting and certainly challenging.

It is a wonderful feeling to know we are safe, but our job was not quite finished. We still have a very seriously wounded man on board. I watch as the medic is working on the wounded LRRP. The wounded man is having a lot of trouble breathing; he has an entry wound in the front of his chest and a large exit wound in his back. One of his lungs has collapsed, he needs a doctor and soon!! My mind starts to wonder again, what the hell just happened? The shock and the terror started to really take hold. I didn't think we had much of a chance of making it out of that LZ.

There had been a few times during my tour that I thought I had a pretty good chance to die, but death seemed a certainty on this day. It was a great relief to have made it out, but then I remember that death has been a certainty for one of our men. One of us didn't make it out and another suffered horrifying, painful and near fatal wounds. I take a brief moment to say a short silent prayer of thanks to God for His merciful protection.

The AC has the airspeed indicator red lined; he's doing everything possible to get our wounded man to a hospital as swiftly as he can. As we approach Tay Ninh, the controller clears us to land and directs us to a MEDEVAC (hospital unit) pad. When we land I can't believe my eyes, the hospital is made of rubber. It is a large inflatable hospital. I'm sure that the doctors are real, but not sure about the nurses. They could be inflatable too (*attempt at humor...no disrespect to our wonderful nurses*). We leave our wounded man in very good hands for some desperately needed treatment.

We return to our initial staging area at the edge of the airfield, for debriefing. The hell with a debriefing, I need a cold beer. We finally shut down the helicopter, and it becomes apparent that the main rotor blades have been severely damaged. The blades have been literally ripped to shreds by the trees in the LZ. The leading edge of one of the blades had started to break away from the rest of the blade. We may have been very near complete rotor failure.

New rotor blades had to be flown in from Cu Chi. The rotor blades had to be changed on the spot, with only a few tools to work with and a lot of muscle powder. The heavy blades had to be lifted into place by hand, just good old human muscle. Then the chopper would be able to fly again and we could get back to our base camp.

Just another day

Many memories of that time and place are just starting to return, my overloaded mind is flooded with these renewed recollections. The Vietnam tour aboard an old and frayed slick helicopter; man, what a trip. I hope you're not looking for a hero here, sorry. I was just an ol' country boy that sat in the back of my chopper and went where the pilots took me. Like the other guys in our outfit, I just did my job. I wish I had the ability to properly describe that experience.

Most of our daily missions were uneventful. A lot of the time slick crews were little more than delivery men. There was always some kind of mission for the slicks; we were always needed by someone, somewhere. Our missions could include almost everything, from dropping illumination flairs at night for the troops on the ground, to the resupply of ammo. Sometimes we would even deliver a hot meal, a little ice, beer and soda to these poor deserving bastards in the field. There were the 10, 12, 16 hour days spent flying and then having to work on your helicopter after your return to base camp. The helicopter always had to be ready to fly the next mission whenever it came. Meanwhile, your pilots and gunner are most likely getting their beauty rest.

The job could be hard, demanding, and sometimes hazardous, but in my opinion it was the best job the army had to offer. It was a job that gave me the opportunity to lay it all on the line, to go get 'em when our men needed help the most.

Everyone is an expert on the Vietnam War. We have been bombarded for years by images from news accounts and the movies. But that media can't really show the emotional side of war. The movies can't convey the true horrors of war, the smells and the images that are burned into your very soul. Everyone's little piece of that war was different. I remember the sounds and smells that came from death and destruction. The smells...to this day I remember that very distinct smell of mangled human tissue and blood, a scent that often filled the inside of a slick helicopter. Those that experienced it can understand what I'm saying, but if you were not there, how can I ever describe the indescribable? No crew will ever forget the stench of burnt human flesh or the experience of flying loads of burned bodies back to base camp. While you are in flight, small bits of burnt human flesh and ash blow all around the inside of the helicopter, covering every part of your exposed skin. The particles of burnt flesh soon begin to get into your eyes, your nose and, yes, even your mouth. Not very much glory in a job like that. I just can't believe that any of this is for real.

Dust-off...the ugly face of war

I will always remember one of my earliest Dustoff missions (medical evacuation). There were many more missions after this one, but I guess I remember it so well because I had never seen anything like it before.

We are scrambled to pick up a load of wounded Vietnamese civilians. We arrive to find mostly women and small children, from a civilian bus that just hit a VC land mine. Many of the injured had arms and legs missing...several are just babies. Some are screaming in agony, while others are silent with eyes fixed into oblivion. I sit there mesmerized by the sight of such carnage. Everything and almost everyone inside the opened door helicopter is soon covered in blood, it's a gruesome site. After we have the cargo department fully loaded, we take off. As the helicopter starts the takeoff run, the nose drops, the helicopter tilts forward. The blood from the maimed and mangled bodies begins to run down the floor of the helicopter. It runs under the pilots' seat and into the chin bubble. As the chopper picks up airspeed and starts to level off, the blood streams out the sides of the chopper, and is caught in the air stream. The blood blows back onto me and my gunner, completely soaking us and our clothing. Just another day as a slick rider...another day closer to going home. Will this nightmare ever end?

Our Dustoff missions were some of our most dangerous missions, but we took great pride in the fact we were very successful at them. D Troop slick crews, in particular, took great pride and satisfaction in that success rate. But there were times when we were just too little, too late. Those are the ones that I will always carry with me. One of those medevac missions still haunts me.

We have just picked up several seriously wounded men. After we are out of the LZ, my gunner (SP4 Adams) and I leave our guns, and move up front to see if we can help the wounded. One man has a severe belly wound. The look on his young face...it's a look of hopelessness. He knows he's dying, but as I look into his eyes, it's like he's trying to say, "Thanks for trying." I try desperately to apply a bandage to his wounds, while holding part of his guts in my hands. I feel so helpless. Damn it, I'm a crew chief and door gunner; I'm not a medic. I try to reassure him, I tell him he's going home and that he's going to be ok. Silently, as he lay on the hard cold floor of my helicopter, he starts to slowly slip away. We have done everything we can, which seems like so very little. I am filled with such a feeling of failure, even though deep down I know that everyone gave it their best. I ask myself, what I could have done differently. Just too little, too late...

Silently I say to myself, at least this war is over for him. I wondered about his family, his mother, his father. Does he have any brothers or sisters? Maybe he has a wife or girlfriend back in the real world. Oh,

I'm so sorry...his family will soon get the heart breaking news. I wish there was some way I could tell them, we did everything we could. Maybe it would give them some comfort knowing that their soldier, their loved one, did not die alone or abandoned. They should be very proud, he gave his life as a brave trooper, and he died with honor and dignity.

Another day and another call.

Another night Dustoff; having to face the demons that wait for us in the darkness. We are aiding an armored convoy that has been ambushed along the MSR (main supply route). The convoy is still under heavy enemy fire. We have to land in the open, on the road. We are now at our most vulnerable point. We are sitting on the ground while they are loading the wounded. Suddenly, there is a tremendous explosion, a VC Rocket Propelled Grenade (RPG) slams into the side of an armed personnel carrier (APC) only a few yards away from our helicopter. I'm not sure if the VC was aiming at the chopper, but that's closer than I ever wanted to be to an exploding RPG round.

I will always remember the day we had to make multiple low level medevac flights into and out of LZ Gold (during the Battle of Soui Tre). Man, that's a story in itself. I remember the day that Spencer, one of our slick gunners, took three rounds off his chest plate, and through the top of his head. He only had a few days left in country and didn't even have to fly. There are so many, so many memories.

D Troop was the best

To someone who hasn't served with an elite, highly disciplined unit like D Troop, I guess some of my stories might sound incredible, almost heroic. These stories are just an account of what seemed like common, everyday actions in our outfit. Many of the men that severed with D Troop have stories that make my tour look like a picnic in the park. Our entire unit always gave maximum effort, and we were all pretty damn good at our jobs. D Troop continually inflicted major damage on the most elite units, of one of the best gorilla war armies in the world. Hey, that's what the Army paid us helicopter crews the big bucks (extra $55.00 per month) to do. I know we all have some pretty amazing stories, and we need to share them. We should all do our part to add to the rich history of our proud unit. Please share your stories before they are lost forever. D Troop, without a doubt, had some of the best helicopter pilots and crews the Army ever assembled.

Though I must admit, I'm far from being an impartial judge. All our pilots were outstanding, and I would have flown into combat with any one of them. But I don't believe our slick drivers (pilots) received nearly as much credit as they deserved. I witnessed those pilots get a helicopter into and out of places that seemed impossible, WO1 F.L. Anderson just to mention one. It was routine for them to make night landings in total darkness, while flying the helicopter completely blacked out. They flew night formations, in groups of 4 or 5 ships (their rotor blades only feet apart). The effects of vertigo during night formation flight can be disastrous. If any part of the rotor blades of one helicopter even touches another set of rotor blades, someone is going to crash and burn.

The stresses from flying 12 to 16 hour days, night flight, poor flying conditions, can be very, very severe. Can you possibly imagine how these flights were made without the aid of any night vision equipment? I don't know how they did it. Amazing! Most of us will never know the level of concentration and the tremendous abilities that were required of these young pilots. As a CE, when we were on a mission, my job was then to be a gunner. That job was mostly defensive, to protect my helicopter and crew. Slicks crews tried to avoid trouble if we could, unlike the gunships, those guys went looking for trouble. And then there are the scout crews; well, let's just say those guys were completely nuts. During my tour, I don't believe I was ever credited with a confirmed enemy kill. I know I never received any awards or recognition for enemy body count, it was not my job. I did manage to burn up literally thousands of rounds of Uncle Sam's 7.62mm ammo, and I did go through a couple of Sam's M-60 machine-guns during my tour. I was very fortunate to be assigned to D Troop, our legs and gunship crews did an outstanding job of handling the offensive work. They kept the chucks (VC) far enough away from us that most of the time my fire power wasn't really needed.

I am certainly proud to have flown with so many good pilots while I was with D Troop. But I have to admit, being a helicopter pilot did have certain benefits, they enjoyed a certain status. The Army made sure that every one of our invaluable pilots was equipped with an armor-plated seat enclosure.

Our esteemed pilots were also provided with the latest model in bullet proof helmets. On the other hand, the lowlife CE and gunner have their jewels parked on a canvas seat and have a plastic helmet to protect their unsophisticated gray matter. But that was ok, all CE's and gunners wanted their pilots to be well protected. When flying, we were always concerned about our pilot's health and welfare. The experience of being a part of D Troop taught me the true meaning of the word "honor". Let those that wish to do so, let them spend their efforts apologizing for that war. I choose to remember the true heroes that I was lucky enough to get to fly with. Men that seemed to never know fear, men that would put their life on the line for you without any hesitation. I am very proud to have been a part of such a special team of soldiers, to have known and served with such a fine group of brave young men.

God Bless...*James M. Vaughn*

(Author's note: While it is certainly possible that some branches of the United States Military had "bullet proof" helmets, it is this author's experience that none of those helmets ever made it to most Army units. Like James Vaughn's Crew Chief helmet, our helmet was simply a place to hold the microphone, earphones and sun visor. Oh, yes, and a cool place to apply paint during your down time. That is pretty much it, our helmets, both pilot and crew, did NOT stop bullets.)

As an added bonus to the reader, James Vaughn sent me the following short stories:

LZ Gold

"The Battle of Soui Tre" - March 21, 1967

Elements of D Troop (Air), 3rd Squadron, 4th Cavalry, 25th Infantry Division, had been temporarily based at Tay Ninh base camp in support of one of their Long Range Reconnaissance Patrols (*LRRP*).

D Troop helicopter 65-09661 (*661*) departed Tay Ninh base camp in the early morning hours of March 21, 1967 on a routine communications check with our LRRP team that had been inserted just the day before. Our crew consisted of Aircraft Commander (*AC*) Capt. Harold Fisher, 1st Pilot Lt. Buck Buxton, Crew Chief (*CE*) PFC Vaughn and Door Gunner Sp4 Adams. The patrols location was north of the Michelin Rubber Plantation and our mission was to get a situation report (*SITREP*) concerning the status of the patrol.

As the crew departed Tay Ninh, AC Fisher observed an area a few miles east of our location of some very intense activity that included heavy artillery and continuous air strikes. Capt. Fisher immediately contacted D Troop operations and requested information on the fighting he had spotted. 661s crew was advised that Landing Zone (*LZ*) Gold was under heavy enemy attack and had scores of wounded (*WIA*) that were in need of immediate evacuation (*DUSTOFF*). AC Fisher, without hesitation, volunteered his helicopter to assist in any way he could with the wounded. He was advised by operations that his helicopter was definitely needed, and to setup in a holding pattern a few miles west of LZ Gold until they could clear us into the LZ.

We continued to circle in a holding pattern waiting for clearance to land at LZ Gold. Because of the low cloud cover our helicopter was required to fly very low (below 500 feet). We were well within the range of enemy ground fire....a fact that had already cost one flight crew their lives.

As we circled the area we began to pick up the frantic radio traffic coming from LZ Gold and the excited radio exchanges became more and more disturbing. We could hear the sounds of immense volumes of automatic weapons fire and large explosions in the background. They were pleading for help as their base camp perimeter had been attacked by wave after wave of VC firing automatic weapons, recoilless rifle and rocket propelled grenades (RPG); they needed immediate help. The waiting, hearing the echoes of the raging battle made us believe we were about to enter the very jaws of hell.

It would have been much easier on our crew to have gone directly into LZ Gold when first informed we were needed. It was very unnerving hearing the troops on the ground describing the fierce battle. They were telling how most of their artillery pieces had been destroyed by VC RPGs, recoilless rifle and mortars rounds. The artillery pieces and their accompanying big shells were burning. The shells were cooking off; exploding white hot shrapnel in every direction.

Continuing to fly in a holding pattern our minds had far too much time to think about what's waiting for us down there in that very hot LZ. When actually engaged in the Dustoffs or other combat mission you are too focused on the mission to worry about anything else. The waiting was always much more difficult than the rescue missions themselves. Sometimes it's better to not know, beforehand, what your about to get into.

Earlier that morning the Stable Boy crew had been tasked to try and locate a downed Forward Artillery Control (*FAC*) 0-1E Bird Dog. The FAC had been shot down by enemy ground fire while flying low over the perimeter of LZ Gold. The crew was shot down soon after their arrival on scene. They were only able to direct one air strike before being downed by heavy machine gun fire.

Stable Boy, commanded by Maj. Fleming, soon located the downed FAC in the heavy jungle canopy not far from LZ Gold. Because of the heavy triple canopy jungle it wasn't possible for them to land to aid the downed crew. PFC Gerald T. Crawford was one of the door gunners on the C&C chopper. Gerald's descriptions of the events concerning their mission was that they had hovered over the crash site, lower a man down on a hoist line, to see if the pilot and observer had survived the crash. While doing so they were sitting ducks from enemy fire. They soon determined both crewmen were dead (*KIA*) and it would be far too dangerous to stay and try to retrieve the bodies at that time. Their helicopter was then directed to fly to LZ Gold for

Dustoff missions as needed.

We could see the ground around LZ Gold was literally covered with VC bodies; some stacked one on top of the other. Capt. Fisher reported that we even had to land on top of some VC bodies during our landing. What an awful sight.

When we turned on final approach into the LZ it was obvious this was going to be a very risky mission to complete. We were committed and we were either going to bring the wounded (*WIA*) out of that hellhole or we were going to join the ranks of the KIAs trying. That was our job and no one on 661s crew was going to hesitate to help those poor men on the ground.

During 661s approach into the LZ, not only did we have to contend with enemy ground fire, the crew had to avoid incoming mortars, outgoing artillery fire and the high performance aircraft as they zipped by dropping their bombs. Normally choppers would stay a few miles away from the jets as they made their bombing runs. They are flying so fast and they can't see the choppers and by the time we see them we can't get out of their way. All this while flying below 500 feet; making us a very tempting target for the enemy gunners. Capt. Fisher and Lt. Buxton had to pilot us through a very tricky and dangerous obstacle course just to get into LZ Gold.

After we landed, our CE left his gunners seat to help load the wounded. Those poor soldiers had endured the battle all night long and were walking around like zombies. It was an unbelievable sight with the jets dropping bombs within 50 meters of the edge of the perimeter, incoming mortar rounds hitting the LZ and artillery rounds cooking off. It was absolute mayhem. After each explosion our CE would duck and hit the ground, but the troops helping to load the wounded wouldn't even flinch. The men of LZ Gold, having suffered through the all night battle, seemed to not even notice the incoming fire and the peril all around them. They just calmly continued to carry the wounded and load them onto the chopper. Each one was walking around with that 1000 yard stare. The look on their faces was that of a person who has been brought to the very edge of their breaking point, but continued to fight on. True American heroes...every damn one of them.

On the flights back to the hospital the CE and gunner had given first aid to some of the severely wounded. One of the wounded soldiers 661 picked up had a very serious gut wound. He had lost a lot of blood and was crying out in agony. He asked gunner Adams for some water because he was extremely thirsty. Adams reached for his canteen to give him a drink. The CE pointed to his belly and shook his head no, reminding Adams that you never give water to a person with a belly wound.

Another soldier had a very large and gaping wound to his upper thigh. He was crying out; just let me die. He said he knew he was going to lose his leg and he was afraid his girl back home wouldn't want him anymore. Both the CE and gunner continued to encourage him; telling him that they had seen much worse wounds and that he was going to all right and he would be going back to the real world soon. Can't help but wonder how life turned out for those guys.

Capt. Fisher asked the CE over the chopper intercom how the wounded soldiers were doing. He told him that the soldier with the gut wound was complaining about being very cold and maybe going into shock. Capt. Fisher quickly removed his own fatigue shirt and Vaughn used it to cover the soldier helping him to feel warmer

Both the C&C crew and 661s crew made multiple successful Dustoff missions into and out of LZ Gold that day. We were very willing and able to assist fellow soldiers and rescue numerous wounded soldiers.

During 1966-67 D Troop Centaurs had established an excellent reputation as far as Dustoff missions were concerned. Their chopper crews never refused, not one time, to make a Dustoff regardless how dangerous the situation. D Troop Centaurs were even called in when other crews refused to go. Soldiers familiar with the Centaurs knew they would go into any hot LZ to pick up their wounded, you could bet your life on that fact.

Contributors: Harold Fisher, Buck Buxton, Mike Vaughn & Gerald Crawford

---

As I get older, particular times, dates & names from the past seem to fade from memory. However, there are some events & people that are hardwired into the deepest recesses of our minds. This is a story of one (and there are many), of the better

demonstrations of pilot skill, concentration & courage, I can remember being a part of.

Lt. Buxton at the Controls

By Mike Vaughn

Date: *Sometime in mid-1967 – Possibly the Rainy Season*

Crew: Aircraft Commander (AC) Lt. Buck Buxton, pilot WO1 Ashabranner, the other gunner (G) was SP4 Adams & I was the crew chief (CE).

My ship was 661 (*tail number*) & our crew had been assigned to dust-off status for that day. It was around mid-day as I remember & it was the time of year that the rice paddies were filled with water ready for planting.

When the klaxon sounded for the dust-off mission WO Ashabranner, the gunner & I all ran to the helicopter to prepare for takeoff. Lt. Buxton went straight to the communications post to learn the location of the unit needing our help.

When Lt. Buxton climbed aboard the chopper, the other crew members were aboard & the chopper was already running & ready for takeoff. Mr. Ashabranner called the tower to get immediate clearance for takeoff. Meanwhile, Lt. Buxton was looking over his maps & calling the artillery advisory to ensure they were not firing into the grid we were about to fly into.

The LZ was not a great distance from our base camp & was near one of the rivers close to our Cu Chi base camp. As we flew toward our objective we started to pick up the radio communication from the unit needing help. The unit consisted of a couple of squads of infantry that had wandered into a heavily booby trapped area & were receiving some sporadic small arms fire. Each time the squad of troops would try to move they would set off a booby trap & add to the wounded.

Lt. Buxton was at the controls as we approached the LZ. It became obvious that there was no place to land our helicopter because of the tree lines & the paddies being full of water. Lt. Buxton headed the chopper for one of the rice dikes as near the wounded troops as he possibly could.

The very small space he put the chopper into was only a couple of meters larger than our ship. He balanced one skid of our chopper on a rice dike while keeping the other skid in midair & holding the chopper straight & level at a partial hover.

At one point I warned Lt. Buxton not to move the chopper aft because of some large tree stumps within feet of our tail rotor. I said to him, "If you backup any further the tail rotor would hit a tree stump & it will come off."

As Lt. Buxton held the chopper steady the infantrymen started to try & make it to our ship to load their wounded. Only a couple of the soldiers were able to assist with the wounded. Some of them were pinned down by sporadic small arms fire & others because of the hidden booby traps.

The infantrymen had to expose themselves to small

arms fire as they carried the wounded across the open rice paddies to get to our chopper. They would only make a few steps & fall because of the grip of the thick black sticky mud in the paddies. It took a lot of effort for them to make even a single step while caring their wounded comrades.

Lt. Buxton continued to perfectly balance the chopper on the rice dike while we anxiously waited for the wounded to be loaded. The men were trying desperately to get the wounded to our chopper...but were tightly griped in place by the thick, knee deep, glue-like, mud. I was thinking that we can't stay on the ground much longer because of the danger to the chopper & crew from possible small arms fire. I knew that Lt. Buxton must consider the dangers to his crew & the chopper & would soon have to make the decision to leave & come back later.

None of the crew wanted to leave the wounded soldiers. I ask Lt. Buxton if he would permit me to leave the chopper & help load the wounded. He gave me permission to help...he's still holding the chopper steady & balancing one skid on the rice dike. Remember that the only protection he & WO Ashabranner had to protect themselves from enemy fire from the front position was a ¼ in of plexey glass. The plexey glass windshield wouldn't even stop a fast pitched rock. For them to hold our chopper in such a delicate position while staring straight ahead, not considering the possibility of hostile fire, took great concentration & skill.

I exited the chopper, stepping onto the rice dike that Lt. Buxton was balancing the ships skid on. I ran as fast as I could toward the wounded men to assist those marred down in the mud of the paddies. I reached the wounded without a lot of difficultly but as soon as I stop moving & picked up one end of a stretcher containing a wounded soldier, I immediately became stuck in the thick mud.

There were four soldiers, including myself, now firmly stuck in the mud trying our best to not let the wounded men fall off of the stretchers into the water & mud. We soon formed a kind chain, handing the wounded off from one to the other. I now have a big problem...I'm the link in the chain that's the farthest from the chopper.

I knew that Lt. Buxton couldn't stick around this LZ much longer because of the danger to our chopper & the need to get the wounded to an aid station. I keeping struggling & fighting trying to make it to the chopper before they have to leave me behind. Lt. Buxton remains very cool at the controls & keeps the chopper in the perfect position with the wounded finally aboard & ready to "un-ass the area" as we used to say.

After what seemed to take forever I managed to make it to the side of the chopper. I was weighed down by my heavy armored chest plate (chicken plate) & my helmet. I was completely exhausted from struggling to help retrieve the wounded & fighting the strong grasp of the thick mud. As hard as I tried I just couldn't muster the strength to lift myself out of the grip of the mud & onto the chopper. My helmet headset was not connected to the chopper so Lt. Buxton & I could not communicate direct with each other. However, it was like we were reading each other's mind. I managed to crawl up as close as I could to the chopper & grabbed hold of the left skid. Lt. Buxton perfectly lifted the chopper straight up a few feet pulling me out of grasp of the mud. He then set the chopper gently back down on the dike, once again balancing one skid on the dike, straight & level, in a partial hover.

I was finally able to standup & climb into the chopper. Lt. Buxton very skillfully lifted our bird straight up out of that very tight & challenging spot. I was physically spent from the struggle with the mud...but I'm sure Lt. Buxton was even more so. Both physically & emotionally spent from having to hold our ship in such a precarious location for what seemed like an eternity.

If not for Lt. Buxton's skill & courage on that day, the mission would not have been such a success. The wounded would not have received the swift aid they desperately needed, & I might have been left behind, without his skilled command of the situation.

Lt. Buxton should have received a military commendation for this mission. But like so many other missions flown by solo helicopter crews, there were no high ranking officers to witness his heroics. No one would have paid much attention to a lowly SP4 crew chief should I have presented the facts of this mission to the higher-ups. Lt. Buxton's efforts were un-commended, but heroic none the less.

Mike Vaughn, his office in the background. Photos courtesy Mike Vaughn.

Mike Vaughn with ammo belts.

Mission 15

The Rescue of 1LT Barry Lloyd

From the 174ᵗʰ Assault Helicopter website.
Reprinted with permission.

The following entry is rather lengthy. Following the below 1968 letter from Major Watke is a recently received personal account of this action by Michael Banek, pilot of the Dolphin helicopter, followed by his DFC award citation and a couple of pictures. Following that is also a recently received personal account of that day from Bill Staffa, a fellow pilot of Lloyd's from the 123rd Battalion. Staffa was also there that day. The following letter is from Major Frederic W. Watke Infantry Commander, Aero Scout Company 123rd Aviation Battalion, Americal Division.

9 April 1968

To: Commanding Officer

14th Combat Aviation Battalion

APO 96374

1. At approximately 1230 hours on 8 April, one of our assigned aircraft was shot down by hostile fire in the area of Quang Nhai. Two of the crewmembers were killed and the pilot severely injured. He is without a doubt alive today only because of an extremely heroic act on the part of a member of your command.

2. The injured pilot, as soon as he was able to talk after extensive surgery, informed members of this unit that he wished he was able to write so he could write this man up for an award. He states that there were at least two fifty caliber machine guns within fifty meters of his location. Heavy fire from these weapons had already shot his ship down, shot up a gunship that had attempted to assist him and prevented our other aircraft from rendering assistance. An aircraft from the 174th Assault Helicopter Company did manage to land and evacuate the injured pilot to Chu Lai.

3. This valorous act is certainly most deserving of an award. 1LT Lloyd, the injured pilot, has specifically requested of me that I do something to get this man an appropriate award.

4. Request that the Distinguished Flying Cross be recommended for the person(s) responsible for this action. It is my desire that this letter serve as a statement representing what 1LT Lloyd saw and knew about the action.

(Following are excerpts from several e-mail messages I received from Mike Banek in May 1997, in response to my request that he provide me some information on the above letter from Major Watke. -- WebMaster)

Mike Banek in front of Shark 137, a UH-1C gunship. Mike was flying a Dolphin UH-1D "slick" the day of the rescue of Lt. Lloyd, and later moved to the Shark gunships.

Mike says, in part... "*I heard Russ Baer died. We saw each other at the '94 or '95 174th reunion in Ft. Walton Beach. He was the door gunner on a Shark the day I tried with a mini-gun to bring down a VC running in the open...after three 2-second bursts, all I did was manage to raise a bunch of spray from the rice paddy...I think Captain Tom Woods was the AC (aircraft commander). From a drift hover, he ordered Russ to stop him...Russ squeezed off two rounds from his upside-down M-60 and wounded him so he could be questioned by advancing troops. I was recounting that story in a crowded motel room when I heard someone from the back say, "Hey, that's my story!" We became fast friends and exchanged cards and letters. My heart goes out to his family...he was a true warrior.*

Russ made me aware of a new perspective that I never realized as a young 20 year old AC...what appears to be heroic as hell in the front seat often looks dumber than hell from the back. Also, twenty-year-old heroes were a dime-a-dozen back then...and it was often the 'back seaters' who laid down supressive fire, left the helicopter to effect a rescue, or pulled an injured pilot from his magnesium grave.

I was the AC of the Dolphin on this mission on 8 April 1968, and I would really like to know who the 174th crewman was when Major Glen Gibson (the 174th Commanding Officer) and I rescued this downed OH-23 Scout pilot. We were leading a huge formation at the time. The citation reads as though I were alone, but the real heroes that day were 1LT Lloyd for faking being dead while VC kicked both his shattered and burned legs, and for clinging to life while waiting for his comrades to take him home...our crew chief for racing out into the open to drag 1LT Lloyd back to the Huey...and those two "magnificent bastards" who hovered in gun-laden Sharks overhead while staring down two 12.75's (also known as .51-caliber anti-aircraft guns). Those Sharks spewed firepower everywhere. They clearly saved my butt that day. Actually, I'll bet the enemy gunners where as much in awe of those gleaming white Shark's teeth as they were of the mini's and rockets!"

UH-1C Shark at what appears to be the Fire Support Base at Minh Long, southwest of Quang Ngai city.

So, as you requested, I am sending a few photos and some info for the home page. Maj. Gibson is far too shy to offer the account...but for my kid's sake, so that they may know some of what "daddy did in the War," I will forgo the humility. More importantly, I would really like to know who the crewman was, our crew chief, because he's the one who unassed the helicopter under file and rescued Lt. Lloyd while Major Gibson and I sank very low in our armored seats and watched while the two gutsy Sharks "hovered" overhead and pedal-turned a hail of protective fire. I think Rex Pearson and Captain Woods were the two Shark AC's, but am uncertain.

As for Major Gibson, when we were first notified of the downed OH-23 Scout, they asked for volunteers from our flight to attempt a rescue. After a long deafening silence, then after asking me if I was up for it, Major Gibson volunteered us. Then, although I was flying as the aircraft commander, I was only a Warrant Officer WO-1 and was flying with my Company Commander, who was also qualified as an aircraft commander. Major Gibson let me fly the helicopter in and out of what was clearly a life-threatening situation. I turned it back to him outbound for Chu Lai. I have never forgotten the leadership and respect he showed me that day. I don't think I would have trusted a 21 year old kid with my life. --Mike Banek, May 1997.

Following is the Award Citation
Dated 9 September 1968
Orders Number 7041

THE DISTINGUISHED FLYING CROSS

Is Awarded To

WARRANT OFFICER MICHAEL BANEK

For heroism while participating in aerial flight evidenced by voluntary action above and beyond the call of duty in the Republic of Vietnam. Warrant Officer Banek distinguished himself by exceptionally valorous actions on 8 April 1968 while serving as pilot on an UH-1D helicopter on an air assault mission in support of the 1st Battalion, 20th Infantry. On that date, Warrant Officer Banek rescued a seriously wounded pilot whose aircraft had been shot down by intense anti-aircraft fire. Other ships that had attempted the rescue had been driven off, badly damaged and with wounded crew members. Pick up of the pilot had to be made from a zone in the middle of an anti-aircraft position and within 50 meters of two (enemy) 50 caliber machineguns. Electing to approach at high speed and low level, Warrant Officer Banek, by expert use of available cover and defilade, was able to surprise the waiting enemy gunners and effect the rescue. Warrant Officer Banek's outstanding display of flying ability, personal heroism, and devotion to duty is in keeping with the highest traditions of the military service and reflects great credit upon himself, the Americal Division, and the United States Army.

Authority: By direction of the President under the provisions of the Act of Congress, approved 2 July 1926.

Mike preflighting the rotorhead of Shark 137

Photo above: Mike after his tour with the 174th AHC when he was flying for Air America. When I asked Mike for more info about the Air America connection, he provided the following: As far as the Air America caption goes, add that I flew for them for 1 1/2 years in Vietnam and Laos. I served as First Officer in "Stretch" B/F model Hueys (had rotor brakes). Had time in S-58 "twin packs," Porters, Volpars, C-46, C-47, Caribou's, etc. I met the actor, Robert Downey Jr., in Savannah in Feb of this year (1997)...he was shooting another John Grisham novel. I told him the part he played in the movie "Air America" was me! He freaked out. I was the proverbial naive kid from the coast, hustled by the CIA with the old line, "Don't worry kid, we don't get shot...we're an airline!" In reality, the pilots were real loony tunes and hardened mercenaries from as far back as Dien Bien Phu. During Vietnam in the 60's, we were in awe of "high-time" combat pilots...remember? Well, at Air America there was one high-timer called "Shower Shoes Wilson" (he refused to wear combat/flying boots and flew with those rubber shower shoes). When asked how much time he had in C-47's (Goony Birds), his favorite ride, he replied, "about 5,000 hours..." The kid scoffed back at him that that wasn't all that much combat time in these parts...to wit he clarified, "Well that's in that one over there." Then, as he pointed to various ships along the flight line, "in that one its 6,000 hours, and that one 3,000, and over there 4,500, and the one in the back..." True story!

Following are excerpts from e-mail messages received from Bill Staffa (Skeeter 6), who flew OH-23 Scouts in the 123rd Aviation Battalion with Barry Lloyd.

This is, for me, truly a "but for the Grace of God, there go I" story. As best I can remember, following are the events that took place that day.

Barry Lloyd was a second-tour guy, his first tour had been with what had been the UTT as a Warrant. (The UTT were early UH-1 Huey helicopter gunship experiments in Vietnam and stood for Utility Tactical Transport.)

Anyhow, we were flying out of (Fire Support Base) Dottie. We flew missions of about 1:15, being limited by the fuel consumption of the "B" Model gunships that accompanied us. Our gunships (Scorpions) were a mixture of "C" and "B" models. Lloyd was the original "Skeeter Leader," and when I came over from A Company he got "out-ranked" and I took the Scouts. Typical military...

On the day of the shootdown, Barry came in from his first mission and told me that he wanted to go back out. He was quite adamant about it. He thought he was on to something. Naturally I wanted to fly the mission, but he convinced me...must have been pretty persuasive, I loved to fly those missions.

A short time later we got a call to launch, that we had aircraft down in the AO (area of operations). The location was at BS545631, almost exactly 10km SW of Quang Ngai City. We took a Scout (me) and two gunships, and were ordered to screen the area west and north of the shootdown to see if we could spot any bad guys before we closed on the crash site.

Lloyd (crewmen were Andreotta and Dutton) had literally had his rotor head smashed by heavy machinegun fire. Barry stated from his hospital bed that he had realized one crewman had been shot in the head just before he impacted. When the aircraft crashed, he was thrown through the front of the bubble. Think about that. In the OH-23 the pilot sat in the middle, directly in front of the console. At the time, and remember this is a doped-up, broken-up, burned-up guy in the hospital telling us, Barry said that he could hear one crewman screaming because the AVGAS (aviation gasoline) had ignited and he was on fire.

Meanwhile, CPT Gerald Walker (Scorpion 6) made an approach in a gunship (the low gunship flew at about 200 feet maybe 1/4 mile behind the scout). He was driven off while hovering up to the wreck, by heavy fire, including one bullet which pierced his right hand and the cyclic...there were no slicks around and both gunships now had wounded on board and were out of bullets...

Somehow they got in touch with a flight of aircraft which turned out to be the 174th, who had their gunships along with them.

Now, somehow, the Dolphin guy just slid in there and picked him up. Not sure how much fire he took, but it took a lot of guts just to start the approach, even if he was contour flying...knowing that those big machine guns were out there. Especially since nobody knew if anyone was alive. Walker had radioed back that he thought they were all dead.

Before the Dolphin got in, the VC walked up to the aircraft and shot what was left of it full of holes. They killed the crewman who was screaming and Barry just laid there. He said one guy nudged him with his boot and looked him right in the eye...didn't seem to think he was worth a bullet. Barry said he had his hand inside his shirt holding on to his St. Cristopher's medal, or crucifix...some religious pendant anyhow...and just squeezed it. The enemy soldier just walked away.

Lloyd couldn't move, he wasn't playing dead, he was in shock. Then the Dolphin swooped in and picked him up. Immediately afterward, probably about 30 minutes after the thing started, we were cleared back over the crash site. We had a FAC (forward air controller) on the line and he could divert any Navy/Marine aircraft returning to Chu Lai with unexpended ordnance. We were going to bomb hell out of them.

Couldn't find beans, and we were real good "finders"...couldn't find anything but expended brass. There were two big machine guns and a .30 calibre in sort of a flat triangle layout. It looked like either a Scorpion or Shark had put a rocket right close to one position, but we couldn't find any evidence that they got it.

This was right on the edge of the foothills and the bad guys were actually on raised ground, so Barry didn't actually get into the triangle. The Dolphin was just as exposed, though...and he managed to get in and out...the Sharks probably had the bad guys heads down some, and I'm sure they were getting ready to hat up. When we got there, the bodies of the two crewmen were still there. One of my observers (I believe it was Larry Colburn who was with Buck Thompson at My Lai) took some pictures. I didn't keep any copies, but I remember you could see the two bodies lying there. Very sobering.

We flew circles around that area the rest of the day...got into some contact, but don't know if it was the same guys...no heavy guns. I logged 6.8 hours that day. Pretty good day in an OH-23G, the collective got awful heavy flying that little helicopter low level all day. Taking off 1.3 hours for my first mission of the day and .7 back and forth to Chu Lai, that means we looked for the little suckers for about five hours.

That Dolphin guy sure had some balls, going in there knowing what he knew and not knowing if anybody was alive to actually rescue.

Something else...that unit (the 123rd) was really tight on awards. A DFC from Watke (or Junius Tanner, his successor) really meant something. I only saw one Silver Star on my whole tour (that was when MAJ Watke was stuck in a burning gunship and ordered his rescuers away...they didn't leave him though), and very few DFC's. A DFC recommendation from Watke was pretty unusual considering the mission we had. Betcha Lloyd would like to meet Banek.

Bill Staffa

20 May 1997

Following is a rather cryptic listing from the VHPA helicopter database on this loss:

On 8 Apr 68, OH-23G, 62-03813, was hit with 12.7 mm in the swashplate and flight controls, killing two and injuring one. The two KIAs were SP4 Glenn U. Andreotta and SP5 Charles M. Dutton with B/123 AVN 23 INF. Records show that the OH-23G was written off on 11 Apr 68 as destroyed by fire. The helicopter was hit while in a right bank at 50 feet and 65 knots. The incident happened at BS545631.

Mission 16

Water and Ammo in,

Bodies Out

By James C. "Bud" Harton Jr.

In early 1967, I was still with the 2nd Platoon slicks, crewing 6982, "Maid Mary." 6982 was a brand new "D" model which the Company got to replace one of our aircraft which had crashed and killed the crew in December. I sweated over it every day, trying to keep it clean, scrubbing the floors out, and a futile attempt to keep the carbon off the tailboom from the jet exhaust.

I had a lot of hours in, was kind of senior in the platoon, when my gunner rotated home. The Platoon Sergeant sent us out to the flight line early one morning for a Combat Assault. He promised me that he would bring my new gunner out to the ship.

I went on out and started getting ready. I popped the cockpit doors open for the pilots who were still being briefed, opened the engine cowling for the preflight inspection and then got my gear ready.

The platoon 3/4 ton truck skidded to a halt and SSG Lawson dropped off a scruffy little guy wearing a boonie hat with the front brim pinned up. He got out of the truck, dropping his flight helmet to the ground, and then stood up and I got a good look at him.

He was OLD, at least 30. As he rambled over to me, I saw he was already wearing the red scarf that we all wore around his neck. As he came up to me, he stuck out his hand and said,

"Hi! I'm Ray Dussault, I'm your new gunner, I just transferred in."

I couldn't believe this, this guy was older than the hills. SSG Lawson came around the back of the truck and grabbed my guns off the bed. He was grinning like a maniac, knowing that I was getting a royal case. "Now you guys have fun, and remember! I'm grading on 'works well with others' today."

And with that he was gone. I watched Lawson pull away and then I turned to Dussault. He was a Sargeant! That meant he outranked me as I was only a Specialist 4.

"Okay, Sarge, here come the pilots, we got to speed it up. Mount the guns and get your gear ready. And say listen, I'm the Crew Chief. Even if you outrank me, this is my airplane and I'm the boss."

He listened attentively, smiling all the time. He nodded his head and then strolled back to the ramp and grabbed the two door guns, carrying them back to the ship. He dropped one off on my side and then disappeared on the other side with his. I figured "what the hell" and went ahead and mounted my M60D machine gun on the mount on the right transmission well. Both pilots showed up and started the preflight.

As I was throwing on my chicken plate, Dussault came back over on my side. "Say, Specialist, could you give me a hand with the gun? I've never mounted one before."

I just stared at him for a second, then followed him back. I grabbed the gun, showed him how to mount it and then started back to my side. I got as far as the cockpit when Dussault said, "Hey, Specialist, could you show me how to load this thing?"

That's when I found out that Ray Dussault had his first helicopter ride late the evening before. He had never crewed, didn't know how to fix his gear, wear his flight helmet, I mean we're talking total cherry here. So I quickly told him what he needed to know just to complete the start up, and then I told the pilots I was going to have to teach all day using the intercom. And that's what happened. He didn't know about clearing the tail rotor, watching for other aircraft or even what the rules of engagement were.

As sure as luck would have it, the first mission was a combat assault carrying 1st Division troops into a landing zone. We picked the troops up in the field. On our arrival, they weren't quite ready, so we shut down; and I had a few more minutes on the ground to teach Dussault. My one thought was to get through the day and then have a "face off" with SSG Lawson when we got home. Dussault kept trying, and he was good at learning everything. But, as the time went on, I kept getting madder and madder.

We finally loaded up the troops and headed for the landing zone. Our formation was staggered trail right, and I was on the inside. That meant I couldn't fire suppression on the way in. The flight naturally drew fire on the way in, and Dussault never got a round off. I found out later that he couldn't figure out where the safety was. On the second and third flight with additional troops, there was no fire. And then the rest of the flight departed, and we got stuck supplying the troops we had just landed with everything they needed.

We called it "ash and trash" and it wasn't our favorite mission. We had inserted an Infantry company, and they had split into platoons and moved out in different directions. Ash and trash meant we brought them water and ammo, if they needed it, or heavy equipment that they couldn't haul. It meant a long day, with the constant whine of the engine in your ears, the helmet squeezing your head, and never enough time to stop and heat up some C-rations.

Late in the afternoon, when it was really hot, one of the platoons got nailed. Their point man spotted movement, opened fire, and then a command detonated mine was blown in their faces. It killed four of them. We got called in to carry the bodies out to graves registration down at 93rd Evacuation Hospital in Long Binh.

The grunts had cut an LZ for us in the foliage. We hovered straight down; and as the skids touched, they started bringing the body bags over. We had carried these guys in early that morning, spent the day resupplying them, and watched as the heat and humidity, the fear and tension, had taken its toll on them as they humped through the triple canopy of the jungle. And now, they were carrying four of their friends to us to take their last ride.

I had to give Ray credit. He moved out of the well into the cargo compartment to help me. I folded the seats up so there was enough room; and we carefully took the rubber bags, one at a time, and gently placed them on the cabin floor. Both of us were silent on the intercom; and we seemed to work as a team, finally. When we were done, I gave the pilot thumbs up, moved back into the well, and then cleared the tail rotor for the pilot as we went straight back up.

It was a pretty quiet flight down to Long Binh. The bodies, exposed to the heat and humidity, had already started to emit that smell that could come from only one source. Blood was leaking out from one of the bags and spraying around. All four of us ignored it.

When we arrived at Long Binh, the pilot called for clearance to the Dustoff pad, and notified them we had KIAs aboard. We hovered into the pad as a team came down the wooden sidewalk to the pad to receive the bodies. I remained in the well as they approached my side of the aircraft. The first medic reached in, gripped one of the handles on the bags, pulled it out of the aircraft, and let it fall to the ground, three feet below.

I couldn't believe it; I was just stunned. I wanted to say something, but I just couldn't seem to get it out. I looked forward and could see both pilots watching as the medic grabbed for the second bag. That's when Ray Dussault became my friend.

I heard him scream, not on the intercom, as he jumped into the cabin. He grabbed an M14 rifle hanging from the pilot's seat and hit the ground on his side. I saw him cross the cockpit as he was jacking a round into the chamber of the rifle; and, suddenly, I wasn't frozen anymore.

I stood up, brought M60 up from the stow position, and pointed at the medics as Ray had them covered from the front right of the cockpit. The pilot was already on the radio, and I heard him distinctly tell the 93rd Evac controller to get an Officer out to the pad because "my crew is going to shoot your medics right now."

The doors flew open and a crowd poured out. By this time, Ray had them on their knees with their hands straight up overhead. Some Doctor cooled everything down, and the medics began to reverently place the bodies on gurneys. Ray and I kept them covered the whole time we were there. When they were finally done and backing away from us, we came up to RPM and left.

We were just as silent going back to Lai Khe as when we headed to the hospital. But once we were on the ground and the aircraft was shutting down, I walked around to Ray's side. He was leaning against his door gun with his head down. As I came up to him, I touched him on the shoulder, stuck out my hand, and then I showed him how to wear the Robin Hood scarf the right way.

SGT RAY DUSSAULT, Robin Hood Doorgunner

James C. "Bud" Harton

Mission 17

"Operation Bright Light"

NOVEMBER RANGER, 75th INF
61ST AHC, 1ST AVN BRIGADE

By Clifford E. White

A few years ago I met Carl Millinder on the Internet while searching for pilots I flew with and trying to make some contact with people I had served with. Carl responded to one of my inquires and we compared notes. Both of us were in country in 1971, Carl with the N Rangers 75th Inf. at LZ English, and myself with the 61st AHC at LZ Lane. I asked if he remembered a mission in Feb. of that year where the Rangers were lifted in to recover some American POW's. Carl said his team was on that mission. We have kept in touch and have decided that this mission needs to be recorded as a part of both units' history.

This mission "Operation Bright Light" took place Feb. 1971. "Bright Light" was a code word used to designate operations and intelligence relating to POW's and down aircraft. To have some idea of the impact of the mission and why I remember it so clearly, first this was a historical mission, or at least it would have been if it had been successful. And secondly, I was on my second tour and the new platoon commander for 2nd platoon. My first tour was in 1968 with Casper Aviation Platoon HHC 173rd ABN. I took some comfort with being familiar with the Area of Operation and supporting the 173rd, but not all that familiar with my new position, or comfortable with being the new guy (FNG) in the unit.

Being woken up at midnight and being told that you have an immediate flight to LZ English, and it is your first mission after the in country check ride the day before, causes some excitement. On the way to operations to find out whom I was flying with and what the mission was it very quickly became apparent that the whole company was awake. I found out that both slick platoons "Lucky Star" and the gun platoon "Star Blazers" were going to LZ English, and we would be briefed on arrival. My AC knew about the mission and was already on the flight line, preflighting the ship and as far as he was concerned I was late. Not a great way to start.

I would be flying right seat "peter pilot (PP)" in the lead ship with, to the best of my memory CW2 Sopko, one of the senior Aircraft commanders. As memory serves, we had two flights of five ships each, four "M" model gun ships. We landed at LZ English on the Crap Table about 2AM and the AC's went in for the mission briefing while the rest waited. Not knowing what to expect made the waiting seem a lot longer than it really was. Some of the crewmembers slept and some ate, I could do neither.

We were briefed on the AC's return. Our mission was to pick up the 75th Rangers at LZ Pony and depart at such time so we would land at first light in an abounded 1st Cav. firebase where an estimated 6 to 10 American POW's were being held by an unknown number of NVA. We would be landing at first light under the cover of the Star Blazers and a heavy drop of CS gas canisters dropped by a Casper ship. Casper also had the Command and Control (C&C) for the mission. After the initial insertion we were to return to Pony and load up the next lift of Rangers who were being held in reserve if the first lift ran into serious trouble. If there was no trouble, and the POW's were recovered we were to return and lift out the first lift.

We were to follow the river West from LZ Pony past LZ Abby turning North at an area called "crows foot' and continue to follow the river. The flight was low level. North on the river there is a large waterfall, about 200-ft. high. I had seen it once before in 68. As we climbed to get over the waterfall we were to continue to follow the river and keep climbing to an altitude so that we could see the LZ, which was to the South of the river.

The waterfall was our IP, Initial Point. The final destination was about 30 miles north of An Khe and about 30 miles West of LZ Pony. I don't know the last time Americans had been in this area. It could have been at least 4 years, truly Charley country. Recon pictures of the abandoned LZ showed old bunkers, down trees and stumps. There were two clearings separated by a row of trees. The first flight would land in the clearing to the right (West Side) and the second flight would simultaneously land in the clearing to the left. There were two large hills, one on the East and the other to the West. They were old volcano vents and were nick named "Witch's Tits".

The Waterfall with cave behind it.

Recon pictures also showed the possibility of machine gun positions on each hill. The most common heavy machine gun used by the NVA was the 12.7-mm (51 cal.). If they were really there they would be able to see us coming and we would be landing below them in a clear line of fire. The NVA typically set the 12.7 up in a triangle so there would have been a third gun that had not been found. First light and coming in fast using surprise would be the only chance to get past the guns and in and out of the LZ before any anti-aircraft guns could be fired. That is if the guns were there or the crews were still asleep.

We were issued gas mask to use during the initial insertion. They were designed for aircrews so had to be plugged into the intercom/radio and the can/filter was on a long hose and strapped to your body or leg. The lens were a thin plastic and hard to see through and in my case there was a wrinkle which distorted the view, such that I could either see two trees where there was one or see none at all without moving my head back and forth. I don't know who was responsible for the gas mask, but there was only enough for two per ship. There were 4 crew per ship and with only two gas masks there was cause for concern. There was no way the mission would be delayed or cancelled, so each ship decided who would wear the mask.

In our case the decision was that I would wear the mask along with the crew chief. The AC would fly the ship into the LZ and as the gas came into the ship and he was affected by it I would take over and fly out. I think Mr. Sopko would have preferred a more experienced pilot with him in the lead ship, however he never said so.

The LZ was tight so to fit all 5 ships in we had to crowd forward so our blades were over lapping an old bunker. It was over grown and we didn't see it till just before we set down. There was an opening in the bunker immediately to my front about 20 feet away. Our orders were not to return fire to prevent accidentally hitting any of the POWs, despite the order I had my .38 out and was ready to shoot thorough the windscreen if I saw any movement in the bunker. The time in the LZ was very short, the crew chief said we were clear, which meant that all the Rangers were out.

We came to a hover and the AC radioed the flight that "lead is up" and I heard trail respond that "the flight is up", there was no other radio talk. As planned the AC said, "you've got it". Excited and still new I pulled pitch, and forgot the left pedal. We listed right and were going out of the LZ sort of sideways, I heard someone, maybe the crew chief or the AC in the intercom yelling "left pedal", which solved our problem.

There were no rounds fired, no one was home. Back at LZ Pony we were waiting for information on our next step. Fly in the reserves, or fly in and pick up the POWs and the Rangers. The call came that there were no POWs and that we were to fly back and extract the Rangers. This was a major disappointment, and the reason why no rounds were fired. Our good fortune of not having a hot LZ was very bad news for the POWs. They had been there, and had been moved as we were coming in. Carl told me that they found the cages they had been kept in. E-mail from Carl, "We knew there were plenty NVA that was supposed to be there. So we were a little concerned. Wrote the goodbye letters and shit. Sorry we didn't find the guys. We knew they were close."
Carl also sent me this: "As I remember the mission, was to have four ranger teams inserted at the Four Corners of a grid square. We were told of sighting of American POWs. The location was never told to us. We practiced the raid for about a week. I remember it was a long flight and we still didn't know where we were going. The piece of map we were issued indicated a waterfall where we would escape and evade to if we had to. About a minute out the grid square would be saturated with CS fired from the Cobras. We donned the protective masks and went in. About 20 to 30 minutes after the insertion, Charlie team discovered bamboo cages, hoochs and

elevated bins that stored rice. The campfires were still hot and fresh human feces were found. No men were seen. No enemy contact was made. They were there, probably underground. I think the mission on the ground lasted about an hour. We were picked up, flew back to English and debriefed. We still never knew where we had gone."

As Carl and I communicated I was surprised to find out that the Rangers didn't know where they were going. Plus that they were expecting to be inserted at the corners of the grid, however there was only one LZ, which would fit in the flights or a single ship and that, was in the old firebase. I was also surprised to find out they had trained for the mission and we had almost no notice.

In one of his e-mail messages Carl said: "I had a guy working on an oil rig 20 years or so ago that was a POW. I told him about the mission, and the water fall. He told me he was one of the guys that built the bridge across the river. I don't remember his name but we called him Snuffy. I didn't remember a bridge at the time. But, I see it in the picture. He told me they had moved underground just before the gas hit. Wow. Gives me chills."

We are left to wonder what the outcome was for the POWs. The Paris agreement for the release of prisoners was that they all were to be released in Hanoi to the Red Cross. Which meant that these POWs and all captured in the South had to walk north, through very rough land, heavy bombing, and with poor food and poorly trained guards. The wounded and sick would have a particularly difficult time surveying. If they could not travel they would be shot and left on the side of the trail. I would like to believe that the POWs made it North and were released. However we may never know that for sure. Carl's experience of meeting "Snuffy" would leave me to hope so.

Carl's and my memory needs some help, so if anyone else in the 75th or the 61st that remembers this mission would like to add to or correct this narrative please get a hold of either one of us. I had most of a full tour left, and as the skills of the peter pilots improved and the current AC's rotated back to the states we became Aircraft Commanders. From my first tour with the 173rd ABN I had gained a great deal of respect for the LURPs, which they were called in 68, but in 71 I got to fly more missions either inserting or extracting the Rangers. I was always in awe of their missions and how they carried them out. The Rangers should know when we knew we were going to be flying N Rangers that the 61st took the missions very serious. The best pilots were assigned, with one of our better ships. These missions always seemed to prove challenging. However most of the time we would be assigned to fly C&C for one of the Battalions and during the day we would find out that a Ranger team needed to be inserted or extracted. At one time or another all our pilots got to fly these missions. Insertions were planned and for the most part went well, however extractions could be the most challenging and some-times were on a TAC-E (tactical emergency) so the closest ship to the team would be sent in. These missions were the bases for many war stories. Not to blow any smoke but I can't think of anyone else that I would rather be flying than the Rangers; they were the most professional troops you could work with.

They knew what they were doing and we knew if the "fit hit the shan" you couldn't be with a better group.

Written By:
Carl Millinder, Charley Team N Ranger, 75th Inf. www.75thrra.com
Clifford White, 2nd Platoon 61stAHC, 1ST Avn. Brigade www.61ahc.org

Clifford White at LZ English.

Mission 18

The Rescue of "Grumpy" Grimaldi

By Charles H. Nesbitt

While I do not recall the exact date of the events written about here, I am certain the date can be determined through aircraft records or the recollections of others involved. I sincerely doubt that anyone who was a part of the mission that day will ever forget it. I will simply say that I believe that the events related herein occurred in late 1968 or early 1969.

All of this occurred during a mission that I was sworn never to talk or write about. I did not speak of this or other related missions for many years after returning from my tour of duty in Vietnam. Early in my tour, I and others raised our right hands and took an oath of secrecy before taking part in these missions, the existence of which was denied from the highest levels of our government. As a result, I only began to speak of these matters after reading several books that detailed a number of the missions from the point of view of some of the Special Forces soldiers.

The weather that morning was not a limiting factor as we took the usual steps necessary to plan a routine extraction of a U.S. Army Special Forces team at the end of their planned mission in Laos.

The fact that we might call such a mission "routine" seems bizarre in retrospect and was an indication of just how inured we had become to the extreme danger we faced during these missions conducted in the areas of Laos and Cambodia that were under the absolute control of the North Vietnamese Army. We did "routinely" face 37mm and 51 caliber antiaircraft fire in addition to small arms (as we would on this mission). Such missions did not often end as planned. Hot extractions, with the enemy in pursuit were the rule rather than the exception, and I had experienced more than my share of in-contact, on the run, McGuire rig team pickups during the months that my unit, the 57th Assault Helicopter Company of the 52nd Aviation Battalion of the 1st Aviation Brigade, had the responsibility to provide aviation support for the mission. The planning session took place, as it nearly always did, at F.O.B. II located on the outskirts of Kontum City, the provincial capital of Kontum Province in Vietnam's Central Highlands. Forward Operating Base II (later referred to as CCC, Command and Control Central) was the home base for the Army's 5th Special Forces in the Central Highlands and the base of operations for the teams made up of U.S. and indigenous soldiers that operated secret missions inside North Vietnamese controlled Laos.

Those soldiers were the best of the best that I encountered in Vietnam. Nearly all of their missions were conducted "across the fence" in Laos or Cambodia, where they surveilled and disrupted enemy activity in enemy base areas and along the Ho Chi Minh Trail. They were highly skilled and incredibly courageous.

We would stage out of Dak To, a remote airfield defended by a brigade of the 4th Division that served as the normal jumping off point for these secret missions. The FAC (Forward Air Controller) would be an Air Force "Covey" pilot accompanied by an experienced Special Forces liaison and flying a push-pull Cessna. A pair of A1E's flying out of Pleiku would provide fixed wing coverage, while a pair of AH-1 "Pink Panther" Cobras from the 361stassault Weapons Company out of Pleiku would provide gunship cover. The actual extraction of the 8 man team on the ground would be performed by a pair of 57thGladiator UH-1H "Hueys" while 2 additional Hueys orbited at altitude and observed from a distance, there just in case something went wrong. I had been flying the UH1H on these missions for some time, graduating from pilot to aircraft commander, from chase ship pilot to insertion and extraction pilot, until I had assumed flight lead status. Members of the unit rotated on the FOB mission, and on the days that I flew it, I most often flew as flight leader, first in the LZ (landing zone) or to drop the McGuire rig. That would not be the case on this mission. We rarely were so certain that a mission would be relatively uneventful (a conclusion drawn from scant information and the knowledge that we were not responding to a "prairie fire", Special Forces code for May Day), so we would give less experienced pilots a chance at performing the extraction and I would orbit above and at a distance as Aircraft Commander of one of the chase ships. My crew would consist of an experienced crew chief, Specialist John Lindsay, Co-Pilot John Howard White who had been in-country for a short time, and a less experienced gunner both there to gain experience on the mission.

Initially, all went as planned. We departed DakTo as a group with the pair of Pink Panther Cobra gunships leading the slicks (our jargon describing the troop-carrying Hueys); I was flying in 3rd position as the first of 2 Huey chase ships. Our formations were loose affairs with different altitudes, intervals and flightpaths used by all, a tactic learned by the unit over time. The jungle provided good cover for us during these transits, made more safely when one did not follow the other over the same spot allowing an enemy gunner to anticipate the trailing aircraft's arrival. We were joined by the Air Force "Spads" in their propeller driven A1Es as we crossed the border into Laos and began taking instruction from the FAC in the Covey who would direct the gunships to the LZ while the slicks staged at a distance.

This part of Laos was completely controlled by the NVA. The famed Ho Chi Minh Trail was so well developed in the otherwise remote, isolated and undeveloped area that it was paved in some sections. The enemy, of whom there were tens of thousands present in the area, had become familiar with our methods and had developed the ability to rapidly respond to our incursions, even assigning watchers to monitor potential LZs and deploying anti-aircraft weaponry to protect their supply routes and encampments. As a result, we knew that every mission had the potential to turn into a life and death struggle at a moment's notice, and they often did. We had the advantage of airpower and airmobility and they had the cover of the jungle, familiarity with the territory and long-planned reactive strategies on their side. Each of these opposing strengths would come into play during this mission.

At the FAC's direction, the gunships approached and located the LZ where they established the classic racetrack pattern that allowed each ship to, in turn, direct its firepower toward the surrounds of the LZ while his trailing partner gave him cover from the rear. I watched from a distance as the first slick then approached the landing zone (a small clearing amongst tall jungle trees) and hovered down to the jungle floor. In minutes he was coming out of the LZ and turning east toward the border. The second ship timed his approach nearly perfectly so that his descent into the LZ began only seconds after the first ships departure.

I began to relax. I'd heard no call indicating enemy fire being received, the first ship was clear and the second ship was reappearing above the jungle canopy and transitioning to forward flight.
Then, for what seemed to be no obvious reason, the second ship crashed into the trees and settled into the jungle. It seemed surreal. I heard "He's down!" from one of the gunship pilots and felt the adrenalin surge as I headed for the crash site. We nearly immediately heard by radio from one of the team members on board that they were off the ship and while there were injuries, everyone seemed to be mobile, a remarkable fact considering that they had just crashed into triple canopy jungle populated with trees that were between 125' and 150' tall.

After confirming everyone's mobility, the FAC directed the downed team and airmen to walk several hundred yards north northeast to an area of elephant grass that was clear enough for our chase aircraft to approach. At about the same time the team reported receiving fire from the south. I waited with the other chase ship east of all of this while the downed men moved to the designated pickup point, which had been quickly chosen after an analysis of the surrounding terrain and conversation between the FAC and me in my role as AC of the first chase (now recovery) ship. The gunships established their racetrack south of the LZ and started laying down covering fire to counter the weapons fire being received by our men.

As soon as the downed men reached the landing area, we moved in to pick them up, hovering into, flattening, and chopping down the elephant grass (10 or likely more feet high) with our rotor blade so that we could get low enough to load them. The grassy area had the additional difficulty of hidden and broken bamboo stumps with the potential to pierce our fuel tank located in the belly of the ship. It was a challenge that demanded coordination of all our crewmembers to get us low enough to load while avoiding the disabling bamboo stumps. Despite the difficulties, we soon had everyone on board and both chase ships lifted off heading east toward the border and safety. I remember the elation. As we climbed out the gunships broke off their racetrack and headed east as well. I had 4 of the 8 men who had gone down and radioed the other chase ship to verify that we had them all. The answer to my question changed everything.

I believe that Warrant Officer Michael Mobley was flying the other chase ship. He replied, saying that he had 3 of the downed men on board. I had 4. That meant someone was still back at the crash site. A feeling of dread crept up my spine. We determined that Specialist John Grimaldi, the door gunner of the ship that had gone down, was the missing man.

There was no question about what would come next; we would do everything possible to recover our missing crewman. This was Laos, our mission was secret, and the only assets available to help would be those sworn to keep it so. Grimaldi, an American soldier, one of us, was down there alone in the enemy's back yard and we would move heaven and earth to get him back.

I radioed the gunships, asking them to return to the crash site as we proceeded to the super-secret Special Forces outpost in Laos, known as Leghorn, where we landed on its small helicopter pad and unloaded our passengers. Leghorn was located on a nearly unapproachable mountain pinnacle where the outpost served as an emergency landing place for the helicopters and a radio relay facility for the teams in the field. It was serving both purposes that day.

From there we flew back to the jungle crash site and commenced a search for Grimaldi. I hovered the Huey right in the treetops and did my best to maneuver in such a way that we could see the jungle floor. We began at the crash site and hovered slowly around the area in an ever widening circle until we had moved some distance from our starting point. We took fire from NVA soldiers on the south side of the crash site and requested covering fire from the gunships. They complied and laid down withering minigun fire while we used the huge jungle trees for cover. We searched and searched and were beginning to run low on fuel having found no sign of Grimaldi.

When it became apparent that our fuel reserves would soon approach the minimum required to allow safe return to Dak To, I made the decision to make a final pass directly over the downed aircraft before breaking off the search and heading back for fuel. I remember the breath-taking moment when on that final pass we found Grimaldi lying beside the aircraft. We were all elated and stunned. How had he gotten there? Was he alive? He laid there motionless. I lowered our Huey into the canopy in an attempt to get down to the aircraft and Grimaldi, but there just wasn't clearance enough amongst the trees and we again received fire from enemy gunners. Someone was going to have to carry him to the elephant grass LZ or we would have to lift him out using a McGuire rig. That meant a return to Dak To for fuel and a Bright Light team.

Word spread quickly as the nature of our dilemma was radioed back to Dak To and our Operations in Kontum. When we arrived back in Dak To, we were met by a heavy fire team of 57th AHC Cougar gunships and additional 57th Gladiator slicks that were needed to carry the Bright Light team to the rescue site. A plan was developed; three Gladiator helicopters would drop the rescue team in the same grassy area that we had used to extract the downed crew and team members. Having delivered my part of the team, I would then hover over the downed ship so the team could use the sound of the rotors coming from our aircraft as a point of reference that would lead them to the crash site. The gunships would suppress enemy fire. When the team had secured the site and determined Grimaldi's condition, they would determine whether it would be necessary for them to carry him back to the LZ or we would take him out by McGuire rig.

A heavy fire team of gunships consisted of 3 UH1-C gunships equipped with the rapid-firing electrically driven "mini-guns" capable of firing at up to 4,000 rounds per minute and high explosive rockets that delivered the explosive power of an artillery shell to a target. A standard gunship team consisted of 2 of these ships. Under circumstances of extreme threat, a "heavy" team of three was used. Such gunships were devastating offensive weapons that were most often used to protect the "slicks" on these operations.

A Bright Light team consisted of Special Forces soldiers whose assignment required them to be on standby at Dak To as a ready rescue force able to be inserted when a team was in trouble, an aircraft was down, or a POW was spotted in the enemy controlled environs of Laos or Cambodia. They were heavily armed, highly trained and fearsome soldiers.

A McGuire rig is a simple construct made up of 4 ropes that are approximately 150 feet in length and equipped with a device that can be attached to a harness worn by the man on the ground. Depending on need one or two of the ropes are dropped out each side of a hovering aircraft through to the jungle floor. Once the soldiers being extracted are safely attached, the helicopter above the jungle canopy lifts them by hovering straight up until the soldiers clear the trees. This maneuver requires interaction amongst a highly skilled and experienced crew who must guide the pilot to safe clearance as the suspended men come up through and eventually clear the trees. A rope tangled in a tree would lead to a tragic result: the death or injury of its passenger(s) and/or the destruction of the helicopter. Crewmen carried knives that would be used to cut the rope and save the ship and crew in that circumstance. Additionally, as they slowly made the initial purely vertical lift, the ships and men performing this type of extremely dangerous extraction are vulnerable to enemy fire as they hang motionless and exposed over 150 feet above the jungle floor.

As a result, this mission would require an experienced and battle-hardened crew that could face the enemy and keep their cool. We all wanted to have the best chance possible to save Grimaldi and survive the experience. The inexperienced co-pilot and gunner who had been with me on the "routine" mission were replaced by Lieutenant Jim McKenzie and Specialist Richard Kleint, a decision that would later prove to be critical to our successful completion of the mission. McKenzie was himself an experienced pilot who I had flown with on many missions. He had proved to be a bright, resourceful and skilled pilot and leader who kept his cool in tough situations. Kleint was a strapping young crew chief who inspired me with his courage and competence every time I flew with him. John Lindsay was a determined and courageous crew chief as well. We had the right crew for the mission as we lifted off with a full load of fuel determined to save our compatriot.

The flight back to the LZ was uneventful. Radio chatter was minimal as we all contemplated the mission at hand. We were flying into an enemy controlled area deep in Laos where the NVA lay in wait for us and the life of our friend and crewmate hung in the balance. The Cougar gunships led the way and set up the racetrack. They immediately received and returned fire. Various types of antiaircraft and small arms fire were now part of the threat. The fight was underway. Our Gladiator slicks dropped into the LZ, hovering into the elephant grass above the dangerous bamboo stumps while the Bright light team unloaded and gathered there.

I then hovered our aircraft from the LZ to the crash site in order to provide an audible guide to the slowly advancing team. When we arrived at our station atop the jungle canopy 150 feet above the crash site, we spotted Grimaldi still lying beside the ship. Then events began to unfold in rapid succession. We began receiving enemy gunfire and saw enemy soldiers moving just yards away from the crash site. I moved the ship behind the cover of the jungle canopy and made a call to our escorting Cougars whose miniguns scattered the waiting enemy and slowed down the NVA's rate of fire. At the same time we alerted the approaching team, letting them know of the presence of the enemy soldiers.

We were on the horns of a dilemma. The team had not arrived and the enemy was directly outside the crash site in position to capture or kill Grimaldi. With the advice of the crew, I made a decision. With the help of guidance provided by our more experienced crew, we would attempt to lower our helicopter into the LZ, chopping limbs with our rotors if necessary, in an effort to get to Grimaldi before NVA soldiers did. I asked for covering fire from the Cougars and

Spads and moved into position. We could hear the bullets popping around us as we began the descent, chopping the light limbs on our way down. But it was no use; we could not risk the helicopter and crew trying to cut through the canopy, it was simply too thick. I hovered back up to the top of the canopy where we sat like a mother hen watching over Grimaldi while Kleint and Lindsay leveled their M60 machine-guns firing at anyone who moved near the clearing made by the downed aircraft.

It seemed like a very long time, marked by the regular passage of enemy bullets heading our way, before the Bright Light team appeared. The team soon secured the LZ and determined that Grimaldi should be lifted out by McGuire rig. Kleint and Lindsay dropped the ropes and a team member fastened the special harness designed for that purpose around Grimaldi's torso. Soon three soldiers from the team and Grimaldi were attached to the ropes and we began the ascent. As noted earlier, there is no hoisting device attached to the ropes. Rather, the pilot, taking direction from the crew must hover straight up until the long ropes completely clear the jungle. This causes the ship to lose the cover provided by the triple canopy and increases the enemies' chance of getting a visual sighting and clear line of fire. The gunships were really working out now, firing constantly in an attempt to disengage the enemy and protect us during our ascent.

We cleared the trees safely. Our experienced crew kept their cool under fire and safely directed me, allowing us to raise the dangling men clear of the jungle. Now we had to fly to the elephant grass area where we would lower and recover our precious cargo. This part of the flight was our most vulnerable. It required slow and precise flying with everyone's lives at stake, while the gunships and Spads gave everything they had to give us a chance to survive.

The crew directed me to a landing spot in the oft-visited elephant grass, calling out altitude and position directions as I made the descent that would put Grimaldi and the team down in the LZ where we could load our injured fellow Gladiator. They called out when our living cargo touched down and proceeded to direct me in descent to a place safely clear of them. Of course I couldn't touch down because of the problem with the bamboo that threatened our fuel tank, so I descended to a hover just above the jagged bamboo stumps. It seemed almost over. Of course, it was not.

We had taken 3 team members out with Grimaldi in the hope that they could help load him once we reached the LZ. Two of them were on the left side of the aircraft and the other was down near Grimaldi about 50 feet from our right side. What was immediately apparent was that the men on the left were struggling to get through the elephant grass to the men on the right while precious time of high vulnerability for us ticked away keeping Grimaldi from the treatment he needed for his wounds. To compound our problem even further, a Vietnamese Air Force CH-34 "King Bee" arrived at that moment hovering in our left rear quadrant about 30 feet above us. The CH-34 carried a Special Forces medic who had the good intention of tending to the injured and wounded Grimaldi. Rotor wash from the larger

CH-34 King Bee was causing the Huey to be right at the edge of control as I tried to maintain a hover and avoid piercing our fuel tank on the jagged stumps below us.

The radios on the CH-34 were notorious among Huey pilots because of the garbling that occurred when we attempted to communicate with them. As a result, the King Bee pilot could not understand my increasingly desperate attempts to communicate the situation to him, nor could I understand his transmissions. Therefore, he remained unaware of the treacherous conditions that we were facing in the LZ. Finally, in a last attempt to avert disaster, I shouted to John Lindsay over the intercom, saying "He can't understand me, wave him away!" Lindsay frantically waved at the intruding ship while I struggled at the controls and monitored Grimaldi's status.

In the middle of all this Rich Kleint and I came to the conclusion that Rich would have to get off the buffeting aircraft and make his way through the elephant grass to help the soldier on the right side of the aircraft carry and load the unconscious Grimaldi. Rich jumped off the aircraft at about the same time that John Lindsay attempted to point his M60 at the culprit hovering above us who was unwittingly about to force us from the air and on to the dangerous bamboo. When Lindsay realized that his gun mount would not allow him to raise the machine gun barrel high enough to threaten the 34, he picked up his M16 and pointed it directly at the pilot. That, as they say, did the job. The King Bee pilot got the nonverbal message and lifted off eliminating the destabilizing rotor wash as he departed.

With the aircraft now fully under control, I watched as Rich Kleint approached carrying Grimaldi. When he reached our helicopter, I soon realized that he could not hoist his precious human cargo high enough to get him in. So, with John Lindsay's guidance, I lowered the ship until it was just touching the jagged bamboo. With Lindsay's help, Kleint then managed to hoist Grimaldi on board. Rich then climbed aboard and we finally lifted off, heading east for Dak To.

After hours of facing down an enemy in his own territory, we had our Gladiator back. He was badly injured, in and (mostly) out of consciousness and in need of medical attention, but he was aboard and we were heading out of Laos. While the rest of the Cougars, Gladiators, Spads and the Covey remained to extract the heroic rescuing Bright Light team, we flew toward safety as fast as the Huey would go.When we finally landed at Dak To, we landed right beside the small medical dispensary that served the troops there. It was the softest landing I ever made in any aircraft. Grimaldi was quickly unloaded and taken inside; we hovered to the revetment area, parked and shut down. The Huey was nearly out of fuel.

We soon learned that Grimaldi was stable and would be flown to the Military Hospital in Pleiku for emergency treatment. 1st Lieutenant Jim McKenzie had maintained absolute composure while he assisted and advised me well during one of the most difficult successful missions performed during my time as a combat pilot. Specialists Kleint and Lindsay had proven to be resourceful and fearless in the face of near constant enemy fire. We had all done what was necessary to bring our Gladiator safely home.

Sometime later I had conversation with a member of the rescuing Bright Light Team, who told me of his belief that the NVA had dragged Grimaldi to the downed ship with the intention of using him as bait for a trap. He believed that only the devastating firepower delivered by the gunships and A1's had foiled their plan. Additionally, he told me that the Bright Light team had wired the downed Huey with explosives. Then, as they withdrew he observed the enemy moving in on the helicopter which was then blown up "in the faces" of the NVA soldiers.

All in all it was a remarkable event carried out over a four hour period by a team of courageous and dedicated men that once again proved the strength of the American military's ethic of "leave no one behind".

Charlie Nesbitt. Photos courtesy of Charlie Nesbitt.

Mission 19

The Noble Warrior: Rescue at Hill 845

by Lieutenant Colonel Gregory J. Johnson, USMC (Ret)

Glancing around at the clutter in my attic recently, I decided it was time to sort through some of the unpacked boxes associated with my military retirement and move to Pennsylvania. A fond smile crossed my face as I gingerly pulled out aging flight logbooks. As I randomly scanned the yellowing pages, I was surprised by the vivid and detailed recall the numerous sorties inscribed on those pages evoked. Aviation seems to have that effect on the mind.

Locked in a trance with my memories, it was the flutter of a small newspaper clipping surrendering to gravity as it fell from between the pages, that snapped the spell of the moment and brought me back to reality. The clipping was a one-line notice from the Navy Times announcing the death of my friend, David Cummings, during 1988. When I first cut out the obituary notice and tucked it away in my logbook, I mentally promised myself that one day I would tell the story of his heroics--in another place and time...

[Vietnam 1969]

It was December. Reconnaissance elements from a battalion-size Viet Cong force probed the hasty defensive perimeter set up by a remote Marine observation team atop Hill 845. From afar, an OV-10 "Bronco" aircraft, responding to an urgent call from the outpost for close air support, swept in low from the south. The confines of adjacent mountain ridges, coupled with a rapidly deteriorating cloud base, made the pending interdiction strike especially hazardous. Monsoon season was well underway and, like the distant thunder, the drone of the Bronco's propellers reverberated off the trees and mountain sides, striking fear in the guerrillas (as wounded VC prisoners would later relate) while providing some semblance of comfort to the beleaguered Marines.

The Bronco pilot and his rear seat aerial observer seemed oblivious to the danger. Directed to the attack by a ground-based forward air controller (FAC), the Bronco pilot focused his attack on a shallow ravine leading into the outpost encampment. Squeezing off two Zuni rockets, he visually tracked the missiles (incorporating a little body language) into a ravine where they exploded in a fury of smoke and fire.

The pilot immediately banked his aircraft sharp to the left to avoid flying debris. Quickly leveling his wings, he simultaneously pulled back hard on the control stick. His Bronco was now pointed straight up. Bleeding off airspeed for rapid altitude gain in an exchange of energy, the Bronco masked itself in the clouds to escape retaliatory ground fire, and to also avoid collision with the mountains. In a matter of seconds, the aircraft punched through the cloud overcast. Leveling off the aircraft, the pilot adjusted the throttle and waited for a radio call to announce the results of his attack. The FAC reported that the attack was successful. Further probing by the enemy had ceased. For the time being a second suppression attack would not be required. In the interlude, the pilot prowled the under-cast looking for an opening that would allow him to venture below in case another request for support was received.

During the siege on the outpost the FAC reported a young Marine had tripped off an enemy booby trap and was seriously injured. Bleeding profusely, he was going into shock. The Bronco pilot was asked to relay a call for an immediate medical evacuation, which his observer did immediately.

Meanwhile, at Landing Zone Baldy, Cobra pilot First Lieutenant Dave Cummings and his aircraft commander, Captain Roger Henry, were standing by on routine medevac escort alert in their AH-1G helicopter gunship. The rear cockpit seat of the Cobra, normally flown by the pilot in command, would today be flown by the copilot, Lieutenant Cummings, as part of his aircraft commander check ride. When the medevac escort call arrived the pilots launched with another Cobra and two CH-46 Sea Knight transport helicopters as part of a standard constituted medevac package. After a smooth join up, the flight headed 40 miles southwest of Da Nang into the Que Son Mountains in Quang Nam Province where they rendezvoused with the Bronco for a mission brief.

Captain Roger Henry, taken during his first tour in Vietnam when he was flying "attack Hueys". Photo courtesy of Greg Johnson.

Weather at Hill 845 had deteriorated badly. Rain and lowering cloud bases made it virtually impossible for the large Sea Knights to get into the area for the pickup. Despite persistent maneuvering, the rescue flight finally retired to the edge of the weather mass where they loitered to wait for another opportunity to come in and pick up the wounded Marine.

After obtaining approval from the medevac mission commander, the agile Cobra flown by Henry and Cummings, proceeded inbound to scout the landing zone in order to facilitate a more expeditious evacuation. The worsening weather, however, prompted Captain Henry, positioned in the higher visibility front gunner's seat, to assume control of the aircraft's more challenging-to-use side console forward cockpit flight controls. Visibility was now practically zero.

In those days, there was a variation of a popular song that "only mad dogs and Englishmen ventured into noonday monsoons!" Undaunted, Henry and Cummings pressed on despite harrowing weather conditions. The two Marines worked their Cobra up the mountain-side amidst severe turbulence generated up and down gnarled mountain slopes. Scraping tree tops at airspeeds that often dipped below 30 knots, or required holding in perilous zero-visibility hovers, the flyers anxiously waited for a call from the outpost giving them either a visual or sound cue that they were above the elusive, ill-defined landing zone. After three hours and five different attempts (with refueling runs interjected in-between), the aviators finally found their mark.

Sporadic radio reports confirmed to Henry and Cummings their worst fear that the injured Marine was succumbing to his wounds. Guiding the Cobra down through tall trees, Captain Henry landed the aircraft on the edge of a bomb crater in a skillful display of airmanship. The helicopter settled to the ground amid swirling debris. The tightness of the landing zone was such that only the front half of the aircraft's skids rested on the rocky outer lip of the bomb crater. While the Cobra loitered in this precarious teeter-totter position, Lieutenant Cummings climbed out of the aircraft to investigate the situation.

Dave Cummings pauses for photo while refueling and rearming during missions in Vietnam. Photo courtesy Greg Johnson

Infantry Lieutenant Dave Cummings in Vietnam. Photo courtesy Greg Johnson.

Torn and bloody, the wounded Marine was drifting in and out of shock. Having served a previous tour in Vietnam as an infantry officer, Lieutenant Cummings was intimately familiar with the situation now confronting him. He had seen the haunting lurk of death in young men's eyes enough times before to know that it was time to get this Marine out immediately. Death, Lieutenant Cummings promised himself, would not visit this Marine today if he had anything to say in the matter.

With the situation assessed, Lieutenant Cummings ordered the casualty lifted into the Cobra. Strapping the semiconscious Marine into his rear cockpit seat, Lieutenant Cummings fastened the canopy shut. As "mud Marines" looked on curiously, Lieutenant Cummings climbed atop the starboard stub wing rocket pod. Straddling the pod and facing aft, Cummings banged his fist on the wing to get Captain Henry's attention before giving him a thumbs up. With a grim smile, Captain Henry nodded and took off. The cloud base, by now, was less than 100 feet above the outpost.

As the Cobra lifted away, the radio airways snapped to life as radio operators in the vicinity broadcast descriptions of the incredible scene they were witnessing. Atop the rocket pod, Lieutenant Cummings flashed a "V" for victory to those remaining in the zone as the Cobra vanished dramatically into the blanket overcast. It was the ultimate stage exit. Marines on the ground stood and cheered. Morale soared.

Watercolor of Hill 845 event by former Sea Knight pilot Captain Jason Drake USMCR.

Leveling off in a cloud mass at 4,000 feet, Captain Henry accelerated the Cobra to 100 knots in order to improve maneuverability. Once stabilized, he glanced over his shoulder to check on the outrider. Lieutenant Cummings flashed him back a sheepish grin. Biting rain, extreme cold at altitude, and the deafening shrill and shuffle-vibration of engines and rotors all mixed to fill his senses. He could hold on only by squeezing his thighs tightly against the rocket pod wing mount. To exacerbate matters, the wind grabbed at the back of Cummings' helmet flexing it forward thereby causing the chin strap to choke him. All the while howling winds taunted him. But at their loudest, Cummings merely glanced at the wounded Marine, and howled back.

The Bronco pilot, still orbiting on patrol, began his return to home base as fuel began to run low. En route, he happened to catch a chance glimpse of the Cobra darting in and out of the clouds in its tenuous race against time. Zooming down for a closer look he was unprepared for the spectacle of Lieutenant Cummings, hanging outside the aircraft, and the bleeding, semiconscious Marine within. In mild disbelief, the Bronco pilot pulled up wide abeam the Cobra, gave a thumbs up and departed. "What a crazy war!" the Bronco pilot quipped to his observer while still shaking his head in disbelief. But in his heart, he knew this was the way of the warriors!

After the twenty-five minute flight through turbulent weather, the gunship descended through the clouds and broke into relatively clear sky at 1,200 feet over a land navigation point called Spider Lake. The Cobra now headed towards a medical facility. Thoroughly exhausted from the strain of the mission, Captain Henry was having trouble discerning the exact location of the medical site when he sensed a series of thumps coming from the starboard wing. Glancing to his right he saw Lieutenant Cummings, much like a prize-winning bird dog, with locked pointed finger directing his attention to their destination below.

After landing, the wounded Marine was whisked into a medical triage for stabilization while Navy Corpsmen, who thought they had seen everything, helped Cummings "defrost" himself off the rocket pod. A short time later, a CH-46 Sea Knight arrived to fly the wounded Marine to Marble Mountain for emergency surgery. Sprinting along through the sky as combat escort with the Sea Knight to the more sophisticated "in-country" medical facility were Cummings and Henry. The two, weary from fatigue, were nevertheless vested in their interest to culminate the safe arrival of the wounded Marine. [The young Marine survived, married, and was last known to be living in Texas.]

Despite the long day and fatiguing limits they had endured, Captain Henry continued the training portion of Lieutenant Cummings' check ride on the way back to home base. Oddly enough, among senior aviators "in-country," there was talk of censure and a court-martial for the outrider affair. The act had overtones, in their opinion, of grandstanding regardless of the fact that the young Marine would have died had he not received medical attention as soon as he did. However, when Henry and Cummings were both personally invited by the Commanding General of the First Marine Division to dine as special guests in his quarters, the issue of court-martial was moot and dead on arrival. For their actions, Captain Henry and First Lieutenant Cummings were each awarded the Distinguished

Flying Cross. Years later when asked about the dining experience with the Commanding General, both pilots readily admit they thought they had a great time. Libations, it appears, were liberally dispensed. And it was reported to the two aviators that they were both transported horizontally into their hooches and gently tucked in their racks by the grunts!

[Epilogue]

When Dave Cummings died unexpectedly in 1988, there were the normal expressions of loss, especially for one so young. But none who first attended his lifeless body, and only a few who were present at his hometown funeral, fully realized the magnitude of his life or the legacy he had left with the Corps.

A native of Woburn, Massachusetts, Cummings enlisted in the Marine Corps during September of 1966. Upon completion of recruit training, he attended Officer Candidate School and The Basic School at Quantico, Virginia. Cummings served several months as an infantry platoon leader with the Second Battalion, First Marine Division in Vietnam. After being seriously wounded in a fire fight with Viet Cong forces, he was evacuated to the States. Cummings had always wanted to fly so it was a thrill, following recuperation, when he was selected for flight training. Earning his "Wings of Gold," Dave Cummings returned to Vietnam during September 1969 to start his combat flying career.

Nineteen years later, Lieutenant Colonel Dave Cummings, en route to attend a special military course in Albany, Georgia, stopped in Atlanta for the night. After a routine workout, he returned to his hotel room where he suffered an apparent heart attack and died. He was 42.

Although Dave Cummings' life spanned a relatively short period of time, he managed to walk a worthy journey. Among his personal military awards were four Distinguished Flying Crosses, four single mission Air Medals, the Bronze Star with combat "V", and a Purple Heart.

In this day and age when the term hero is used so loosely, it is comforting that I can say I actually have known some true ones in my lifetime. Dave Cummings was a man who set the example. He was a guy who displayed courage that all of us who knew him hoped we could muster if the call came. Dave Cummings was a special piece of the Corps' past, a large measure of its tradition, and maybe, more importantly, a sizeable chunk of its soul. He will not be easily forgotten. Semper Fi, Dave.

About the author: LtCol Johnson served 20 years as a Marine Corps aviator, amassing 4350 hours of flight time with 2000-plus helicopter hours (primarily in the CH-46) and another 2000 in fixed wing aircraft. Following retirement, Johnson continues to serve as a research administrator at Penn State University's Applied Research Laboratory--a U.S. Navy University Affiliated Research Center sponsored by the Office of Naval Research

Greg Johnson in front of Marine CH-46 Sea Knight. Photo courtesy of Greg Johnson.

Dave Cummings in front of AH-1G Cobra. Photo courtesy of Greg Johnson.

Cummings in the Aircraft Commanders seat, back seat, of AH-1G Cobra. Photo courtesy of Greg Johnson

Mission 20

The Rescue of
Lady Ace 7-2

By Rex Gooch

My Best Friend, Russ Miller

For some time, I have carried a story in my mind that I felt compelled to share. This story is about my best friend, Russ Miller, and what he experienced in Vietnam in 1972. As I began writing this story, I could almost hear Russ's voice recount all the details to me. I soon found myself totally immersed in those events from long ago. Then, in the middle of my writing, this story took a fortunate turn: it would involve many others who were personally involved in the event. Read on...

Russ Miller and I were stick-buddies (pilots-in-training paired with an instructor) in the Primary Phase of U.S. Army Helicopter School at Fort Wolters, Texas. The stress of learning to fly a tiny, complicated training helicopter, offset by the humor and good times we shared, resulted in a bond of friendship that would remain unmatched in other life endeavors.

After graduating from flight school in September 1971, Russ and I received our orders for Vietnam. Upon arrival in "Nam," I was assigned to C Troop, 3/17 Cavalry, call sign Lighthorse, flying out of Vinh Long in the Delta. Russ was assigned to F Troop, 4th

Cavalry, call sign Centaurs, flying out of Lai Khe, west of Saigon. Although we were flying in different units, we kept in touch whenever possible.

In Vietnam, Russ became a skilled and highly effective Cobra gunship pilot flying with the F-4 Air Cavalry. The Centaurs typically flew in "Pink Teams" with two small helicopters flying at treetop level, seeking out enemy ground forces. Once the helicopters took fire or visually located the enemy, two Cobra gunships rolled in from high above, firing rockets for the kill.

Many years later, Russ and I would meet at Vietnam Helicopter Pilots Association (VHPA) reunions and reminisce about our flying days. On one occasion, Russ told an amazing story that captivated me. His story involved the heroic actions of F Troop, 4th Cavalry, in the courageous rescue of a downed U.S. Marine helicopter crew. Several times, I suggested that Russ or someone in his unit document this story. Unfortunately, my best buddy Russ died in 2011. I was heartbroken by the loss of my best friend and later decided that I would write this story in his honor.

As I researched the events surrounding the July 11, 1972, rescue, I discovered that this daring night extraction was an extraordinary example of flying skill and bravery. And the story expanded beyond my buddy, Russ. The heroic actions of the Centaur pilots of F Troop, 4th Cavalry, on that day were truly remarkable and worthy of sharing. This is their story.

To understand what happened that day, I must first

tell of the events leading up to the rescue. Step back in time with me to the spring of 1972.

1972 Easter Offensive

In March 1972, the North Vietnamese Army (NVA) staged the largest invasion of South Vietnam since the Tet Offensive of 1968. The Easter Offensive was a radical departure from previous NVA assaults because the North Vietnamese advanced their forces with not only infantry but also armor and heavy artillery. Their intent was to gain as much territory and destroy as many Army of the Republic of Viet Nam (ARVN, the South Vietnamese army) units as possible to gain an advantage at the Paris Peace Accords. Invading South Vietnam from the north, the NVA easily overran the ARVNs and captured the city of Quang Tri in I Corps (northernmost U.S. Military quadrant of South Vietnam.) In II Corps, the NVA advanced toward Kon Tum, the provincial capital, with a planned drive to the sea that would have split South Vietnam in two. The sheer size of this massive assault caught the U.S. High Command by surprise.

In April 1972, F Troop, 4th Cavalry was tactically relocated from Lai Khe to Phu Bai and later to Tan My in I Corps to support the Easter Offensive counterattack strategy. In their new area of operations, Russ Miller and the other Centaur pilots found themselves in the midst of almost daily combat engagement with the North Vietnamese Army.

Lam Son 72—Phase II

In July 1972, the U.S. and South Vietnamese commands developed a counteroffensive strategy to recapture the city of Quang Tri. This strategy was code named "Lam Son 72." In accordance with the Vietnamization policy, the U.S. provided aviation support, while the South Vietnamese army provided and commanded the ground forces. Phase II of this strategy was to insert a reinforced battalion of South Vietnamese Marines behind enemy lines north of NVA-occupied Quang Tri with the objective of retaking the city. The aviation support was a joint tactical operation of U.S. Air Force, Marines, and Army aviation units.

The preparatory fire plan for this mission included early bombardment of the landing zone (LZ) with carpet-bombing from U.S. Air Force B-52s and artillery fire from offshore U.S. Naval gunships. After the bombing ceased and just prior to the troop insertion, Vietnamese Air Force (VNAF) A1-E Skyraiders were to cluster-bomb the trench lines of the north bank of the Song Vinh Dinh River.

The preparatory fires appeared to be the crucial area where the mission went awry. It was later reported that the U.S. Air Force cancelled (or possibly relocated) the B-52 strikes for supposed "humanitarian reasons" because the landing zones were in open areas containing Vietnamese cemeteries with mounds and tombstones. Additionally, it was uncertain whether the U.S. Navy guns fired on the LZs. Army pilots flying the mission stated that there was no evidence that B-52s or Navy guns prepped the landing zones because Navy five-inch guns and 500 lb. bombs leave huge craters.

Finally, the VNAF Skyraiders arrived late, and apparently, their cluster-bombing mission was cancelled. As a result, the NVA were unscathed and able to react promptly when helicopters entered their area. To make matters worse, neither U.S. Army nor Marine pilots were advised of the lack of preparatory fires for their mission.

Marine Insertion Mission

On the morning of July 11, 1972, 34 U.S. Marine helicopters flying off the USS Okinawa and USS Tripoli picked up 840 South Vietnamese Marines and 12,000 rounds of ammunition/equipment and headed for LZ Blue Jay and LZ Crow, 2,000 meters North of Quang Tri City (see map page 284). The Marine aircraft were a combination of CH-46 Sea Knight and CH-53D Sea Stallion helicopters. All helicopters were instructed to fly 60 to 90 knots and 50 feet off the ground on their approach to the landing zones.

At 1150 hours, Captain (Capt.) Fred Ledfors and First Lieutenant (1st Lt.) Pete Holmberg of F Troop, 4th Cavalry, each flying an OH-6A Light Observation Helicopter (LOH, nicknamed "Loach") led the initial assault into LZ Blue Jay. Following the two Loaches were six Cobra gunships from F/79 Aerial Rocket Artillery (ARA), call sign Blue Max, as they laid down suppressing fire along the approach path to the LZ. The Blue Max Cobras were instructed to make a single pass and expend all ordinance. Pete Holmberg later commented, "Canary (Capt. Ledfors) and I led the Blue Max Cobras in an all-aircraft-on-line, single-pass, 100% dump. It was awesome!" The six Blue Max Cobras, flying abreast, blasted the LZ approach path with 2.75-inch rockets, 40mm grenades, and 7.62 mm mini-gun fire.

As the Blue Max Cobras exited to the northeast, the two Loaches circled back to meet the first sortie of Marine helicopters and led them to the landing zone. Flying fast and low, with erratic evasive maneuvering, Ledfors and Holmberg marked the northern boundary of the LZ with smoke grenades and exited to the east. Behind the two Loaches, 18 U.S. Marine helicopters in three sorties (groups) flew toward the colored smoke that marked the LZ. On the left flank, three Cobra gunships from F Troop, 4th Cavalry, provided covering fire as they escorted the Marine transport helicopters inbound. My good buddy, 1st Lt. Russ Miller, was flying one of the Centaur Cobras, and Chief Warrant Officer 2 (CW2) Chuck

O'Connell was piloting another. Three Cobras from the 48th Assault Helicopter Company, call sign Blue Stars, covered the right flank.

When the vulnerable transport helicopters began their final approach to LZ Blue Jay, the NVA opened up with intense crossfire from AK-47s, 23mm and 37mm anti-aircraft guns, .51 caliber machine guns, rocket-propelled grenades (RPGs), and Strela SA-7 heat-seeking missiles. With their door gunners continually returning fire, the Marine helicopters settled into the landing zone, offloaded the Vietnamese Marines, and quickly exited north, turning east toward the coast. An observer from afar commented, "There were so many helicopters in the air, it looked like a school of sharks swarming."

LZ Crow, "Hot as Hell"

Three minutes after the last helicopter departed LZ Blue Jay, Capt. Ledfors and 1st Lt. Holmberg rendezvoused with the first of three sorties of Marine helicopters (16 total) flying to LZ Crow, about 500 meters southeast of LZ Blue Jay. By this time, the enemy fire was described as "hot as Hell," and the element of surprise had vanished. The NVA were dug-in and stood ready to unleash a torrent of fire on any aircraft in the vicinity of the two LZs. Flying fast and low, with severe evasive maneuvering, the two Loaches led the Marine helicopters toward LZ Crow. The enemy fire was extremely intense, and at one point, two RPG rounds passed between the two Loaches.

Arriving at the second LZ, Ledfors and Holmberg marked the northern boundary with smoke grenades and flew toward the south end of the landing zone. Upon turning outbound, Holmberg saw an NVA soldier on one knee with an SA-7 heat-seeking missile aimed directly at him. Flying in an extreme 120-degree right turn, Holmberg violently banked left in an opposite 120-degree left turn. The evasive maneuver worked, and the SA-7 missile passed approximately 15–20 feet from his aircraft. Holmberg and Ledfors, now low on fuel and ammo, returned to their base at Tan My to rearm and refuel.

Crash of Lady Ace 7-2

Marine First Lieutenant Bruce Keyes of HMM-165, from the USS Tripoli, was flying a CH-53D (Sikorsky Sea Stallion) helicopter with the call sign Lady Ace 7-2. His aircraft was among five helicopters flying the last sortie into LZ Crow. Lady Ace 7-2 followed behind the lead aircraft that carried a sling load of ammunition and supplies. Onboard were the co-pilot, Marine Captain Henry Bollman, the crew chief, another crewman, two U.S. Marine door gunners, and a U.S. Marine combat photographer. They were transporting 50 South Vietnamese Marines to be dropped at LZ Crow.

As the last sortie of Marine helicopters began their final approach to the LZ, they flared to slow and began their descent. The enemy fire from the tree lines and dug-in fighting positions was extremely intense. Anti-aircraft fire, RPGs, and small arms fire was coming from all directions. U.S. Army CW2 Chuck O'Connell, flying a Centaur Cobra gunship, was initiating his gun run in a northerly direction from the south side of the Song Vinh Dinh River when he saw a Strela SA-7 heat-seeking missile erupt from the river's edge to his right. Chuck stated, "When I glanced to the right, I saw a smoke trail coming up the river, ninety degrees to my flight path and holding steady at my altitude of about 100 feet. As it approached, I could clearly see the missile and thought, 'This is going to pass right between us.' Then, to my surprise and horror, it did a 90-degree turn right in front of me and into one of the CH-53s." That CH-53 was Lady Ace 7-2.

The SA-7 missile made a direct hit on the starboard engine of Lady Ace 7-2, sending engine turbine fragments down and forward into the passenger compartment. The aircraft immediately burst into flames, filling the cockpit with a rush of fire and smoke. Miraculously, 1st Lt. Keyes and his co-pilot, Capt. Bollman, were able to continue flying the aircraft to a controlled crash landing. While the aircraft was descending, the heat and fire continued to ignite the ammunition and fuel, causing a series of explosions within the fuselage.

The burning helicopter touched down hard. The surviving crewmen and passengers rushed to escape the intense inferno. The crew chief was on fire as he exited the helicopter wreckage. The pilot and co-pilot, who were already out of the burning hulk, extinguished the fire on the crew chief while pulling him to safety. The two pilots, the injured crew chief, another crewmember, and the combat photographer sought shelter in a nearby bomb crater. The two U.S. Marine door gunners and all but seven of the 50 ARVN Marine passengers perished in the burning aircraft. The seven surviving ARVN soldiers evaded enemy forces and made their way to friendly Vietnamese units already engaged in combat.

The five Lady Ace crewmembers huddled together in the bomb crater, awaiting rescue. As the battle raged around them, the Sea Stallion's wreckage burned until all that remained was a portion of the rotor blades and the mast. After the crash remains cooled, the Americans watched North Vietnamese soldiers as they poked through the twisted wreckage and ashes. Fortunately, the Marines' hiding place remained undetected.

Lam Son Counteroffensive 11 July, 1972 - Area North of Quang Tri City

Rescue Attempt

Minutes felt like hours as the Lady Ace crew hunkered down in the bomb crater while intense fighting erupted all around them. Roughly two hours passed as the survivors desperately attempted to transmit a distress signal on their PRC-90 survival radio. Around 1400 hours, U.S. Army Capt. Gary Knapp, call sign Vanguard 216, flying an RU-21 reconnaissance aircraft (a modified Beechcraft King Air), heard an emergency beeper on the "guard" frequency. Knapp responded to the call and began talking to the Marine survivors in the bomb crater. He relentlessly tried to locate their position from the air, but there was so much smoke from fires in the area that any use of smoke grenades was futile. He asked if there was another way to mark their location, and the crew put out an orange marker panel. Knapp spotted them immediately and marked their location with his onboard inertial navigation system, at grid coordinates YD350550.

Capt. Knapp contacted "King 26," Air Force Search and Rescue (SAR) Command (flying a C-130 aircraft,) and asked for assistance in rescuing the Lady Ace crew. Two Sandy Skyraiders and a Super Jolly Green HH-53 helicopter were dispatched for the rescue.

> Note: The Air Force 602nd Special Operations Squadron, call sign Sandy, was based in Thailand and flew Douglas A1-E Skyraiders, a powerful, single-engine attack bomber used extensively in the Korean War. Sandy's rescue mission was to conduct a general search for the downed aircrew, talk to the survivors by radio, determine their exact location, and escort the rescue helicopters. The A-1s, equipped with guns, bombs, and rockets, suppressed any hostile forces in the rescue area prior to the arrival of the Super Jolly Green helicopter.

Knapp met the Air Force rescue team on the coast and led them inland to the crash site. When they arrived in the vicinity of the survivors, the NVA opened up with intense anti-aircraft fire from multiple locations. The two Sandy Skyraiders immediately dived to engage the anti-aircraft guns with rockets as the rescue helicopter turned away. Running low on fuel, Knapp returned to his home base, saddened that they could not make the rescue while he was on station. He left wondering whether the Marine aircrew would be rescued later that day.

After several attempts by the Sandy Skyraiders to silence the anti-aircraft guns, they realized that the

NVA anti-aircraft fire was overwhelming and that the Super Jolly Green could not get close enough for a rescue attempt. Eventually, the Air Force SAR aircraft returned to their home stations to rearm and refuel.

At 1530 hours, a reconnaissance (recon) platoon of the ARVN Marines reached the crash site and found the survivors. Because of imminent danger in the extremely hostile area, the survivors were relocated to a more defensible location near the Song Vinh Dinh River. During this relocation, the Sandy Skyraider lost visual contact and spent a frustrating two hours attempting to locate the Lady Ace crew.

Meanwhile, on the ground, the ARVN recon platoon led the survivors to a defensible area of dense shrubs and trees, approximately 30 meters wide. Night was fast approaching, and as the darkness began to settle over them, the Americans were losing hope and fearful of being captured. The odds against a successful night rescue were overwhelming. It was becoming increasingly evident that the Lady Ace crew would have to wait out the night before a rescue could be attempted. This was unwelcome news, made more so because three of the survivors were badly burned and desperately needed medical attention.

At 1815 hours, the Sandy Skyraider located the survivors' new position (note: sunset was at 1829 hours). Considering the double threat of a nighttime operation and the intense anti-aircraft fire, Sandy decided not to dispatch the Air Force SAR helicopter for another rescue attempt.

Centaurs to the Rescue

At 1845 hours, King 26 contacted F Troop, 4th Air Cavalry of the U.S. Army and requested their assistance in the rescue of the five crash survivors. 1st Lt. Frank Walker and Capt. Fred Ledfors volunteered to attempt the rescue with their two OH-6A (Loach) helicopters. After a quick briefing on the intensely hostile situation, Walker and Ledfors launched their aircraft and headed for the downed Marines.

Walker was accompanied by Specialist 4 (Spc. 4) Randy Baisden, crew chief/gunner, and Sergeant (Sgt.) Joseph Beck, observer/gunner. Capt. Ledfors' Loach was equipped with a side-mounted 7.62 mm mini-gun, so he flew with a single crew chief/gunner, Sgt. Leon Ring. Following the Loaches and flying cover were 1st Lt. Russ Miller and CW2 Chuck O'Connell in AH-1G Cobra gunships. Capt. James Elder, F-4 Cavalry Commanding Officer, in a UH-1H Huey, flew at a higher altitude, providing command and control of the rescue operation. Two additional Cobras and another Huey orbited at Twin Steeples (navigation landmark, 12 miles southeast of Quang Tri) as backup aircraft should they be needed.

Nightfall had significantly reduced visibility when F-4 Cavalry received a second update on the enemy situation at the recovery site. An ARVN ground unit in the vicinity was engaged in hand-to-hand combat with a main force of NVA regulars supported by armored vehicles, tanks, and artillery. Multiple 23mm and 37mm anti-aircraft guns, 51 caliber machine guns, and SA-7 missiles were fired on any aircraft approaching the area. The downed crew was being protected by the ARVN Marine recon platoon that was also actively engaged with NVA forces.

Dismissing the extreme dangers, 1st Lt. Walker and Capt. Ledfors chose to continue the rescue mission. Shortly thereafter, Sandy 08 intercepted the F-4 Cav Team at a location several miles from the recovery area and offered to lead them to the pickup zone (PZ). The four helicopters descended to near ground level with Ledfors in the lead. Walker trailed behind Ledfors and the Cobra gunships followed behind on each side, covering the flanks. Sandy 08 descended to an altitude of about 600 feet and lowered its flaps to slow its airspeed. Following Sandy 08, the four helicopters slowly flew nap of the earth, using terrain and foliage to conceal their aircraft.

It was completely dark as the Cav Team cautiously proceeded to the recovery area. I asked Frank Walker how he was able to navigate when it was so dark with no moonlight. He replied, "It was God, adrenaline, and my 24-year-old eyesight that enabled me to see with no light, in that order."

Approximately one mile from the recovery area, all four aircraft and Sandy 08 began receiving heavy AK-47 and 23/37 mm anti-aircraft fire. Since they did not know the exact position of friendly forces, the helicopter crews could only return fire for fire at positively identified targets. Walker's crew chief, Spc. 4 Randy Baisden, stood on the Loach skids outside the aircraft returning fire with his M-60 machine gun and guiding Walker around terrain features. Baisden later stated, "The NVA were all around us, entrenched in fighting positions. As we continued our approach, they fired AK-47s, RPGs, and anti-aircraft guns. At one point, we passed three NVA tanks, and the tank crew started shooting at us with AKs and 51 calibers. We were so low and so close to the enemy that several times I had to ask Lieutenant Walker to go 'blades up' on the right side so I could return fire."

The Rescue

Traveling northwest, the Cav Team approached the Song Vinh Dinh River. Miller and O'Connell, in Cobra gunships, broke left and remained on the south side of the river, entering a low-level racetrack (oval) pattern. At this point, the two Loaches ventured unprotected into a known enemy stronghold. They crossed the river and turned 90 degrees left, continuing their slow and deliberate approach parallel to and near the river's edge. As they got closer to the pick-up zone (PZ), it became evident that the Marine survivors and their ARVN protectors were surrounded by the NVA. As Randy Baisden commented, "We had to fight our way in and fight our way out. The NVA were on all sides of the pick-up zone, and the enemy fire intensity increased on our departure."

As the Loaches closed on the recovery area, Sandy 08 dropped a flare to mark the location of the stranded Marines. A short time later, the two Loaches lifted up and over a hedgerow and settled into the PZ. Walker told his gunners to cease fire as he maneuvered his aircraft to land within a few feet of the Lady Ace aircrew. He positioned his Loach to shield the survivors from enemy fire as they were loaded onto his aircraft. Baisden, on the right side of Walker's Loach, quickly loaded Marine 1st Lt. Bruce Keyes, Staff Sgt. Clyde Nelson, the severely burned crew chief, and a badly burned South Vietnamese Marine onto the Loach.

Now carrying six people, Walker's Loach was extremely overloaded. (Note: Ledfors' Loach picked up three Marines and was now carrying a total of five people.) Walker instructed his crew chief and gunner to "lighten the load" by offloading boxes of grenades and all but 200 rounds of ammunition for the return flight. Then he deftly lifted the Loach light on its skids, but it was too heavy to hover. Walker slowly inched the overloaded aircraft forward, bumping along the ground as he tried to get "clean" air through the rotor blades for lift. It was so overweight that Walker ran out of left pedal and the overburdened Loach crabbed to the right. Walker "nursed" every bit of available power from the straining engine until he slowly gained altitude and airspeed, all the time receiving a hail of enemy fire from all directions.

Taking the lead, Walker chose a southeast departure, hoping to minimize and evade enemy fire. This departure path would once again cross the Song Vinh Dinh River at a location about 1,000 meters south of the first crossing. Directly ahead, on the riverbank, was a 15 to 20-foot tall embankment covered with mangroves and other vegetation. Just prior to reaching the embankment, Walker's Loach entered translational lift (extra lift from the horizontal flow of air across the rotor blades), giving the aircraft additional power. The timing could not have been better. Walker raised the Loach up and over the embankment, barely missing the tops of the mangrove trees, and swooped down over the river, all the time gaining airspeed.

Upon reaching the other side of the river, Walker and Ledfors resumed flying nap of the earth (10–15 feet of altitude), evading the enemy and trying to maximize airspeed on their exit. Suddenly, on their right flank, two Strela SA-7 heat-seeking missiles came streaking through the night sky in their direction, passing above Walker's Loach. Fortunately, the missiles were fired from such close range that they were not yet armed (SA-7s arm at 120 meters) and were well past the Loach before they could lock onto the heat signature of the Loach turbine engine. Baisden, standing on the skids of the Loach, saw the SA-7 crew at about 30 to 40 yards. He promptly reacted with a rapid burst of fire from his M-60 machine gun, taking out the NVA rocket crew.

Cobra Shoot-out with Anti-Aircraft Gun

Seconds later, the two Cobras flown by Miller and O'Connell reunited with the Loaches for their departure. Russ Miller joined up with Walker's Loach, passing by high on Walker's right side. Suddenly, NVA 37 mm anti-aircraft fire erupted from their left flank, passing in front of Walker and Miller's aircraft. Walker recalls seeing Miller's Cobra begin to shudder as he quickly flared, standing the Cobra almost vertically on its tail. Simultaneously, CW2 Terrance Hawkinson, Miller's co-pilot-gunner, engaged the anti-aircraft gun with a hail of fire from his 7.62 mm mini-gun. Walker recalls it looking like a battle scene from a *Star Wars* movie. The night sky was filled with 37mm tracers from his left and 7.62 mm tracers from his right. As Walker's Loach continued, Miller brought his Cobra to a standstill, swinging its nose 90 degrees left to engage the anti-aircraft gun. From a hover, Miller and Hawkinson unloaded 2.75-inch rockets and 7.62 mm mini-gun fire into the gun emplacement in the tree line. Chuck O'Connell was trailing Miller and witnessed the maneuver. Chuck said, "It was great. Russ totally obliterated the anti-aircraft gun." Later, it was reported that the Cobras silenced two anti-aircraft guns and destroyed at least one armored vehicle during their departure.

Walker continued flying low and evasively in a general southeast direction, choosing his path based on the terrain and vegetation. They continued to receive heavy enemy fire from the NVA, who were well established in fortified fighting positions. Baisden stated, "At times, we flew directly over NVA gun emplacements, and I found myself firing my M-60 straight down between the skids."

On Capt. Ledfors' Loach, a different dilemma was playing out. In the rush to load the three survivors into his aircraft, Sgt. Leon Ring wasn't able to connect his safety harness. When they crossed the river and started receiving intense enemy fire, Ring was holding on for dear life as Ledfors put the Loach into extreme evasive maneuvers. Ring later said, "The enemy fire was much more intense on our departure. We had rockets and anti-aircraft fire coming from all directions. I was holding onto the door frame to keep from falling out while firing my M-60 at the same time."

Marines Returned to Their Ship

Once the Cav Team was clear of the intense hostile fire, it was decided that, because the Loaches were so heavily overburdened, the rescued survivors should be transferred to the Hueys. They spotted a dirt road running through a rice paddy, and Walker started his approach. Walker was concerned about the landing because he knew that his overloaded Loach was too heavy to hover and decided that he must make an approach directly to the ground. When the Loach descended through the last 10 feet of altitude, a dense cloud of dust erupted from the road and obscured all visibility. Unable to see, Walker held steady on his approach and soon felt the skids hit the ground, and the struts bottomed out from the load.

The two F-4 Cavalry Hueys landed on the road adjacent to the Loaches. The rotor wash from the Hueys kicked up a massive sandstorm from the road. Realizing how painful this must feel, Spc. 4 Baisden huddled two Marines and himself around the severely burned Marine crew chief to shield him from the stinging sand blast as they escorted him to the waiting Huey. The six rescued survivors (five U.S. Marines and one badly burned South Vietnamese Marine) were transferred to the Hueys, and the four helicopters took off to join the other Centaurs for the return trip to their home base at Tan My. Upon arrival at 2000 hours, the survivors were given emergency medical treatment for their burns and other injuries. Later that night, the U.S. Marine aircrew was loaded aboard a Marine CH-46 helicopter and returned to their home ship, the USS Tripoli.

Afterward, while discussing the mission, Frank Walker stated, "We flew the night rescue because we realized our fellow soldiers were stranded deep inside enemy territory and their chances for survival were slim if we didn't get them out soon. Bringing back those Marines was definitely worth the risk!"

The daring rescue was an outstanding success,

especially considering the volume and intensity of enemy anti-aircraft fire and the task of locating the survivors in near-total darkness. Several days later, Marine 1st Lt. Bruce Keyes wrote in his report of the rescue, "Heavily overloaded, we took off into the night for friendly lines, maneuvering and evading a withering hail of enemy fire with an aeronautical skill unequalled by anything I have ever witnessed. The coordination between the two Loaches and their Cobra gunship escort was uncanny."

Combat Awards

The following day, Major General Howard H. Cooksey, U.S. Senior Advisor, I Corps, and Marine Brigadier General Edward J. Miller, Commander of the 9th Marine Amphibious Brigade, visited F Troop, 4th Cavalry to recognize the heroic actions of the pilots and flight crew who rescued the stranded Marines. In presentation formation, General Cooksey and General Miller addressed the F-4 troopers, acknowledging their bravery and thanking them for saving the Marine aircrew. General Cooksey awarded Impact Awards (field awards to recognize valor in combat) to the Centaur pilots and crewmembers, and General Miller congratulated and thanked the Centaur Troopers for rescuing the Marines.

My good buddy, 1st Lt. Russ Miller, learned that the general was awarding five Silver Star Medals; the remaining awards were Distinguished Flying Crosses and Air Medals. The general started down the line awarding Silver Stars, the higher award, first. Russ did the mental math and determined that he was going to be the last to receive a Silver Star Medal. Standing to Russ' left and positioned to receive a

Distinguished Flying Cross was Walker's crew chief, Spc. 4 Randy Baisden, the brave trooper who stood on the skids while providing cover fire for Walker's Loach. As the generals proceeded down the line presenting awards, Russ quickly traded places with Randy, who received the Silver Star, and Russ received the Distinguished Flying Cross. As a result of this realignment, the Loach pilots and crew received the Silver Stars and the Cobra pilots/co-pilots flying their cover received the Distinguished Flying Cross.

In August 1972, 1st Lt. Frank Walker and Capt. Fred Ledfors were recommended to receive the Medal of Honor. In October 1974, the Department of the Army awarded Wesley F. (Frank) Walker the Distinguished Service Cross, the next highest award. In February 1975, Frederick D. Ledfors was awarded the Distinguished Service Cross.

In July 2008, the Army National Guard of South Carolina named a weapons range at Columbia's Fort Jackson the "1st Lt. Wesley F. Walker Range." The naming of the range recognized Frank Walker's status as one of the most highest-decorated soldiers to retire from the South Carolina National Guard since World War II.

To Russ Miller: Hey, good friend, the rescue story is out there now. You and your fellow Centaurs are highly commended for your selfless dedication to saving some of our own and for your unfaltering courage in the face of extreme danger. I miss you, buddy.

©**2013, Rex Gooch** Longknife 23
C/3/17 Air Cavalry, Vietnam 1971-72

Note: In July 2005, the rescued Marine pilot, Bruce Keyes, reached out and contacted the pilots of F Troop, 4th Cavalry at a Vietnam Helicopter Pilots Association (VHPA) reunion in San Francisco. In an emotional meeting, they revisited the details of the dramatic 1972 rescue. Since then, Bruce Keyes has attended the VHPA reunions and sat with F Troop, 4th Cavalry as an honorary member of the Centaurs.

My sincere thanks to the following people whose interviews and email messages contributed so much to the writing of this story:

- Randy Baisden   F Troop, 4th Cavalry
- Bob Greene   121st Assault Helicopter Company
- Brian Harrison   F Troop, 4th Cavalry
- Pete Holmberg   F Troop, 4th Cavalry
- Jim Dan Keirsey   F Troop, 4th Cavalry
- Gary Knapp   138th Aviation Company
- Wayne Moose   F Troop, 4th Cavalry
- Jon Morales   US Marines, nephew of Capt. Henry Bollman
- Chuck O'Connell   F Troop, 4th Cavalry
- Leon Ring   F Troop, 4th Cavalry
- Rick Waite   D Troop, 3/5 Cavalry
- Frank Walker   F Troop, 4th Cavalry

Crash site grid coordinates (YD 3478 5524) verified by the JTF-FA Case 1999 Excavation Report

F Troop, 4ᵗʰ Cavalry

F Troop, 4ᵗʰ Cavalry, call sign Centaurs, operated as an independent Air Cavalry Troop and was one of the last U.S. Army units to depart Vietnam when the war ended in 1973. The Centaurs' primary mission was flying in support of South Vietnamese military units in I Corps, near the Demilitarized Zone (DMZ.) F Troop served with distinction accumulating many unit and individual awards. First designated D Troop, 3/4 Cavalry, the troop's designation changed to F Troop, 4ᵗʰ Cavalry in February, 1971, when the 25ᵗʰ Infantry Division departed Vietnam and returned to Hawaii.

"Loach"

The Army OH-6A Light Observation Helicopter (LOH nicknamed "Loach") flew the scout mission for air cavalry units in Vietnam. This egg-shaped, highly maneuverable aircraft flew at treetop level, seeking out and engaging the enemy. Often, the Loach flew so low that the pilot could follow a set of footprints to find the enemy's location. A single pilot and two door gunners, one on each side of the aircraft, typically manned the Loach. The door gunners fired hand-held M-60 7.62mm machine guns. It could also be fitted with the M134 six-barrel 7.62mm minigun and, in this configuration, only one door gunner. The Loach was a tough little aircraft. It could absorb an extensive amount of small arms fire and still bring the crew home safely. It was also very crashworthy with many stories of crewmembers surviving catastrophic crashes with minimal injuries.

Cobra Gunship

The Army AH-1G Cobra helicopter, nicknamed "Snake," was the Army's first dedicated attack gunship. This sleek two-person helicopter was fast with a Vne (Velocity never exceed) speed of 190 knots (219 mph) and a cruising speed of 150 Knots (172 mph). It had stub-wing pylons on each side of the fuselage for attaching an assortment of armament, including 2.75-inch rockets and wire guided anti-tank missiles. The co-pilot, sitting in the front seat, controlled the steerable nose turret that contained a 7.62mm Minigun, capable of firing 2,000/4,000 rounds per minute and a 40mm grenade launcher. The pilot, in the rear seat, aimed the Cobra at the target and fired rockets or missiles. This deadly aircraft was highly effective in attacking both personnel and mechanized vehicles.

"Pink Team"

A "Pink Team" consisted of two Loaches paired with two Cobra gunships. Flying slow and low, the Loaches flew at treetop level, "trolling" for the enemy. Meanwhile, the Cobras flew high above in a racetrack (oval) pattern as they covered the Loaches on the ground. When the Loaches received enemy fire, they called "Taking Fire" to their Cobras protectors, marked the target with a smoke grenade and quickly departed the area. Immediately, the Cobras signaled "Inbound" on their radios and dived from high, firing 2.75-inch rockets, 40mm grenades and 7.62mm minigun fire into the smoke-marked enemy location.

Lady Ace 7-2 Crew:

- Pilot: 1st Lt. Bruce G. Keyes
- Co-Pilot: Capt. Henry C. Bollman
- Crew chief: Staff Sgt. Clyde K. Nelson (died a month later from burns)
- Crewman: Cpl. Lester E. (Sonny) Cox (burns)
- Marine Combat Photographer: Lance Cpl. Stephen G. Lively (suffered burns and shrapnel wounds)
- Door Gunner: Staff Sgt. Jerry W. Hendrix (died in the crash)
- Door Gunner: Cpl. Kenneth L. Crody (died in the crash)

Captain Bollman in the crater awaiting rescue. Photo courtesy of Rex Gooch. Note charred helmet at top right and left.

OH-6 from F Troop, 4th Cavalry Division. Photo courtesy of Rex Gooch.

F Troop, 4ᵗʰ Cav AH-1G Cobra. Photo courtesy of Rex Gooch.

Rex Gooch. Photo courtesy of Rex Gooch.

Mission 21

Medals of Honor

Major Patrick Henry Brady

I started this book off with the loss of Major Charles Kelly, the unofficially recognized "Father of Dustoff", in Mission 1. I am giving you now in Mission 21, this book's next to last Mission, the results of the legacy of Kelly; those who were awarded the Medal Of Honor for their actions in rescuing America's warriors in time of combat.

I first met Patrick Brady while he was an instructor and I was a student at Fort Sam Houston in San Antonio, Texas. By this time, a combat veteran, he was instructing us young Warrant Officer Graduates as to the "art" of flying Dustoff in Vietnam. We knew of his past and greatly respected him.

Then a Major, now a 2-Star General, Patrick Henry Brady was better known as Dustoff 5-5 flying out of Chu Lai with the 54th Medical Detachment. January 5, 1968, was the middle of the monsoon season in southern I Corps where the 54th was based. Days and even nights were often punctuated during the monsoon season with heavy rains, heavy clouds and heavy fogs...sometimes all at the same time. Thus were the conditions on this day for Major Brady and his crew: Lieutenant Foust, copilot, Specialist Brian Browick, crew chief, and Specialist Travis Kanida, medic.

Their first mission of the day was for injured South Vietnamese soldiers who had been wounded the night before. Two attempts that evening by other Dustoff crews proved fruitless, as it was impossible for them to find the landing zone during these monsoon conditions. The next morning, the 6th, Brady and his crew volunteered to make an attempt, with fog still shrouding the Landing Zone where the wounded were waiting. Brady knew that he could hover along a trail that led to the wounded, a technique he had perfected the previous November. Locating the trail was the easy part. With his newly found skill of flying in the fog, he was not able to follow the trail flying normally by looking out the windshield. However, he knew that by lowering his door window, he could fly sideways by looking out the window with the crew in the back keeping him clear of helicopter grabbing obstacles. Hovering along not much faster than a man could walk, and only able to see a few feet at a time, Dustoff 55 finally reached the wounded and landed between the inner and outer defensive wires, a difficult landing under any conditions. With his wounded on board, he performed an instrument takeoff, lifting straight up through the fog and into clear air for his flight to the hospital. Unknowingly to Major Brady and his crew, his day was just beginning.

They had no longer shut down the aircraft before they received another call. For several hours, North Vietnamese troops have been firing on an American unit of the 198th Light Infantry Brigade. Dozens of casualties were on the ground in need of medical attention and extraction. Another aircraft of the 54th had tried to make it into the landing zone, but the same "zero-zero" weather conditions had thwarted their attempts at rescue. Also, two other helicopters had been shot down trying to resupply and support the Americans on the ground. Knowing the gravity of the wounded soldier's situation, Major Brady took along a medical team to triage the wounded on the ground.

Using the same tactics as earlier in the day to get through the fog and clouds, and again being familiar with the area, Brady repeated his sideways hover along a road and a stream that he knew would lead him to his wounded. Drawing enemy fire along the way, the fog apparently created a situation where the enemy, certainly surprised by a helicopter in these conditions, was firing only at this sound of the Huey without being able to see their target. Getting close to the landing zone, but now out of landmarks to follow, Brady needed the troops on the ground to guide him in by the sound of the helicopter, now trusting *them,* in addition to his own crew to keep him clear of obstacles.

Immediately upon landing, the medical team began to determine the most seriously injured troops and within a few minutes the helicopter was fully loaded for the trip to the hospital. Again, an instrument takeoff straight up was required to safely leave the area. Knowing that there were many more wounded on the ground, he flew to a firebase to unload the wounded at an aid station where his patients could be stabilized and taken to hospitals by other Dustoff aircraft while he returned to the landing zone. Brady briefed four other Huey pilots on how to locate the wounded, and they followed Brady back to the general area. However, the dense fog and enemy fire forced them out of their approaches. Only Brady continued to penetrate the white-out conditions for more wounded.

Again, he was able to locate the wounded and once more, with a full load of wounded, proceeded out of the area and back to the same firebase where the patients were stabilized for back-haul to hospitals. But there were more wounded, and being the only pilot able to locate the battle zone, he once again picked up wounded, returning to the fire base for the third time. And he did it a fourth time, for a total of 39 men from one landing zone which was shrouded in heavy fog and clouds.

Ah, but the day of Dustoff 55 and crew was not even close to being over. A call for more wounded American soldiers sent them into the air again, this time to another landing zone under fire. No longer protected from enemy view by fog, they took heavy fire going in and because a helicopter on the ground is a very high value target for the enemy, they took even more fire upon landing. In fact, the enemy fire was so heavy that the soldiers on the ground refused to leave their cover to load the wounded. Brady called them on the radio and insisted they get their wounded to the aircraft but they refused. Rather than continuing to sit on the ground, Brady left the landing zone, again taking more fire as they flew away. Another radio call to the troops on the ground brought a promise to him that if he returned they would get their wounded to the aircraft. Brady did return to the landing zone, again taking fire, but this time the guys on the ground loaded the wounded and Brady had two more patients to add to his total for the day, flying them to the 2nd Surgical Hospital at Chu Lai for treatment.

Dustoff 55 was still not done this day. Patrick Brady obtained a fresh aircraft and a fresh copilot. Another company of the 198th Light Infantry Brigade was in trouble. The enemy had laid an ambush for one of the platoons of the 198th. Enemy fire and land mines had taken their toll of the platoon, killing six men and wounding the rest. Warned to wait for enemy fire to subside, Brady elected to continue to the battle regardless, knowing that the men on the ground needed them. Landing as close as possible to the wounded, this put them in the center of a minefield.

With the wounded scattered about the minefield and surrounding area, the crew chief and medic, Jim Coleman and Ron Tweed, immediately began scrambling around, assisting the wounded onto the aircraft while disregarding their own safety; and also disregarding the mines and enemy fire. As one wounded soldier was being brought to the helicopter by the crew chief and medic, a mine exploded only a few yards from the aircraft hurtling the men into the air and sending hundreds of shards of shrapnel into the helicopter. Fortunately, the men were virtually unhurt and loading continued until all were on board. Again with a full load of wounded troops, he returned to the 2nd Surgical Hospital. (Jim Coleman, for his actions this day, has been enshrined in the Army Aviation Association of America Hall of Fame.)

A *third* helicopter was obtained upon his return to base, his second aircraft now was also badly in need of repair because enemy fire on the previous mission had damaged some of the control mechanisms. Two more urgent missions that day required Dustoff 55 to fly well into the night, finally bringing an end to their rescues. Major Patrick H Brady, Commanding Officer of the 54th Medical Detachment, and his *many* crews on this day, had gone through three helicopters, taken over 400 hits including shrapnel, and rescued 51 warriors. The Department of the Army recognized these actions in the life of a Dustoff crew by awarding Major Brady with the Congressional Medal of Honor, the first ever awarded to a Dustoff crew member.

Major Patrick Brady in country. Photo from the internet.

General Patrick Brady. Photo from Gen. Brady.

Warrant Officer
Michael J. Novosel, Sr.

You have already been briefly introduced to Mr. Novosel in Mission 6. Novosel distinguished himself on 2 October 1969. His citation reads thus:

For conspicuous gallantry and intrepidity in action at the risk of his life above and beyond the call of duty. CWO Novosel, 82d Medical Detachment, distinguished himself while serving as commander of a medical evacuation helicopter. He unhesitatingly maneuvered his helicopter into a heavily fortified and defended enemy training area where a group of wounded Vietnamese soldiers were pinned down by a large enemy force. Flying without gunship or other cover and exposed to intense machinegun fire, CWO Novosel was able to locate and rescue a wounded soldier. Since all communications with the beleaguered troops had been lost, he repeatedly circled the battle area, flying at low level under continuous heavy fire, to attract the attention of the scattered friendly troops. This display of courage visibly raised their morale, as they recognized this as a signal to assemble for evacuation. On 6 occasions he and his crew were forced out of the battle area by the intense enemy fire, only to circle and return from another direction to land and extract additional troops. Near the end of the mission, a wounded soldier was spotted close to an enemy bunker. Fully realizing that he would attract a hail of enemy fire, CWO Novosel nevertheless attempted the extraction by hovering the helicopter backward. As the man was pulled on aboard, enemy automatic weapons opened fire at close range, damaged the aircraft and wounded CWO Novosel. He momentarily lost control of the aircraft, but quickly recovered and departed under the withering enemy fire. In all, 15 extremely hazardous extractions were performed in order to remove wounded personnel. As a direct result of his selfless conduct, the lives of 29 soldiers were saved. The extraordinary heroism displayed by CWO Novosel was an inspiration to his comrades in arms and reflect great credit on him, his unit, and the U.S. Army.

Chief Warrant Officer Michael J. Novosel (left) and Michael Jr, both Army helicopter pilots. Photo from the Internet.

Chief Warrant Officer Michael J. Novosel. Photo from the
Internet.

Chief Warrant Officer
Frederick Edgar Ferguson

While serving with the 227th Aviation Battalion, 1st Cavalry Division (Airmobile), Mr. Ferguson's citation reads thus:

For conspicuous gallantry and intrepidity in action at the risk of his life above and beyond the call of duty. CWO Ferguson, U.S. Army distinguished himself while serving with Company C. CWO Ferguson, commander of a resupply helicopter monitoring an emergency call from wounded passengers and crewmen of a downed helicopter under heavy attack within the enemy controlled city of Hue, unhesitatingly volunteered to attempt evacuation. Despite warnings from all aircraft to stay clear of the area due to heavy antiaircraft fire, CWO Ferguson began a low-level flight at maximum airspeed along the Perfume River toward the tiny, isolated South Vietnamese Army compound in which the crash survivors had taken refuge. Coolly and skillfully maintaining his course in the face of intense, short range fire from enemy occupied buildings and boats, he displayed superior flying skill and tenacity of purpose by landing his aircraft in an extremely confined area in a blinding dust cloud under heavy mortar and small-arms fire. Although the helicopter was severely damaged by mortar fragments during the loading of the wounded, CWO Ferguson disregarded the damage and, taking off through the continuing hail of mortar fire, he flew his crippled aircraft on the return route through the rain of fire that he had experienced earlier and safely returned his wounded passengers to friendly control. CWO Ferguson's extraordinary determination saved the lives of 5 of his comrades. His actions are in the highest traditions of the military service and reflect great credit on himself and the U.S. Army.

Warrant Officer Frederick Edgar Ferguson. Photo from the Internet.

Warrant Officer Frederick Edgar Ferguson. Photo from the
Internet.

Captain Ed W. "Too Tall" Freeman

The Medal of Honor citation for Captain Freeman reads thus:

Captain Ed W. Freeman, United States Army, distinguished himself by numerous acts of conspicuous gallantry and extraordinary intrepidity on 14 November 1965 while serving with Company A, 229th Assault Helicopter Battalion, 1st Cavalry Division (Airmobile). As a flight leader and second in command of a 16-helicopter lift unit, he supported a heavily engaged American infantry battalion at Landing Zone X-Ray in the Ia Drang Valley, Republic of Vietnam. The unit was almost out of ammunition after taking some of the heaviest casualties of the war, fighting off a relentless attack from a highly motivated, heavily armed enemy force. When the infantry commander closed the helicopter landing zone due to intense direct enemy fire, Captain Freeman risked his own life by flying his unarmed helicopter through a gauntlet of enemy fire time after time, delivering critically needed ammunition, water and medical supplies to the besieged battalion. His flights had a direct impact on the battle's outcome by providing the engaged units with timely supplies of ammunition critical to their survival, without which they would almost surely have gone down, with much greater loss of life. After medical evacuation helicopters refused to fly into the area due to intense enemy fire, Captain Freeman flew 14 separate rescue missions, providing life-saving evacuation of an estimated 30 seriously wounded soldiers -- some of whom would not have survived had he not acted. All flights were made into a small emergency landing zone within 100 to 200 meters of the defensive perimeter where heavily committed units were perilously holding off the attacking elements. Captain Freeman's selfless acts of great valor, extraordinary perseverance and intrepidity were far above and beyond the call of duty or mission and set a superb example of leadership and courage for all of his peers. Captain Freeman's extraordinary heroism and devotion to duty are in keeping with the highest traditions of military service and reflect great credit upon himself, his unit and the United States Army.

(Author's note: The Battle of the Ia Drang was the battle portrayed in the movie "We Were Soldiers Once" starring Mel Gibson.)

Captain Edward W. Freeman with OH-13 Soiux helicopter. Photo from the Internet.

Edward W. Freeman receiving the Medal of Honor from President Bush. Photo from the Internet.

Major Bruce Perry Crandall

Major Crandall's citation reads:

For conspicuous gallantry and intrepidity at the risk of his life above and beyond the call of duty: Major Bruce P. Crandall distinguished himself by extraordinary heroism as a Flight Commander in the Republic of Vietnam, while serving with Company A, 229th Assault Helicopter Battalion, 1st Cavalry Division (Airmobile). On 14 November 1965, his flight of sixteen helicopters was lifting troops for a search and destroy mission from Plei Me, Vietnam, to Landing Zone X-Ray in the Ia Drang Valley. On the fourth troop lift, the airlift began to take enemy fire, and by the time the aircraft had refueled and returned for the next troop lift, the enemy had Landing Zone X-Ray targeted. As Major Crandall and the first eight helicopters landed to discharge troops on his fifth troop lift, his unarmed helicopter came under such intense enemy fire that the ground commander ordered the second flight of eight aircraft to abort their mission. As Major Crandall flew back to Plei Me, his base of operations, he determined that the ground commander of the besieged infantry battalion desperately needed more ammunition. Major Crandall then decided to adjust his base of operations to Artillery Firebase Falcon in order to shorten the flight distance to deliver ammunition and evacuate wounded soldiers. While medical evacuation was not his mission, his disregard for his own personal safety, he led the two aircraft to Landing Zone X-Ray. Despite the fact that the landing zone was still under relentless enemy fire, Major Crandall landed and proceeded to supervise the loading of seriously wounded soldiers aboard his aircraft. Major Crandall's voluntary decision to land under the most extreme fire instilled in the other pilots the will and spirit to continue to land their own aircraft, and in the ground forces the realization that they would be resupplied and that friendly wounded would be promptly evacuated. This greatly enhanced morale and the will to fight at a critical time. After his first medical evacuation, Major Crandall continued to fly into and out of the landing zone throughout the day and into the evening. That day he completed a total of 22 flights, most under intense enemy fire, retiring from the battlefield only after all possible service had been rendered to the Infantry battalion. His actions provided critical resupply of ammunition and evacuation of the wounded. Major Crandall's daring acts of bravery and courage in the face of an overwhelming and determined enemy are in keeping with the highest traditions of the military service and reflect great credit upon himself, his unit, and the United States Army.

Major Bruce Crandall in country. Photo from the Internet.

Bruce Crandall receiving the Medal of Honor from President Bush.

Specialist 4 Gary G. Wetzel, Helicopter Door Gunner

Specialist 4 Gary Wetzel was the only Enlisted helicopter crewman to receive the Medal of Honor. His citation:

Sp4c. Wetzel, 173d Assault Helicopter Company, distinguished himself by conspicuous gallantry and intrepidity at the risk of his life, above and beyond the call of duty. Sp4c. Wetzel was serving as door gunner aboard a helicopter which was part of an insertion force trapped in a landing zone by intense and deadly hostile fire. Sp4c. Wetzel was going to the aid of his aircraft commander when he was blown into a rice paddy and critically wounded by 2 enemy rockets that exploded just inches from his location. Although bleeding profusely due to the loss of his left arm and severe wounds in his right arm, chest, and left leg, Sp4c. Wetzel staggered back to his original position in his gun-well and took the enemy forces under fire. His machinegun was the only weapon placing effective fire on the enemy at that time. Through a resolve that overcame the shock and intolerable pain of his injuries, Sp4c. Wetzel remained at his position until he had eliminated the automatic weapons emplacement that had been inflicting heavy casualties on the American troops and preventing them from moving against this strong enemy force. Refusing to attend his own extensive wounds, he attempted to return to the aid of his aircraft commander but passed out from loss of blood. Regaining consciousness, he persisted in his efforts to drag himself to the aid of his fellow crewman. After an agonizing effort, he came to the side of the crew chief who was attempting to drag the wounded aircraft commander to the safety of a nearby dike. Unswerving in his devotion to his fellow man, Sp4c. Wetzel assisted his crew chief even though he lost consciousness once again during this action. Sp4c. Wetzel displayed extraordinary heroism in his efforts to aid his fellow crewmen. His gallant actions were in keeping with the highest traditions of the U.S. Army and reflect great credit upon himself and the Armed Forces of his country.

Specialist Gary Wetzel in country. Photo from the internet.

Gary Wetzel, official Medal of Honor photo. From the Internet.

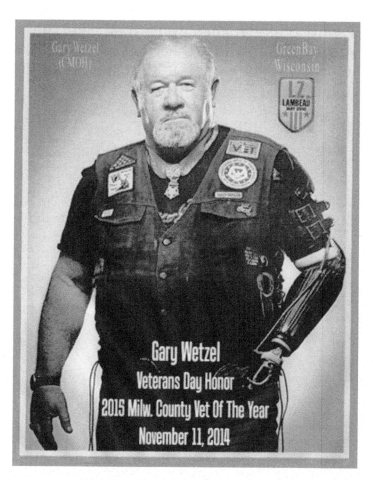

Gary Wetzel. Photo from the Internet.

All of the Medal of Honor, MOH, stories of these 6 helicopter crewmen are available in greater detail on the web and printed publications other than this one. It is not my intent to "reinvent the wheel" by reproducing their complete experience, only to expose you to them and their stories. It is this author's recommendation that if you have any interest about the lives of these 6 men, you should search for their Medal Of Honor descriptions and learn just what it is to be awarded the MOH. You just may learn why these 6 men, and men like them, were revered by the warriors that we supported, the men on the ground who were the REAL heroes of the War in Vietnam.

Mission 22

The Last 11

It was this author's good fortune to be in attendance at a presentation by one of the very last 11 Marines in Vietnam. We shall call him Sgt. Smith as he declined to be interviewed later by me. There was nothing unusual in this Marine's background as far as enlistment or reason for joining the Marines. However, what was a little bit unusual, was the fact that he was assigned to Consulate duties in Vietnam.

Because of his assignment, and the dates of his service in country, this Sergeant was one of the Marines tasked with the orderly evacuation of Vietnamese civilians as the North Vietnam Army was rolling into Saigon with their tanks and other heavy equipment. The evacuations were taking place not only on the lawn of the Consulate but also the rooftop. During the evacuation, which became very famous with photos such as the one on the next page, his commanding officer, a Captain, was called to the Ambassador's office. During this visit to the office he was given the telephone and to his surprise, President Gerald Ford was on the other end. His direct orders from Mr. Ford were to stop the evacuation of civilians and get his Marines out on the next helicopters. It was 30 April 1975.

With these orders from the President, the Marines began destroying sensitive paperwork including their own personal files. While this was taking place, other Marines began to close off access to the rooftop. A high priority was the evacuation of the Ambassador, his family, the Assistant Ambassador and his family.

As the next helicopters came in, the Assistant Ambassador, a rather large man, decided that he was going to enter the CH-46 Boeing Vertol twin rotor helicopter through the forward crew door rather than the ramp at the back of the aircraft. Carrying his briefcase and due to his larger size, this gentleman was having trouble climbing up into the aircraft, so Sgt. Smith heaved him from behind, very unceremoniously sending the assistant ambassador tumbling into the aircraft. (Years later, both of these men were assigned to a European country where they recognized each other. Our Marine was very concerned that there would be bad repercussions from this recognition due to his manhandling of the Assistant, and sure enough Sgt. Smith was called into the Assistant Ambassador's office. Upon entering the office, Sgt. Smith was given a big hug and told "Thank you. I want you to be my personal bodyguard while I am here. When I am gone, I want you to stay in my home and keep an eye on things for me. You are welcome to enjoy anything that I have there." Sgt. Smith stated to his audience "The ambassador had very good liquor and food.")

While the last of the Vietnamese refugees were leaving by helicopter, those still waiting for a flight began to climb the perimeter walls and the gates of the compound. Seventy seven remaining Marines barricaded the building and made their way to the rooftop. With the last of the civilians evacuated, the commanding officer chose the next 66 men to leave with the two approaching helicopters. Eleven Marines soon would be the last 11 Americans in Vietnam. With the arrival of the two helicopters, the Marines began to receive sniper fire from the enemy. The two helicopters safely departed for the fleet which was anchored just off shore and the last 11 began to pile sandbags on the rooftop for protection. Through some form of miscommunication, the helicopter pilots thought that they had evacuated all of the Marines left on the rooftop and as such reported that they were inbound for landing with the last of the Embassy guard. The fleet then immediately set sail for the Philippines as the helicopters were still inbound.

Before long, it became obvious to the Captain in command and the other 10 Marines that they were not going to be evacuated; minutes became hours. They continued to receive sporadic sniper fire and as such, they were now laying on their backs, behind the hastily erected low wall of sandbags with their weapons on their chests. Back on board the evacuation fleet, it was finally realized that there were still Marines at the embassy. The fleet commander advised President Ford of the situation, that there were still Marines in Saigon, and incredibly the reply from the man in the White House was something to the effect of "They are expendable, do not go back to get them."

It is this author's opinion that a President with a military background would never give an order such as that. Only a politically correct President with a civilian background who perhaps got hit in the head one too many times playing college football would give an order like that. Let me assure the reader that the Marines would never leave anyone behind. Disregarding the orders of the commander-in-chief, a CH-46 helicopter headed west, back to Vietnam. Back on the rooftop, the Captain was apologizing to his men, telling them he was sorry that they were the ones he asked to stay behind but they were all going to die together and take out as many of the enemy as they possibly could. They were Marines!

Sgt. Smith, still on his back with his weapon locked and loaded with the safety off, noticed what he called "an ant" directly above them high in the sky. Soon it became apparent to him that it was a Marine helicopter circling the compound for landing. Upon approach and landing, the aircraft, like the Marines on the rooftop, began taking fire from the North Vietnamese troops. Wasting no time, the last 11 scrambled aboard the aircraft and according to Sgt. Smith the aircraft just sat there. "I could see bullet holes appearing in the skin of the aircraft as we sat there. I yelled to the flight engineer 'Why aren't we leaving?' and his reply was 'The pilots have a bet that we can sit here for 1 min. before we leave'" Incredible! But that was what Sgt. Smith remembered.

With a final liftoff from the American Embassy in Vietnam, one Marine helicopter headed offshore for the fleet that was already steaming east. Its cargo was the very last 11 Americans to leave Vietnam. Close one more chapter in the history of the United States of America. While not the prettiest chapter ever written, it was one where many lessons should have been learned but unfortunately were not. Again, it is this author's opinion, and that of many of my comrades, that this country continues to make the same mistakes over and over. If you are going to put "boots on the ground", you need to let the military run the show, not the politicians. Politicians need to be involved *before* there is conflict, not *after*. We had to fight the Communists in Vietnam with one hand tied behind our backs, just as we are doing in Iraq and Afghanistan. Want to know how to win a war? Read about how General Norman Schwarzkopf, Jr. kicked the Iraqis out of Kuwait. President George Bush the first, a Navy veteran, knew how to win a war and did it the right way; he let the military have the reins, not Congress.

From the Author:

Many years after returning from Vietnam, my wife and I attended a Christmas party with several other adult couples, most of which I had never met. In a small group of these attendees, our host introduced my wife and I and mentioned to them that I was a helicopter pilot in Vietnam. Immediately one of the younger women said to me "Oh, you're a warmonger." I couldn't believe my ears, she had no idea that I was there to save lives, not take them, and that I had been wounded while rescuing other wounded soldiers. I was taken aback for a second or two and all I could think to say was "Ma'am, you will never meet anyone more antiwar than someone who has been there." I took my wife's arm and we walked away from the group, avoiding the ignorant woman for the rest of the evening. One should hate the war but you have to love the warrior.

END

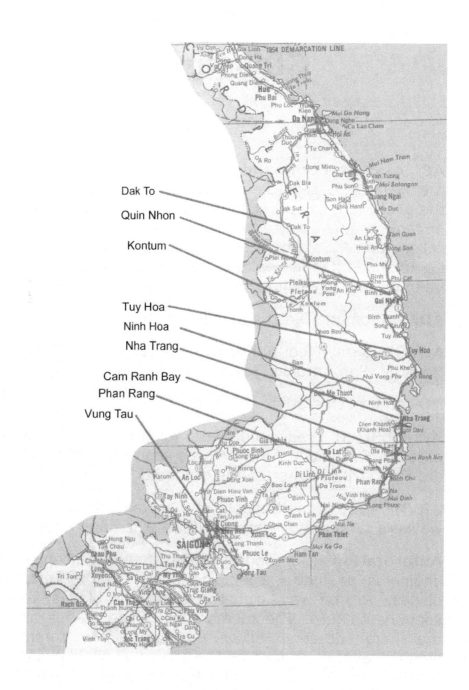

Dak To

Quin Nhon

Kontum

Tuy Hoa

Ninh Hoa

Nha Trang

Cam Ranh Bay

Phan Rang

Vung Tau

343

Glossary

AC- Aircraft Commander. The man in charge of the helicopter, regardless of rank. Virtually always the pilot more experienced in the aircraft, regardless of rank or age. Written orders were required to be called an AC, otherwise, he was the Pilot In Command, PIC. The epitome of flying helicopters in Vietnam was to be made an AC.

ADF- Automatic Direction Finding radio.

AMEDD- Army Medical Department based at Ft. Sam Houston, San Antonio, Texas.

AO- Area of Operation

Arc-Light- The radio code word for a B-52 bombing mission. One did not want to be anywhere near an arc-light strike, either on the ground or in the air.

ARVN- Army of the Republic of Viet Nam. The troops we were supporting. Also known as "The good guys".

Autorotation- the good news is, when a helicopter engine is no longer supplying power to the rotor blades, a one-way clutch allows the blades to continue to turn. The momentum of the blades as the aircraft descends allows a skilled pilot to safely land the aircraft as long as there is an available safe landing area. The bad news is that the pilot only gets one attempt to do this.

Beeped Up, Beeped Down- A button on the collective pitch control allows the pilot to increase or decrease the engine RPM within a few hundred RPMs. This button regulates the fuel control governor and is operated by the left thumb. Pushing the button up increases the engine and rotor speed, pulling back the button decreases those speeds. A helicopter operates at a constant RPM at all times; the pilot does not "rev up" the engine to take off and "throttle down" to land as one might observe in Hollywood movies.

Black Syph- A mythical, incurable venereal disease conjured up apparently to scare soldiers away from fraternizing with the local populace. Supposedly, those GIs who caught the disease were banished to an off-shore island, never to return home.

Boonies- See "Humping"

C&C, C&C Ship-Command and Control aircraft, normally flying in the area of combat with a Commissioned commanding officer on the radios overseeing the conflict while directing and organizing aircraft operations with the ground troops.

Chalk- In a multi-ship flight, the lead aircraft is "Chalk 1" and the others are numbered back to the last aircraft...Chalk 1, Chalk 2, etc. The term comes from the grunts taking a piece of chalk and writing the number on the side of the aircraft so each trooper would know which aircraft to get on when making an assault. Of course, when it came to depart an LZ to come back to base, any helicopter would do. The term probably started during World War II with the paratroopers loading into assigned aircraft. Also known as "Chock". The Marines called it "Dash".

Charlie, Charles, Chuck, Dink, Gook- All terms (some not politically correct) identifying the enemy. The NVA, North Vietnamese Army, the "regulars" and also the Viet Cong, VC, the guerilla fighters. All terms were meant as the "bad guys". "Charlie" coming from the military's phonetic alphabet for "VC", Victor Charlie.

Charlie Model Gunship- a Huey with the shorter fuselage but wider rotor blades and more powerful T53-13 engine than was used on the original Alpha and Bravo model Hueys that used the same, shorter fuselage. The Charlie and Mike model Hueys were used primarily as gunships due to their increased lifting power.

Chicken Plate- A very heavy vest of cloth covered lead that protected the chest and stomach only. Because there was absolutely no protection to the pilots from the front of the aircraft, many wore a chicken plate that merely rested on the lap and was held in place by the safety harness shoulder straps or it may surround the torso and stay in place with Velcro straps. It could stop small arms fire, but that's about all.

Chicom- Chinese Communist

Clicks- See "**Kliks**".

Chock- See "Chalk"

Cobra- AH-1G attack helicopter, only about 3 feet wide, using a Huey powertrain, but developed for the Vietnam War strictly as a gunship. It was crewed by two pilots only, sitting in tandem like a fighter airplane.

DEROS- Date of Expected Return from OverSeas.

THE date that every warrior in Vietnam knew, when they were due to go home, back to the Real World.

Didi'd- Pronounced *"dee' deed"*. *A truncated version of the Vietnamese phrase for Di Di Mow (Mow, like "Ow, I hurt myself.") Loosely translated it means getting the heck put out of someplace. i.e. "When the rockets started pouring in, the enemy di di mowed the area."*

Fast Movers- Jets

FNG- "Funny" New Guy. Most substitute the word "Funny" with a different "F" word. Any person new to a unit, regardless of rank.

GI- Comes from Government Issue, any soldier, Sailor, Marine etc. (Not Gastro-Intestinal)

Ground Pounder- See Grunts

Grunts- A non-offensive term used to designate the guys on the ground. Those who did the "grunt work". Probably a term coined by the grunts themselves, a description of the sounds they made carrying heavy equipment while "humping the boonies".

Guard Frequency- When a radio call is made on this frequency, any and all aircraft for miles around can hear it, as long as the listening aircraft have their radios set to "Guard Receive." In combat, aircraft in flight virtually always are monitoring Guard in case someone gets in trouble. See "Mayday".

Happy Hour- Late afternoon time when drinks are at a reduced price in the Club. Not necessarily lasting only one Hour but definitely Happy!

Head shed- Could be either Flight Operations or the Orderly Room of the Commanding Officer.

Hellhole- The 2 seats on either side of a Huey cargo compartment which face outward at the back of the aircraft. So named because in many configurations, once one is seated on the back two seats, they can move nowhere else in the cargo area without exiting the aircraft. Normally where the crew chief and gunner sit when the Huey is outfitted with M60 machine guns.

Hooch, Hootch- Living quarters, usually a "bare-bones" wooden structure of 2 by 4 studs and plywood with a tin roof. Sandbags would be placed on the roof to hold the sheet metal down during monsoons.

Hot Mike- A position on the aircraft intercom system. In normal operations, a crewmember had to push a button to transmit within the aircraft, but in the "Hot Mike" position, the microphone was constantly open, relieving the crewmember from pushing the button, leaving both hands free.

Hue- Pronounced "whey". A beautiful, centuries old, walled city with a moat surrounding, it was the old Imperial Capital city of Vietnam. Roughly located at the geographic center of Vietnam.

Humping (the Boonies)- Walking through the jungle, likely in enemy territory.

I Corps- South Vietnam was divided into 4 Corps, running North to South. I Corps (pronounced "eye" Corps, rather than "1" Corps) and 2, 3 and 4 Corps.

IFR- Instrument Flight Rules- While we, as Army Aviators, had Instrument Flight Training in Flight

School, the inside joke among we students was that we learned just enough to kill ourselves while flying in bad weather, fog and clouds. The blessing for our efforts and training to be IFR qualified was a pink piece of cardboard known as a Tactical Instrument Ticket. MANY aircraft and crew losses occurred during attempts to complete these IFR missions because many of us lacked the experience necessary to safely complete the rescue. Many crews survived inadvertent and even known IFR conditions purely by luck and the grace of God. See VFR.

JP- Jungle Penetrator. A rather heavy device with fold up seats at the end of the hoist cable. A pointed end allowed the penetrator to descend through the foliage to the ground, at which time the seats would be opened for the ride up to the hovering helicopter. Troops were taught to let the penetrator touch the ground before grabbing it, as the build-up of static electricity would release quite a jolt if not grounded first.

KIA- Killed In Action.

Kliks, Klicks- Kilometers, 1 Kilometer equals about 6/10 of a mile. Navigation maps were laid out in 1 kilometer squares with location coordinates.

Lam Son 719- (Pronounced "lamb-sahn") Named for an attempt to cut the so-called Ho Chi Minh Trail that ran through Laos and Cambodia, a supply trail used to bring troops and weapons from North Vietnam into the South. American helicopters and American crews transported and supplied South Vietnamese troops into Laos; no Americans were to be on the ground. The enemy was waiting and a lot of good men and a lot of good aircraft were lost during what many call a very ill-conceived incursion.

The 719 came from the year 1971 and 9 from the East West Route 9 that was utilized that ran from South Vietnam to Laos.

LZ- Landing Zone. Any area used to pick up patients or insert/pickup troops; improved areas or not.

LOH, Loach- Hughes Aircraft Company OH-6 helicopter. A Light Observation Helicopter, LOH, that resembles a flying egg and is highly crashworthy. Mostly used to locate the enemy and often used as bait for the Cobra gunships flying overhead cover for the LOH; pronounced "Loach". Other observation aircraft such as the Bell OH-58 might be called Loaches, but the only true Loach for a Vietnam Vet is the Hughes OH-6.

Mayday- When an aircraft is going down, the pilot is trained to say the word 3 times, usually over the Guard Frequency, and them immediately give out location and any other pertinent information as briefly as possible. The pilot then must concentrate on attempting as safe a landing as possible. The use of the word comes from a French phrase that sounds much like the English word "Mayday" but apparently translates from "Oh, crap, I'm in big trouble" or something like that.

Minigun- A 6 barreled, electrically fired machine gun carried on helicopter gunships. With a normal fire rate of about 3,000 to 4,000 rounds per minute when fired in tandem, the rate could be stepped up to 6,000 rounds of 7.62 per minute when fired singly. An improvement over the Civil War Gattling Gun. Therefore, a single pass by a helicopter gunship firing miniguns can put one round in every square yard of a football field. Devastating.

Niner- No, that is not a typo for "nine". Over the radio, the numbers "five" and "nine" can sound a lot alike, so flight crews learned to say "niner" for "nine" to avoid confusion.

OJT- On the Job Training. Many of our crew chiefs learned advanced first aid from our medics; more first aid than was given to new recruits in Basic Training. Thus, OJT.

Peter Pilot- The co-pilot. Being called Peter Pilot as a new aviator in country was an incentive to become an Aircraft Commander, and thus, no longer a new guy. See FNG.

PIC- Pilot in Command. A pilot who has yet to receive Aircraft Commander, AC, orders but may be in command of an aircraft on a (usually) non-combat flight. PICs were usually high time Peter Pilots who were close to receiving Aircraft Commander orders.

Pink Team, White Team, Red Team- White was the observation helicopters and Red was the gunships. A Red team was 2 or 3 Cobras working out, a White Team was two Scout birds (Loachs) , a Pink Team was a Loach and 1 or 2 Gunships working together.

POL- Petroleum, Oil, Lubricants. Our refueling point, often only a huge rubber bladder laying on the ground, sometimes fed by a pump to the aircraft or simply gravity fed from uphill of the pad. Normal procedure was to keep the aircraft running with only the Aircraft Commander at the controls with the Crew Chief doing the actual "Hot Refueling". This was also an excellent opportunity for the crew members outside the aircraft to relieve themselves on the immediate surrounding area.

Prairie Fire- All heck is breaking loose and our guys on the ground are in big trouble! Kinda like your local fire department and EMTs responding to a multi-alarm fire or emergency.

Pucker Factor- The whimsical notion that the cheeks of one's buttocks can pucker up tight enough to grab the seat they are sitting on, thus, no need for a seat belt. A high pucker factor means a very dangerous or potentially very "hairy" situation.

R&R- Rest and Relaxation. "Vacation" time away from the day to day stress of combat. This relaxation could be taken in Viet Nam at a few secure destinations such as Vung Tau in the South or China Beach in the North of South Vietnam, or the time could be taken out of country to exotic places such as Bangkok, Thailand or Sydney, Australia. Married combatants often opted to meet their spouses in Hawaii for this brief respite. Usually, no more than 2 weeks. Transportation was provided by the US Government but all other expenses were paid by the individual Warriors.

Red X- When filling out the aircraft log book after flight, the Aircraft Commander notes any discrepancies in the helicopter. Those discrepancies that affect safe flight are designated with a red "X", thereby deeming the aircraft unsafe to fly until corrected.

RFPF- Regional Force, Peoples Force. The local Vietnamese militia. Also called Ruff Puff.

RPG- Rocket Propelled Grenade, I have also seen it referred to as a Rifle Propelled Grenade.

Rucksack- A military backpack.

Slicks- Troop carrying Hueys with no external armament, thereby a "slick" profile. May or may not have door guns but virtually always did. Even with door guns, it was still called a "slick".

Tac Push- Tactical Radio Frequency, usually the FM radio for air to ground communications.

Urgent/Urgents- Those patients who required immediate medical attention. Missions were classified as Routine, Priority and Urgent. Many aircraft and crews were lost while attempting to rescue Urgent patients. Also, many missions were called in by the ground troops as Urgent which were actually Routine or Priority. Called in as Urgent apparently for fear that if they weren't called in as Urgent, they might be ignored. No mission was ever ignored that this author is familiar with.

VFR- Visual Flight Rules- In a nutshell, the crew can see the horizon and the ground, or at least the ground. Let's go flying! Oh, yeah, don't run into anything. See IFR.

VOR- VHF Omni-directional Range radio.

WIA- Wounded In Action.

World- Home, the REAL world...the good old USofA. Land of pizza, flush toilets, real hamburgers and round eyed women; not necessarily in that order. Viet Nam was definitely *not* the real world to us.

Please be sure to read the Author's other books, "DMZ Dustoff Vietnam", which documents 22 missions flown by the crews of the 237th Medical Detachment, and "Dustoff & Medevac Vietnam" which documents missions flown by all Dustoff and Medevac units.

If you have any comments or if you have a Vietnam Dustoff or Medevac mission that you would like to include in the next Volume of "Helicopter Rescues Vietnam", please contact the author at DMZDustoffVietnam@yahoo.com